THE HOME MAINTENANCE MANUAL

First published in Great Britain by
Sphere Books Ltd 1983

Illustrations by Will Giles, Tony Hannaford,
Dave Parr and Hussein Hussein

SPHERE

Set in Helios by Colset Private Limited,
Singapore

Printed and bound in Great Britain by
Hazell Watson & Viney Ltd, Aylesbury, Bucks

Introduction

This book is for the not-so-handy handyman – for the man, or woman, who would like to do many of the repair and maintenance jobs around the house or flat that crop up from time to time but lacks the basic knowhow to tackle such jobs with confidence.

There are four good reasons why the house-owner should be able to look after his or her property whether old or new; firstly there is the time factor, as it can take weeks to get a plumber, electrician or builder to call; secondly there is cost; repair bills can be high and the average householder has no way of knowing if the price for the job is fair; thirdly there is the tremendous satisfaction that comes from doing a job yourself; and lastly it is a fact that most jobs around the house are not **that** difficult if tackled properly.

Obviously there are some jobs that require special skills and knowledge if they are to be done competently and safely. This book deals only with the sort of thing that can be mastered with a little practice and some commonsense and tells you the jobs for which the experts must be called in; but make sure they **are** experts. Avoid the 'cowboy' firms who offer a cheap quick job – often they employ unskilled casual labour. Always employ firms who are members of an appropriate trade association – in Britain these include the Master Builders' Federation, the Electrical Contractors' Association and the Associated Master Plumbers and Domestic Engineers.

Simon James

Contents

Basements and cellars

Lining a basement wall

You will need: hammer; bolster chisel and club hammer; crosscut saw; bitumen-impregnated lath; masonry nails; 2 in × 1 in (50 mm × 25 mm) wood batten; plaster or plasterboard

Many older properties have basements or cellars which may be used either as extra living space or for storage. Because they are below ground, dampness in the walls can be a problem. Small areas of damp will show as dark stains in the plasterwork. These can be treated with a water repellant liquid, such as Aquaseal or Storma. Firstly it is important to clean the affected areas thoroughly to remove the discolouration and any mould growth that may have occurred. Apply the liquid by brush or spray, extending about 6 in (150 mm) beyond the affected area, and allow to dry.

If you want to redecorate the wall, you can use a special cellar paint which can be applied on a damp surface. If a whole wall, or large area of it, is damp then it should be lined with bitumen-impregnated lath, obtainable from a builders' merchant. The lath is corrugated to provide insulating cavities on the side fitted to the wall, and to provide a key for plasterwork on the outer surface. Any existing plaster on the damp wall must be removed. The wall will continue to be damp, so it is worthwhile painting the brick with fungicide to sterilize the surface.

Lath sheets, such as Newtonite, are nailed to the wall from floor to ceiling, with a 1 in (25 mm) gap at the bottom to prevent damp rising, and then plastered or dry lined with plasterboard.

1. A damp basement wall can be lined with a pitch-impregnated fibre lath. First remove all plaster back to the brickwork.

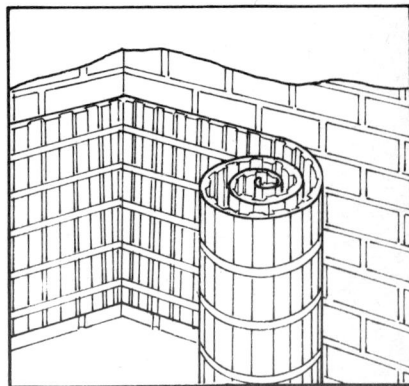

2. The lath is supplied in rolls. Unroll the lath along the wall. Allow a 1 in (25 mm) gap at the bottom if the floor is solid.

8

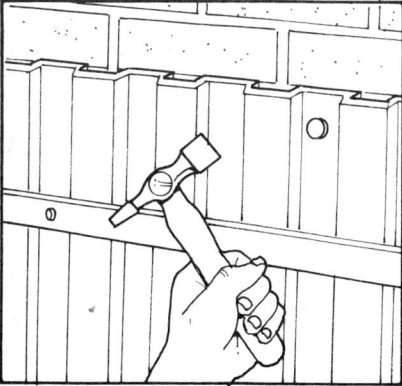

3. Nail the lath to the wall, using clout nails hammered into the mortar joints; alternatively use masonry nails driven through the metal strips.

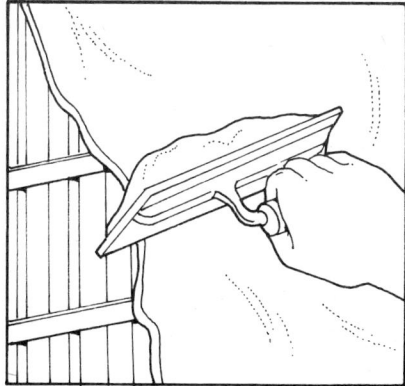

5. Apply two coats of plaster, first a light coat to fill the corrugations and then a finishing coat. Allow several weeks before decorating.

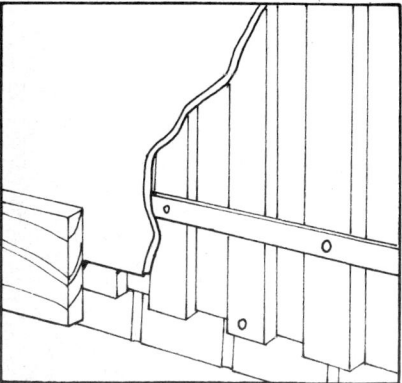

4. On a solid floor, maintain the gap all the way around, and leave a slight gap to allow ventilation if you fit a skirting board.

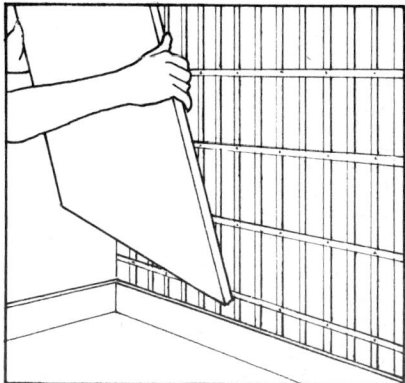

6. If the wall is to be decorated immediately, line it with plasterboard instead of plastering. Use dabs of plaster to hold the board in place.

Ceilings

How ceilings are constructed

There are two types of ceiling found in most houses – plasterboard; and lath and plaster.

Most modern houses have plasterboard ceilings, which consist of boards nailed to the underside of the ceiling joists. The boards are made of gypsum plaster faced on both sides with a tough paper, and are cheap, fireproof and easy to replace. The thickness of the boards depends on the joist spacing; $\frac{3}{8}$ in (9.5 mm) thick boards are used where the joists are 16 in (40.6 cm) apart, and $\frac{1}{2}$ in (13 mm) boards are fitted to joists (45.5 cm) 18 in apart.

The old method found in prewar houses consisted of laths nailed to the joists with a gap between each lath. Plaster, bound together with animal hair, was then spread over the laths and forced up between them, so that it oozed over the laths and keyed on to them when it solidified. Lath and plaster ceilings are easily recognized from above by this rough-cast appearance. As with a plasterboard ceiling, lath and plaster was finished off with a finishing plaster to give a smooth surface.

Both methods provide a good ceiling if they are properly maintained by regular cleaning and decorating. **Fixings such as light fittings or curtain tracks should always be attached to the joists because plaster will not support heavy weights**.

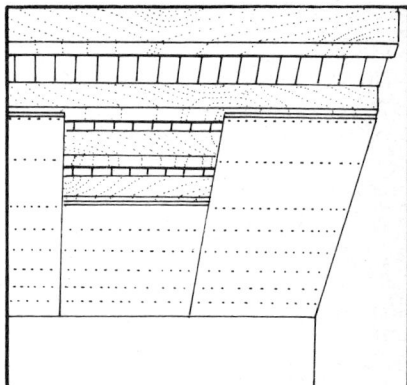

Plasterboard is the modern method of ceiling construction. The boards are nailed to the joists and are staggered to avoid continuous joints.

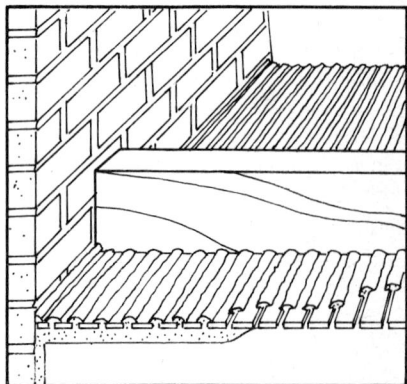

Lath and plaster In older houses, laths are nailed to the joists, with gaps between the laths which are filled with a mixture of plaster and animal hair.

Filling a hole in a lath and plaster ceiling

You will need: filling knife; bolster chisel; club hammer; trowel; filler; medium grade sandpaper; expanded metal or wire mesh; paintbrush; plaster

Problems and cures

The two most common problems with ceilings are **cracks** and **stains**. Both are easily dealt with if they are treated quickly. Hairline cracks can be filled with a proprietary filler and then sanded smooth when dry. Cracks at the join between the wall and ceiling can also be filled in this way, but will often reappear due to a slight movement of the ceiling joists. Often a better cure is to conceal the cracks with coving.

Before treating a stain, look for and eliminate its cause. In a bedroom ceiling this could be a leak from the water tank in the loft or a leaking pipe. Check that any dampness in the ceiling has not spread to the joists or laths and caused them to rot. If it has, treat or replace the damaged wood (see pp 196-201). Paint the stained area with aluminium sealer and then repaint or repaper.

Holes in the ceiling up to about $\frac{1}{2}$ in (13 mm) in diameter can be filled with plaster, but larger holes will require a backing for the plaster to key into. On a plasterboard ceiling, lay a piece of expanded metal or small wire mesh across the top of the hole and hold it in place with a few blobs of filler. Then apply two coats of plaster to the underside (see pp 190-191). Use wire mesh or expanded metal also to bridge a hole in lath and plaster, but in this case hold the mesh in place.

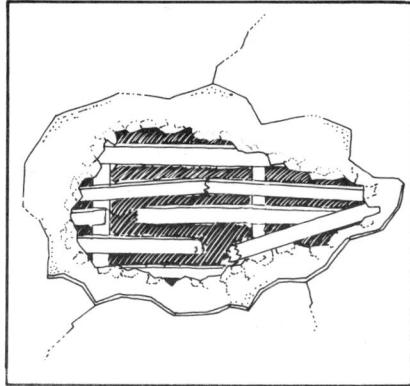

1. Damage to a lath and plaster ceiling can be repaired by filling the hole with fresh plaster or a proprietary filler, with some support for broken laths.

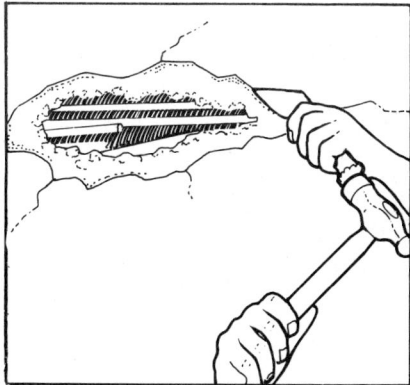

2. First chisel away all loose plaster around the hole, working to the full extent of any cracks radiating from it. Brush out any remaining matter from the laths. *(continued)*

11

Ceilings

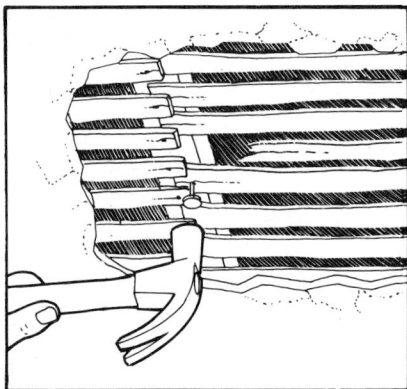

3. Secure any laths that have pulled away from the joists, using small nails or tacks.

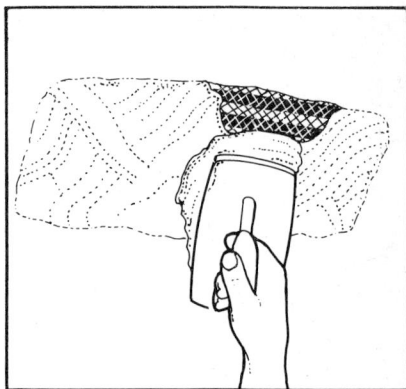

5. Apply the plaster or filler with a trowel, working it into the mesh and between the laths. Finish with a wet trowel for a smooth surface.

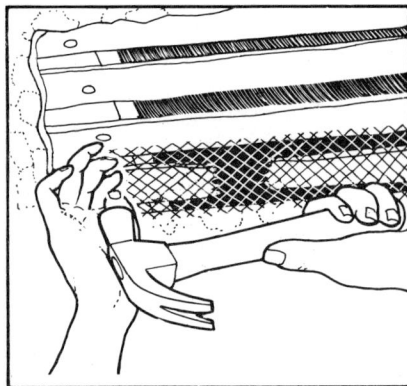

4. Cover broken laths with expanded metal. Cut the metal to length with tin shears and nail each end to a joist.

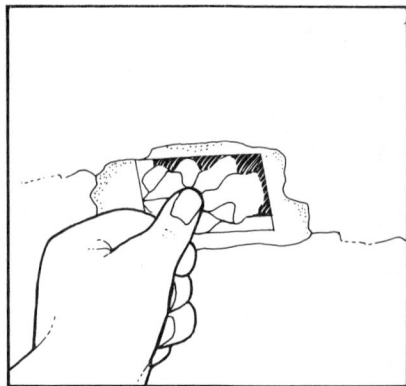

6. For a small hole, use a plug of paper soaked in plaster. Press the paper in firmly to about $\frac{1}{4}$ in (6 mm) below the surface. Apply plaster as in 5.

Filling cracks

You will need: trowel; filler; paintbrush

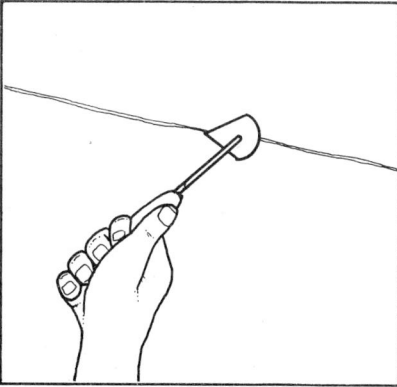

1. Cracks often occur at the angle between wall and ceiling, especially in a new house as it dries out. Scrape away loose plaster and widen the crack to about $\frac{1}{16}$ th in (2 mm).

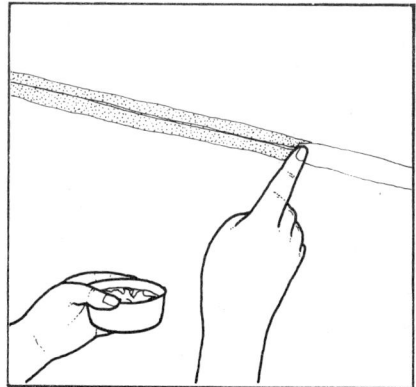

3. Mix a small amount of a proprietary filler to a thick, workable consistency and press it firmly into the crack.

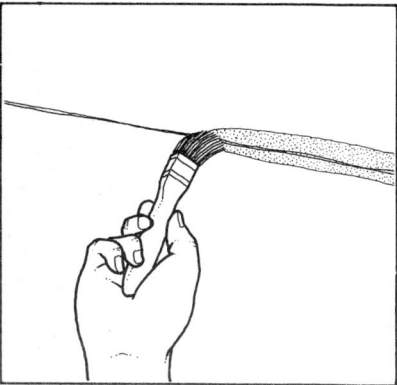

2. Use a paintbrush dipped in clean water to moisten the plaster along both sides of the crack and inside the crack itself.

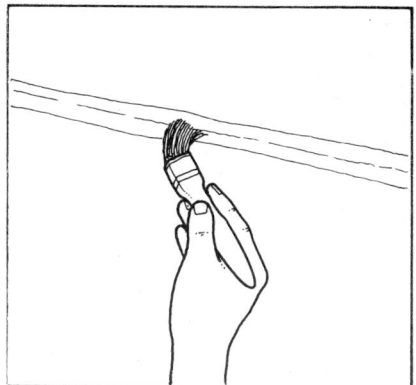

4. When the filler has set but not fully hardened, use a damp paintbrush to clean off the excess. Allow a few days before touching in paintwork.

Repairing a plasterboard ceiling

You will need: filler knife; plaster; metal float; scrim cloth

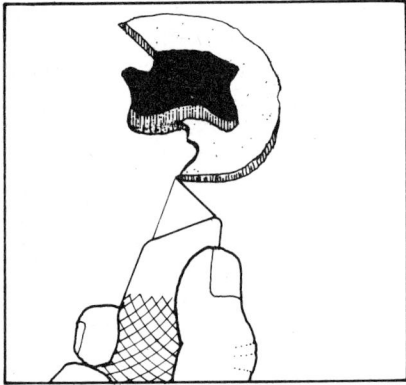

1. To fill a large hole in plasterboard, first cut a ledge around the hole about $\frac{1}{2}$ in (13 mm) wide and $\frac{1}{4}$ in (6 mm) deep.

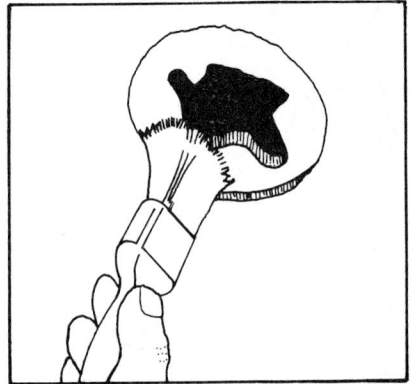

3. Moisten the plasterboard around the hole with clean water. Then mix a small amount of plaster and press a few dabs around the ledge.

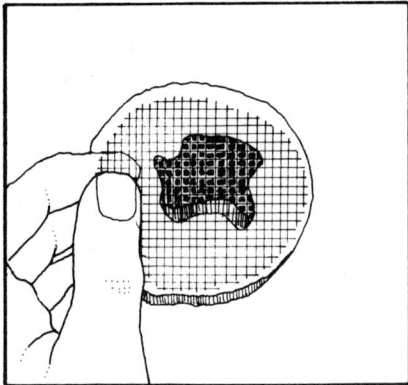

2. Cut a piece of scrim cloth to fit over the hole and inside the ledge. Trim the cloth to the shape of the hole.

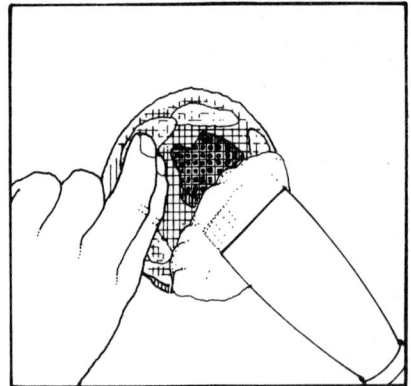

4. Press the scrim onto the dabs of plaster and hold it in position while applying a thin coat of plaster with a filler knife.

Finishing a ceiling

You will need: (for painting) roller and tray; 1 in (25 mm) paintbrush; emulsion paint; (for papering) scissors; paste brush; hanging brush; scaffolding board and 2 step-ladders; pencil; string; chalk; rule; cardboard tube; paper and paste

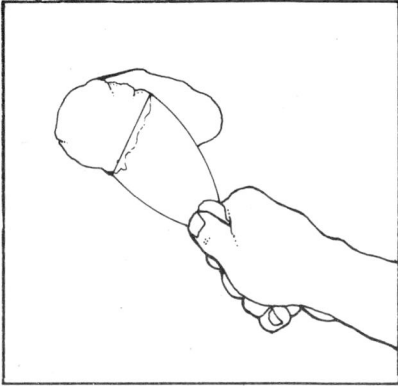

5. Allow the plaster to half set, then apply further layers until level with the surrounding surface.

6. Just before the final coat is fully set, moisten it with water and smooth it with a metal float.

Any repairs to a ceiling will show, however careful you are, so always finish off with a coat of paint, or by papering.

The easiest way to paint a ceiling is with a roller, but first paint in the edges the roller cannot reach with a 1 in (25 mm) paintbrush. Hold the brush edge-on to get a clean line in the angle between the wall and ceiling and then use the brush flat.

When this is done, paint across the ceiling firstly with diagonal strokes of the roller, and then finish off with straight strokes working towards the window. If you are using textured paint, a low density foam roller will give a good textured finish.

To paper a ceiling you will need a scaffolding board placed between two step-ladders, so you can hang a length in one go. Hang ceiling paper working from the window inwards. First measure the width of the paper and subtract $\frac{1}{4}$ in (6 mm) for the overhang at the wall angle. Mark off this measurement from the wall on both sides of the room, and stretch a chalked length of string between the two marks. Snap the string so that it leaves a chalked line on the ceiling and lay the first length of paper to it.

Paste the paper and fold it into a manageable width. Support the folded paper with a length of cardboard tube, or a spare roll of paper, and unfold one pleat at a time as you move across the room. Brush the paper on to the ceiling.

Central heating

Central heating is fast joining such items as washing machines and vacuum cleaners as being essentials for comfortable living. The most widely used central heating system employs the 'wet' system, in which water is heated by a central boiler and is then pumped to radiators which feed the heat into the rooms. The main components in the system are the boiler, circulating pump, radiators and a feed and expansion cistern.

The water can be heated by gas, oil or solid fuel. A room thermostat maintains an even temperature by automatically switching the pump on or off, and a thermostat on the boiler controls the water temperature. Individual thermostats can also be fitted to the radiators. In some systems, water from the boiler passes through tubes in the hot-water storage cylinder to heat the water supplied to the taps. Alternatively an electric immersion heater serves this function.

In any system, however, the water in the central heating circuit is entirely separate from the main hot water supply. The same water circulates continuously, and is topped up by water from the feed and expansion cistern in the roof space.

Fast gaining popularity in the UK is the Electricaire system in which warm air is circulated throughout the house. The heat comes from a storage block — heated by electricity during off-peak periods — and is blown through ducts by a fan.

Storage heaters, which are also heated by off-peak electricity and disperse their heat during the day, are another form of heating, though this system is not strictly 'central' since each unit is a heat source in itself. The heaters can be controlled in several ways — some release their heat at a greater rate at the end of the day by either manual or automatic controls; some are fan-assisted and some have a thermostat-controlled fan.

There is little to choose in the cost advantages of fuels for central heating — all are subject to price fluctuations, especially oil. But gas and electricity have major advantages over oil and solid fuel in two other respects; the fuel does not have to be stored on the premises and it is not prone to shortages caused by international incidents.

The electricity board in the UK claims that electrical central heating is more efficient, stating that in any 'wet' system much of the heat goes out through the boiler flue, and that it needs no maintenance. The Electricaire system, however, is unsuitable for installing into older houses unless as part of a major modernization scheme. Mostly it is found in new houses with built-in fan ducting.

Storage heaters can be installed quite easily though the work should be done by a qualified electrician.

A typical central heating system

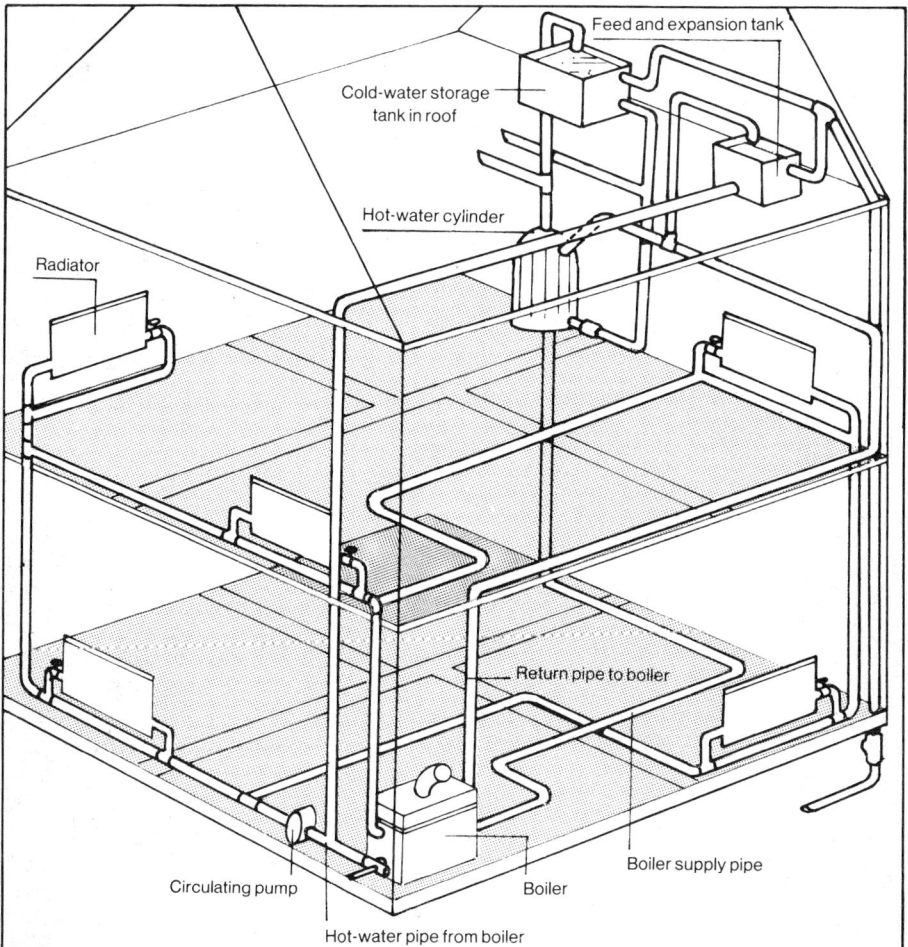

Feed and expansion tank

Cold-water storage tank in roof

Hot-water cylinder

Radiator

Return pipe to boiler

Boiler supply pipe

Circulating pump

Boiler

Hot-water pipe from boiler

The most widely used type of central heating has hot water as the heating element, the heat being fed into the rooms by radiators. Water is heated in a central boiler which may be gas, oil or solid-fuel fired.

Central heating

Maintenance of a 'wet' system

To get the best out of a central heating system, whether gas or oil-fired, take advantage of the maintenance schemes offered by your gas authority and by some oil suppliers. A solid-fuel boiler should be cleaned every six months and the flue and chimney once a year, preferably in the spring. To ensure maximum efficiency use only recommended fuel.

There is much the householder can do to keep the central heating trouble-free and running at maximum efficiency. During the summer, turn the pump on once or twice to keep it free, and operate the radiator valves or taps occasionally. At least once a year, go into the roof space and see that the ball valve in the feed and expansion cistern pivots freely. A smear of grease on the pivot will keep it free and prevent corrosion.

With an oil-fired system, clean the filter unit regularly. First turn off the oil supply at the tank and switch off the electrical ignition system. Remove the screws holding the filter unit cover and check that the control float moves freely. Lay newspaper under the unit to catch any drips; remove the drain nut and filter. Wash the filter thoroughly in petrol and let it air-dry before refitting.

On no account try to make repairs or adjustments to a gas-fired boiler. At the first sign of trouble, notify the gas board.

Problems and cures

You may find sometimes that radiators are cold at the top while hot at the bottom. This is caused by **air locks** in the system and the fault is easily cured. First switch off the circulation pump and then open the bleed screw at one end of the top rail of the radiator. You will need a special key for this which fits over the squared end of the screw. Hold a container such as a jam jar beneath the bleed screw. At first there will be a rush of air, and if you place a hand on the radiator you will feel the heat begin to rise. When the air stops and water begins to flow, tighten the bleed screw.

If there are **cold patches** on a radiator, this means that there are blockages and the radiator must be removed and flushed out.

Air locks may occur in other parts of the system, such as in the pump or in the flow pipe from it. To bleed air from the pump, slacken the grub-screw in the pump body and close it when water begins to flow. To release air from the flow pipe, use a small spanner to open and close the bleed nipple.

To remove a radiator, either to flush it or replace it, you may be able to isolate it by turning off the valves at each end. If the radiator has only one valve the entire system must be drained. For flushing, connect a garden hose to one inlet.

Two types of thermostat

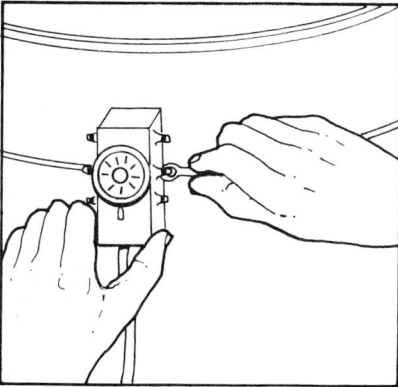

Adjusting an immersion heater thermostat

You will need: small screwdriver

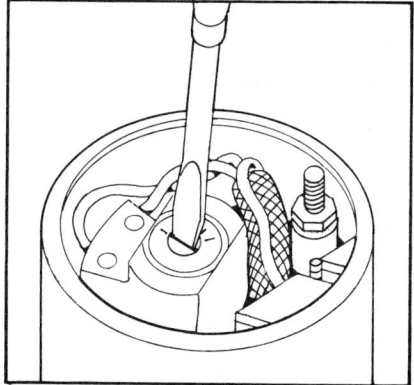

A thermostat is used to control the temperature of the water in the hot-water cylinder. This type is held by a strap around the cylinder.

An electrical immersion heater may be fitted in a hot-water cylinder to supply hot water to the house taps when the central heating is not in use. The water temperature can be adjusted by varying the thermostat control beneath the element cap. Switch off the power supply at the main fusebox and remove the element cap, which is secured by a single screw. Adjust the temperature control with a screwdriver – the settings are marked on the outer ring. Do not set the temperature above 180° F (82° C). Replace the cap before switching on the power supply.

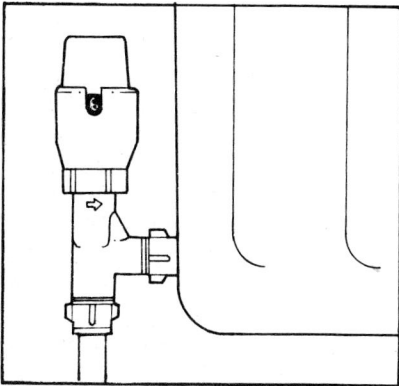

Individual thermostats can be fitted to radiators. They can be adjusted to operate at a given room temperature, which can be varied from room to room.

Adjusting a pump

Clearing an air lock in a pump

You will need: small screwdriver

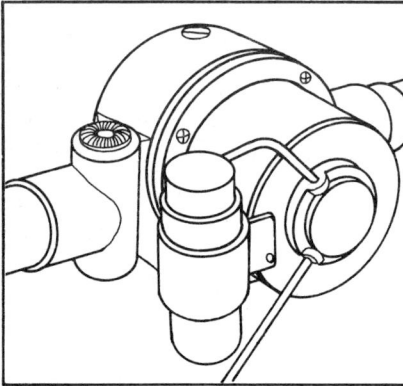

1. The circulating pump is fitted near the boiler and is operated electrically with its own switch.

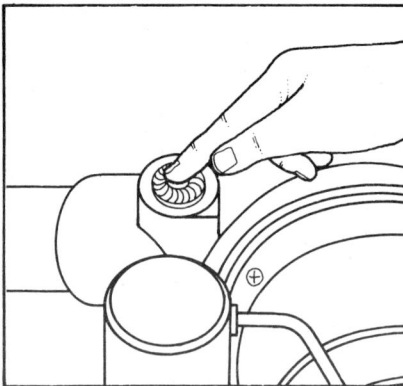

1. If water is not circulating properly, there may be an air lock in the system. Open the vent plug on top of the pump and close it when water begins to flow.

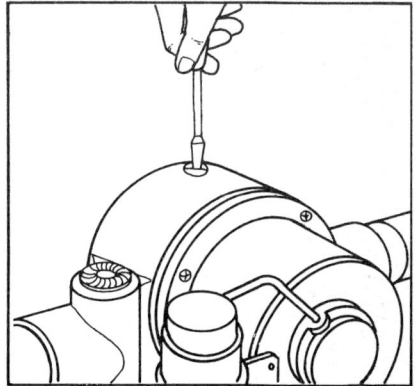

2. The pump should adequately supply all radiators in the system. If it does not, the flow can be adjusted by turning the regulator on the side of the pump.

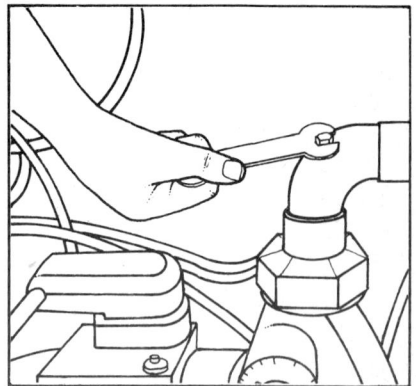

2. There is also a bleed nipple in the flow pipe. Open it with a small spanner to release air and close it when water starts to flow.

Clearing an air lock in a radiator

You will need: bleed valve key; jam jar; screwdriver; small spanner

Flushing a blocked radiator

You will need: adjustable spanner; screwdriver; jointing compound or ptfe tape; garden hose

1. Switch off the circulating pump. Hold a cloth under the bleed valve and insert the bleed key.

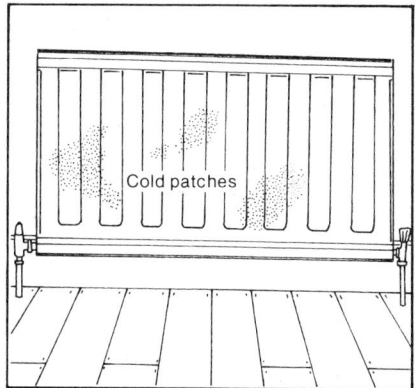

Cold patches

1. Cold patches in a radiator are caused by blockages which are cleared only by removing the radiator and flushing it with clean water.

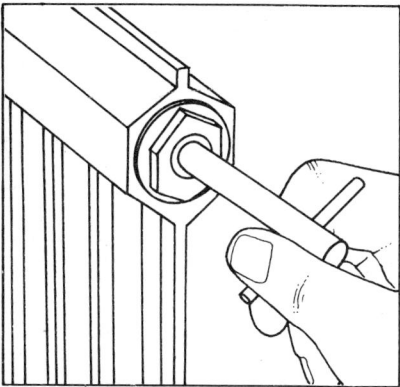

2. Open the valve to expel the air and allow a little water to flow before closing the valve.

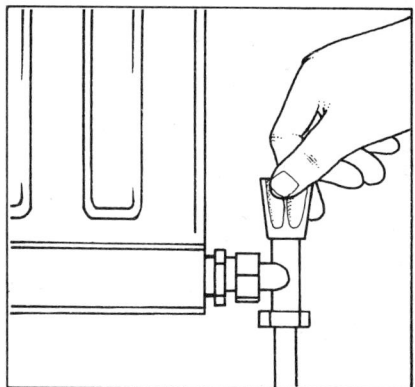

2. First make sure that the central heating system is switched off. Close the control valve at the bottom of the radiator. *(continued)*

Central heating

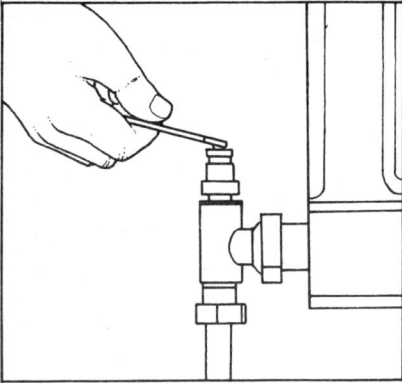

3. If the radiator has a lock-shield valve, at the other side, remove the cover and close the valve, counting the number of turns.

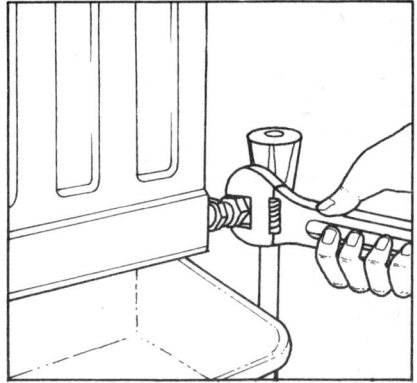

5. Place a bowl under the joint and disconnect the radiator at both ends.

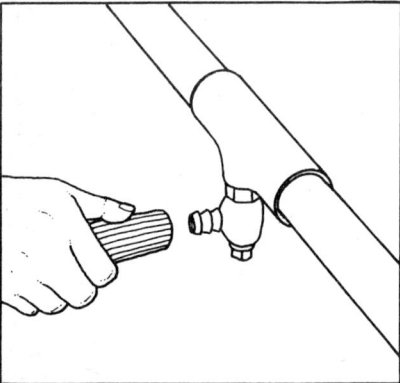

4. If the radiator has no valves, or only one, the system must be drained (see p 25).

6. Disconnect the radiator from its fixing brackets and lift it off. Some radiators can be lifted off without being disconnected.

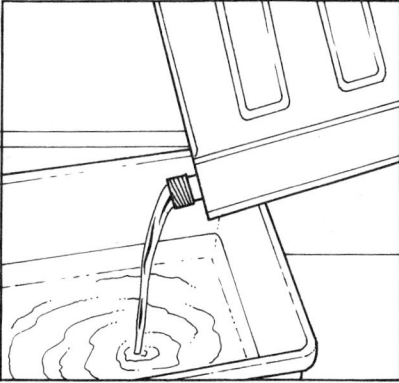

7. Tilt the radiator to empty out any remaining water into the bowl.

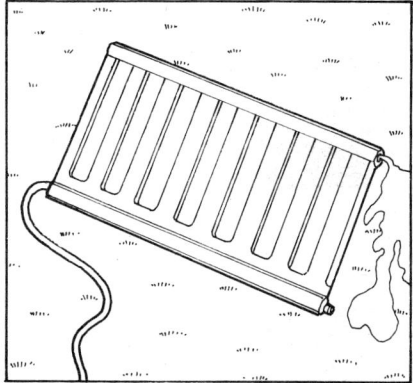

9. Lay the radiator flat outside. Put a garden hose into the open end of the bottom rail. Flush until clean water flows from the bleed valve.

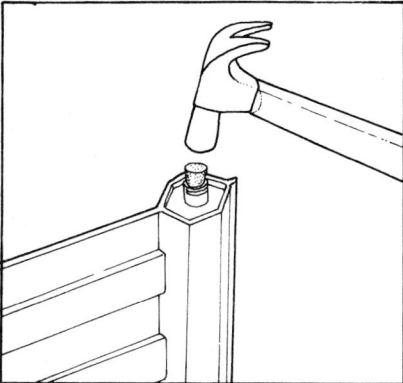

8. Remove the bleed valve assembly at one end of the radiator top rail. Fit a cork or wood bung in the end of the bottom rail at the opposite corner.

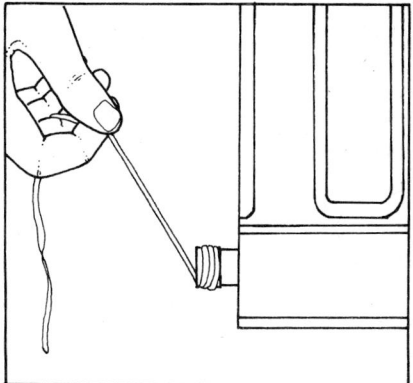

10. Wrap ptfe tape around all threads, including the bleed valve assembly. Refit the bleed valve.

(continued)

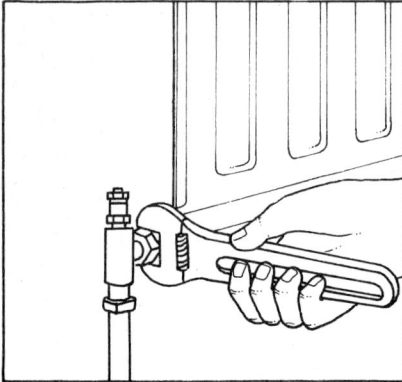

11. Rehang the radiator. Reconnect and tighten both supply pipe joints.

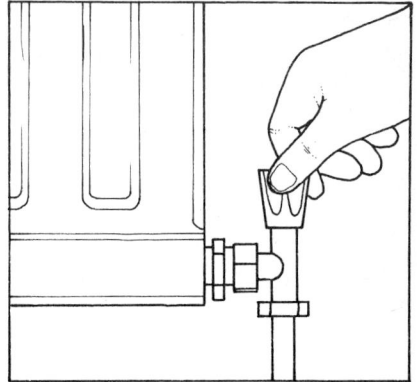

13. Fully open the control valve. Refill the system if it has been drained.

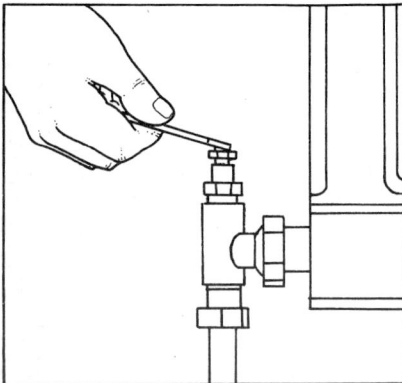

12. Open the lock-shield valve by the same number of turns taken to close it.

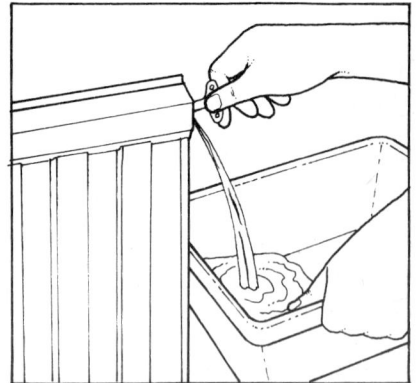

14. Open the bleed valve and hold a bowl underneath until all the air has been expelled and water begins to flow. Close the bleed valve.

Draining and refilling the system

You will need: adjustable spanner; jointing compound or ptfe tape; garden hose

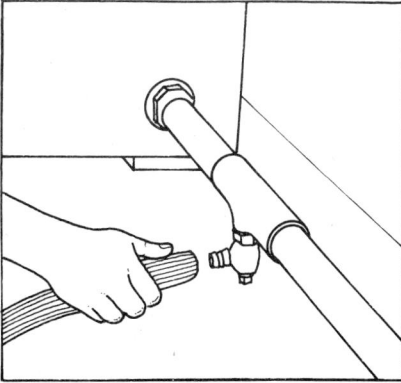

1. First turn off the water at the expansion tank stop valve, or tie up the ball valve. Fit a garden hose to the drain cock on the boiler return pipe.

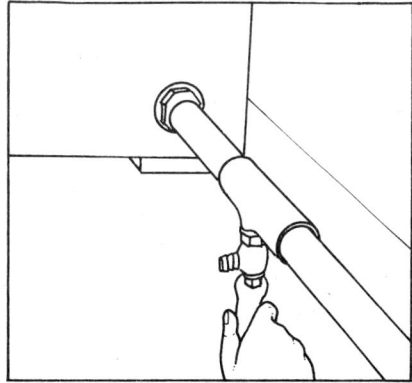

3. Before refilling the system, remove the drain cock and wrap ptfe tape around the threads. Replace the cock and tighten with a spanner.

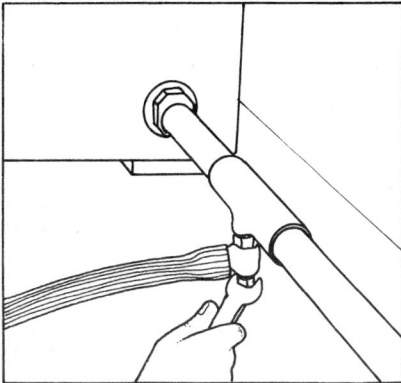

2. Run the hose out to a convenient drain and open the drain cock with a spanner. Allow the system to empty.

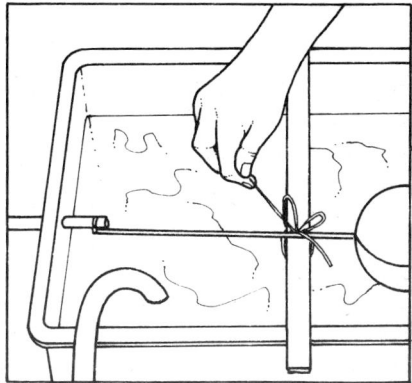

4. Refill the system by opening the expansion tank stop valve, or by releasing the ball valve. **Do not refill too quickly or air locks will occur.**

Chimneys and fireplaces

Sealing around a chimney flashing and capping a chimney

You will need: ladders, scaffolding and crawler boards; pointing trowel; bitumastic sealant; mortar

Because of their exposed position, chimneystacks are more prone to damage by wind and weather than any other part of the house. Mortar joints crumble, weakening the brickwork, and chimney pots become loose in their flaunching (the cement bed in which they are set). **A chimney in a poor state of repair can be very dangerous and should be rectified**.

Examination of a chimneystack is difficult without ladders and scaffolding, but a preliminary check can be made from the ground. Look also for gaps around the flashing; this is the seal at the point where the chimneystack protrudes through the roof and is usually made from zinc sheet, lead or bituminous sheet. Evidence of faulty flashing will also occur inside the roof space.

All these faults can be tackled by the handyman. **But never attempt to do any work on a chimneystack without the proper ladders and scaffolding**. You will also need crawling boards if the chimneystack is at, or close to, the roof apex. These are specially designed boards with crossbars for foot and handholds.

Crumbling mortar joints can be repointed (see p 158), flaunching repaired and flashing sealed — but if the brickwork is loose or a chimney pot broken it is best to have the work done by professionals.

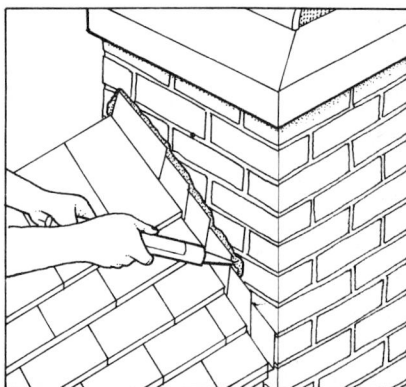

1. If a gap occurs between the lead flashing and brickwork, seal it with a bitumen-based weatherproofing sealant. Build up to about $\frac{1}{4}$ in (6 mm) to ensure a good seal.

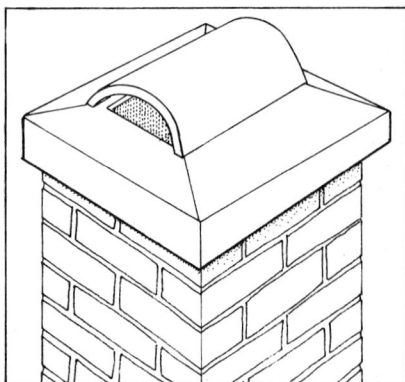

2. If a fireplace has been removed, cap the chimney with a half-round tile embedded in mortar. Make sure there is also an aperture in the fireplace covering (see p 33).

Replacing a broken tile

You will need: cold chisel; hammer; trowel; tile adhesive; applicator; grouting mixture

Fireplaces

Many houses, even those converted to central heating, may still have at least one open fireplace. For most of the time they need little maintenance other than regular cleaning, but eventually the fireback may crack and weaken, the chimney brickwork.

Cracks can be filled easily with a special fireclay obtainable from a builders' merchant, but if the fireback is badly damaged replace it.

Fireplace surrounds should be maintained in accordance with the material used; clean brick surrounds with a solution of 1 part of spirits of salts to 15 parts of water; clean wood surrounds with warm, soapy water; wash marble, stone or tiles with water and a detergent. Brick surrounds are prone to mortar crumbling through the action of fumes and can be repointed (see p 158).

Removing a fireplace, either to replace it by a more modern design or to do away with it altogether, is a simple task. It may be a bit messy, however, if the surround is of brick or tile as this will probably collapse into a heap of rubble as it comes away.

After removing a fireplace, close the hole either by bricking it in or by panelling across the opening. **In either case, always fit a ventilator, or an air brick, in the closure or condensation will form inside the chimney.** You will also need to cap the chimney pot.

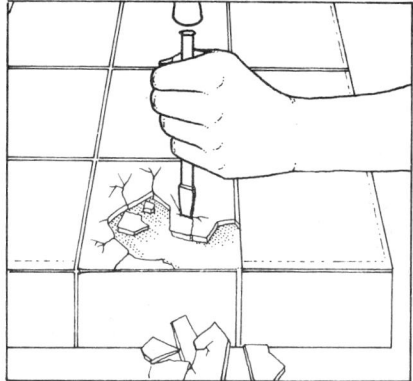

1. Start from the centre and break up the damaged tile with a cold chisel and hammer. Remove the broken pieces.

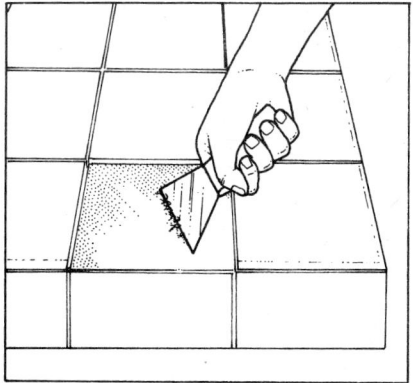

2. Use a paint scraper to remove the old mortar or adhesive from the tiling base. Brush out with a soft brush.

(continued)

27

Repairing a cracked fireback

You will need: stiff brush; trowel; fireclay

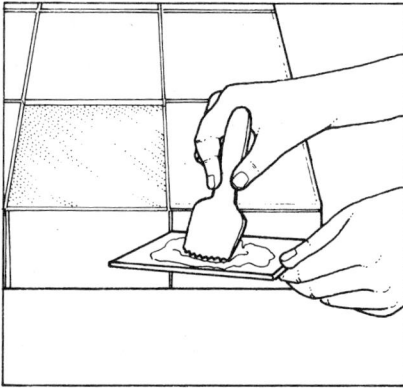

3. Apply tiling adhesive to the back of the new tile with an old paintbrush, or alternatively with an applicator supplied with the adhesive.

1. A badly cracked fireback is unsightly. It is also dangerous as it will allow heat to penetrate to the brickwork behind.

4. Press the tile firmly into place. Wipe off the surplus adhesive with a damp cloth or sponge.

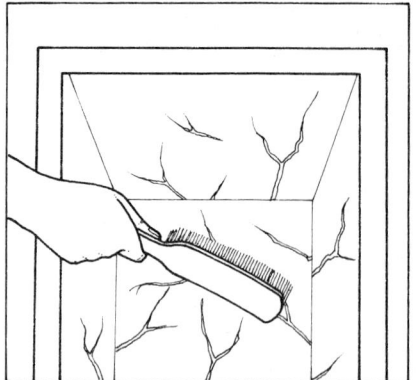

2. First brush out all soot and loose dirt with a stiff brush – a wire brush is ideal. This may reveal other cracks which were previously hidden.

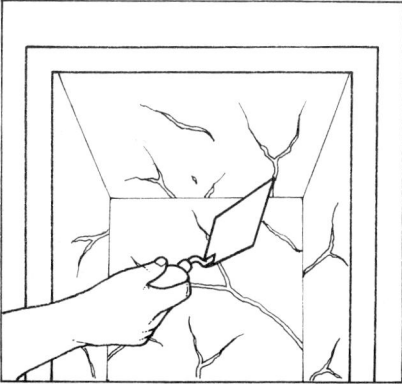

3. Rake out the cracks with the tip of a pointing trowel. Brush the cracks clean with a soft brush.

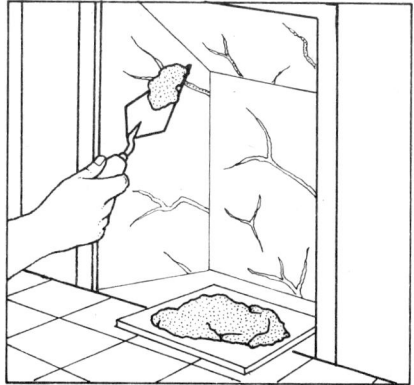

5. Use plastic fireclay, obtainable from a hardware or builder's merchant, to fill the cracks.

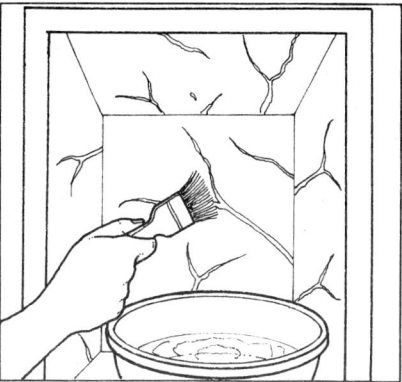

4. Immediately before filling the cracks, dampen them thoroughly with clean water.

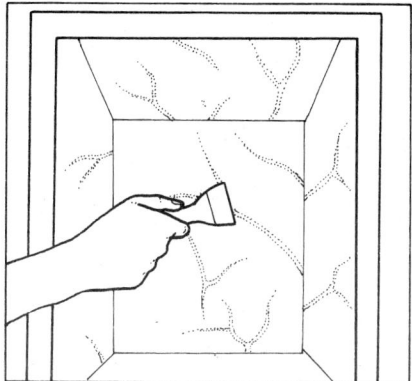

6. Use a plastic spreader to remove surplus fireclay while it is still moist.

Fitting a new fireback

You will need: bolster chisel; trowel; club hammer; cement

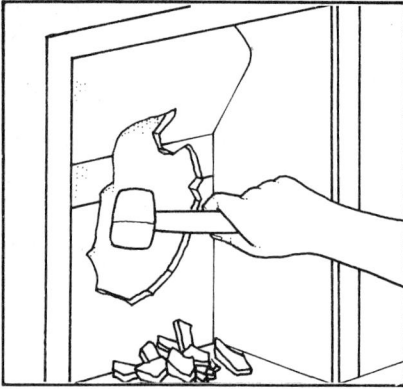

1. It may be possible to remove the old fireback in sections, but it is easier to break it up with a club hammer.

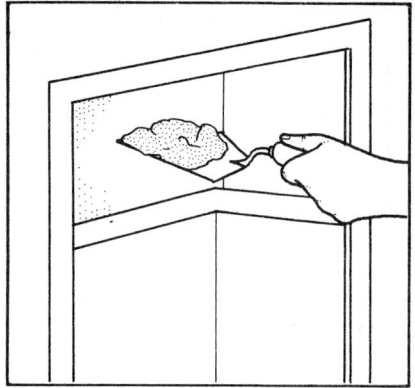

3. Fill the gap behind the fireback with a weak mortar mix. The mix should be fluid enough to fill all cracks and gaps.

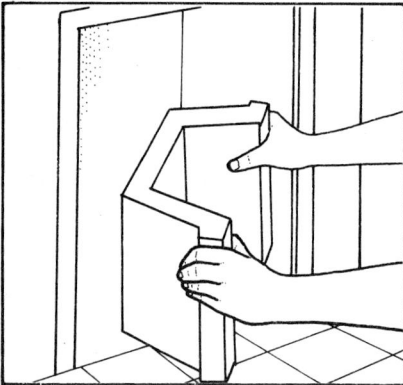

2. Clean out the fireplace thoroughly and fit the lower half of the new fireback. Make sure to check to see that it is square and central.

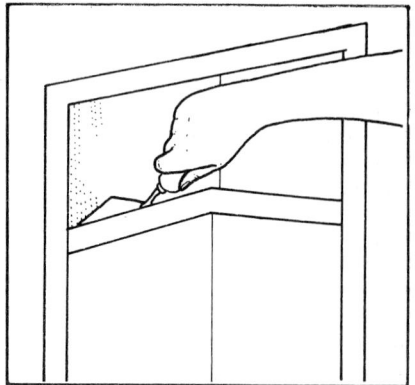

4. Tip the mortar behind the fireback with a trowel and add more until the space is completely filled.

30

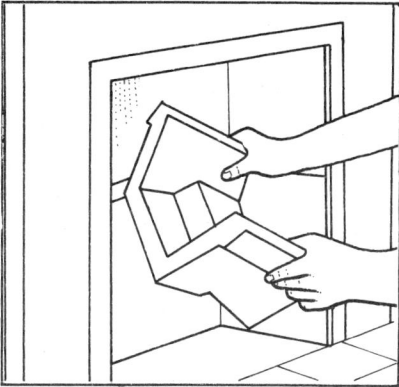

5. Place the top section of the fireback into position. Make sure it is in line with the lower section.

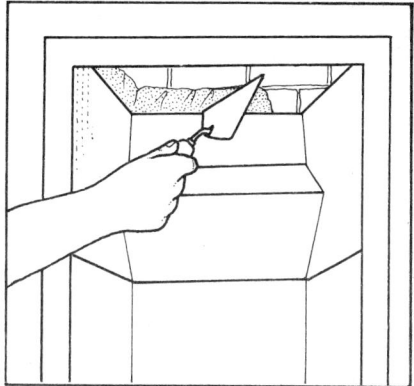

7. When the cavity is filled, seal the fireback top to the brickwork with a cement mix – 1 part cement, 4 parts sand.

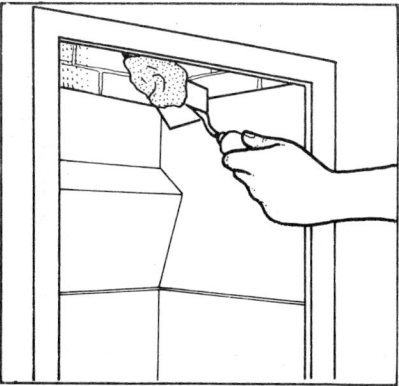

6. As with the bottom section, fill the cavity behind the fireback with a weak mortar mix.

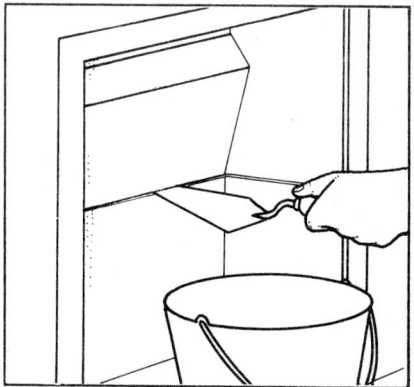

8. Dampen the joint between the two sections with water, fill the joint with plastic fireclay and level the join with a plastic scraper.

Removing a fireplace

You will need: large screwdriver; club hammer; chisel; levering bars (eg) crowbar or car tyre lever

1. A tiled or brick surround is usually fixed to the chimney breast by lugs at the side of the surround. First chisel away all plaster with a bolster chisel.

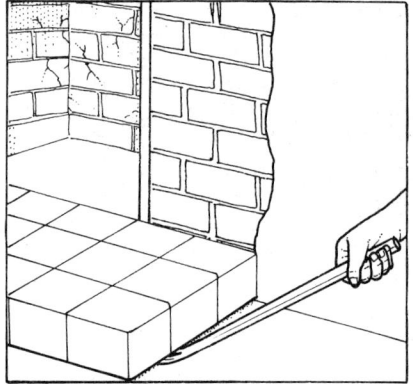

3. Remove the surround in one piece if possible, or break it up into manageable pieces. Use the crowbar to lever up the hearth front.

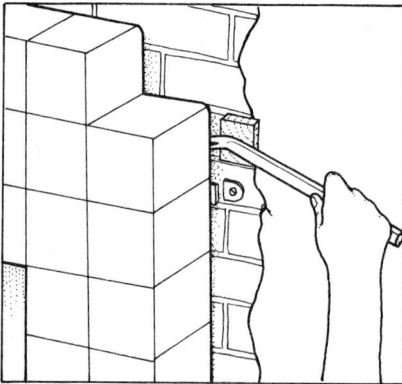

2. When the lugs are revealed, take out the fixing screws. Use a crowbar, (with a block of wood for leverage) to prise away the surround.

4. Remove the fireback (see pp 30-31) if the fireplace is to be left open. Brush down the brickwork and repoint if necessary (see p 158).

Closing a fireplace

You will need: (for bricking up) trowel; mortar; bricks; plaster (for panelling) masonry nails; round nails; timber battens; asbestos sheet; plaster

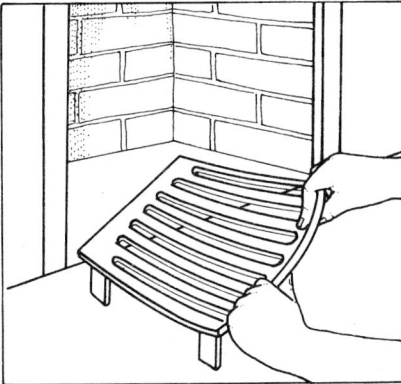

1. Remove the fireplace surround (see opposite page) and the fireback (see pp 30-31). Take out the metal grate.

3. Cut a piece of hardboard or plywood to cover the aperture. Cut out a rectangular section to take a ventilator grille.

2. Cut 2 in × 1 in (50 mm × 25 mm) battens to fit the aperture. Fix the uprights with masonry nails and wedge top and bottom members for a tight fit.

4. Screw or nail the cover to the frame. Glue the grille into the aperture. The ventilator is essential to prevent condensation in the chimney.

Doors

House doors are made in standard sizes; the height is 6 ft 6 in (198 cm) with widths of 2 ft (61 cm), 2 ft 3 in (68.5 cm), 2 ft 6 in (76 cm) and 2 ft 9 in (84 cm) for interior doors. The standard thickness is $1\frac{3}{8}$ in (35 mm). Exterior doors are made in widths of 2 ft 6 in (76 cm) and 2 ft 9 in (84 cm) with a thickness of $1\frac{3}{4}$ in (45 mm).

There are two main types – flush and panelled. Flush doors are used mostly indoors and consist of plywood sheets on a wood frame. Flush doors for exterior use are usually solid wood.

Panelled doors have a solid frame, with inset panels of plywood or glass. There are a number of designs; some have four panels in quarters, some have two panels and others have three or four panels with one, two or three cross rails.

Interior door frames consist of strips of wood inside the doorway, called jambs, onto which $\frac{1}{2}$ in (13 mm) door stops are nailed. The gap between the jamb and the wall is covered by a wooden moulding called an architrave. Exterior door frames are much heavier and more robust. The jambs are fitted with steel lugs which are cemented into the wall, and the top bar of the frame extends into the walls. In cavity walls the jambs fit where the cavity between the outer and inner wall is closed, and a vertical damp-proof course is placed between the walls.

Door hinges are made in steel, brass and aluminium. They are measured by their length and by their width when fully open. A 3 in (75 mm) hinge, 2 in (50 mm) wide, is suitable for most household doors, but larger sizes are available if the door is exceptionally heavy.

The fixed pin is the type of hinge commonly used; it has its two leaves, the opening halves, permanently fixed to the pivot pin. Another type has a loose pin which can be tapped out so that the door can be removed without taking off the hinges.

Even more practical is the lift-off butt hinge which is in two halves, so that the door can be lifted off with one half of the hinge still attached to the door and the other attached to the frame.

The rising butt hinge is also in two halves, with a curved pivot point so that the door rises as it opens. This allows the door to clear fitted carpeting taken right up to to the doorway. This type of hinge also allows the door to be lifted off easily.

Door hinges should be lubricated occasionally with a few drops of light oil. Drop the oil onto the head of the hinge and be ready to wipe off any surplus with a rag. Rising butts should be oiled every month. The friction between hinge and pivot is greater than in a straight hinge and rapid wear will take place if the pivot is allowed to become dry.

Two types of door and a selection of hinges

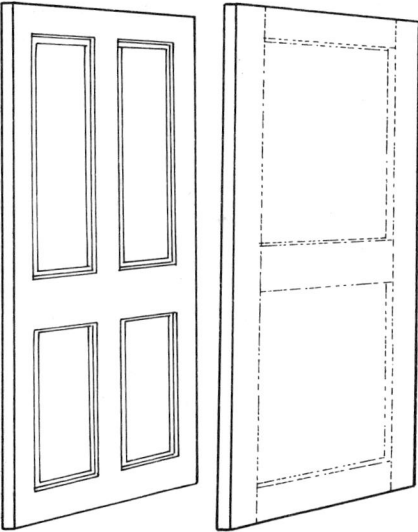

Fixed pin. A standard hinge suitable for most types of interior or exterior door.

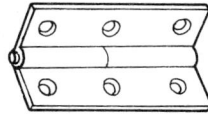

Lift-off butt. The swivel pin is fixed in one half of the hinge, so that the door can be lifted off.

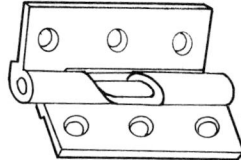

Panel doors have a timber frame with a number of inset panels of plywood or glass.
Flush doors consist of a light timber framework clad with sheets of plywood or hardboard.

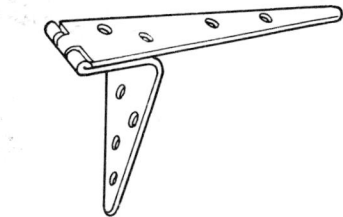

Rising butt. The hinge lifts the door as it opens to clear floor covering.

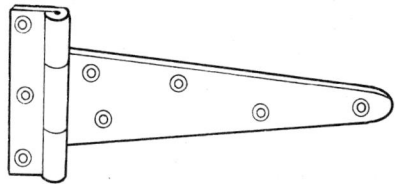

Box hinge. Useful on doors too thin to take a butt hinge.

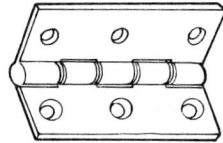

Tee hinge. Used for ledged doors, such as in a garden shed, and for garden gates.

Problems and cures

Most of the problems that occur with doors are easily cured, though usually the door will have to be removed from the frame. This is a simple enough task if the door will lift off from the hinge pivot pin.

Loose hinges cause a door to sag, preventing it from closing properly and throwing the catch and striker plate out of alignment. First rock the door on its hinges to see where the looseness is. It may be that the pivot pins have worn (in which case replace the hinges) or possibly the screws have worked loose. If the screws will not tighten, remove them and plug the holes with a wooden plug — then refit the screws.

When fitting new hinges, make sure they are the same size as the old ones. But there may still be slight discrepancies which will cause a gap either at the hinge side or closing side of the door. In the latter case, pack out the hinges with a piece of card or a thin piece of wood. If the gap is on the hinge side, remove the hinges and deepen the hinge recesses with a wood chisel.

A badly distorted door must be replaced, but slight distortion causing the door to stick can be rectified by planing. Mark the point where the door is fouling the frame — it should be possible to see the rubbing marks on the paintwork — and remove the door. Use a finely set smoothing plane or a surform to shave off a small amount, then rehang the door. If it still sticks, remove more wood — it is better to use this 'trial and error' method than to take off too much wood and leave an unsightly gap.

All doors, however well they fit, have a small gap all the way round which will let in **draughts** — particularly exterior doors. There are a number of excellent draughtproofing methods available; some are designed to fit on the door, others are attached to the frame. One of the most effective is the V-shaped seal, consisting of a sprung-metal strip which adjusts itself to fill the gap when the door is closed. Some V strips can be fixed to the frame with adhesive, others are nailed to the frame with small panel pins. The strip fits all the way around the frame, and the bottom of the door can be fitted with a plastic strip to give 100 per cent draughtproofing.

Draughts beneath exterior doors may be caused by a rotted or badly worn wooden sill. A large, uneven gap is difficult to cover even by fitting a weatherstrip to the bottom of the door; and filling a rotted sill is impracticable because the filler will not stand up to wear and tear. It is better to replace the sill which can be bought from a builders' merchant, or you can make one yourself.

Door locks and latches should be oiled regularly to keep them working well, especially on exterior doors.

Curing a sticking door

You will need: screwdriver; smoothing plane or surform

Curing a sticking door

A door that sticks in its frame can be annoying, and if not cured may result eventually in the door being weakened by continual forcing. There are three principal reasons for a sticking door – each with its own particular remedy.

A common cause is loose or badly fitted hinges. Sometimes all that is required is a few minutes' work with a screwdriver – if the screws will not tighten, remove them and plug the holes with wood dowels and then refit the screws. Badly fitting hinges can be adjusted by packing the recess with thin strips of wood, or by deepening the recess with a wood chisel.

In some cases the door joints may have become loose, causing the door to sag. Remove the door and clean out the joints with a scraper or old kitchen knife, then reglue using PVA adhesive (see pp 184-185). Bind the door with rope or straps to hold the joints firm until the glue has set.

On exterior doors, swelling due to damp may cause sticking, and may occur only during wet weather. To cure bad swelling, plane the door edges down by about $\frac{1}{8}$ in (3 mm) and treat with paint or weather-proof varnish. It may also help to fit a weatherstrip around the door (see p 40).

For slight sticking, try one of the two cures described opposite.

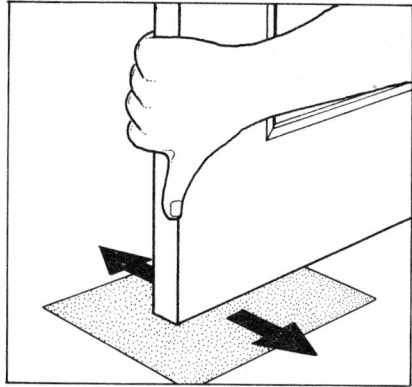

1. If a door binds at the bottom, place a sheet of coarse sandpaper or glasspaper underneath and swing the door across it several times.

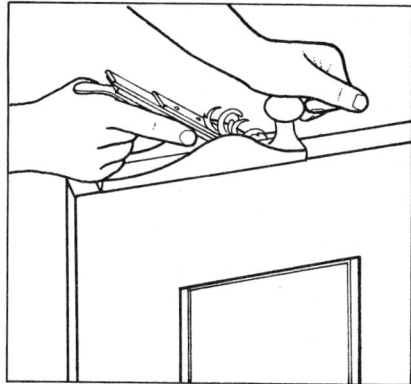

2. If a door binds at the top look for the high spot, where the wood is smooth and shiny, and plane it down.

Hanging a door

You will need: screwdriver; panel saw; plane; wood chisel; hammer; bradawl; hinges; screws; try square

1. Hold the new door against the door frame, on the opening side, and from the other side mark with a pencil line where the door is too high or too wide.

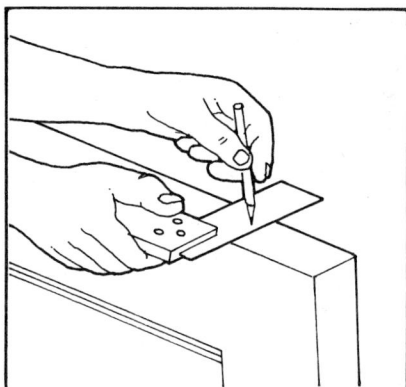

3. Measure where the hinges are to fit and use a try square to mark two lines, the length of the hinge apart.

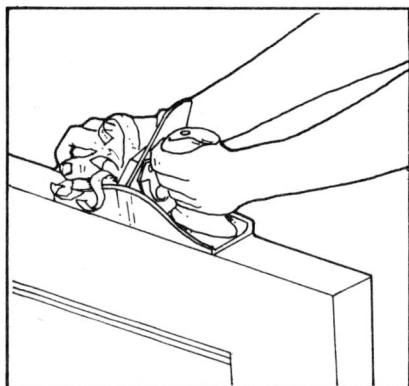

2. Plane down to the pencil lines, or use a saw and finish with a plane if the amount to lose is more than $\frac{1}{2}$ in (13 mm).

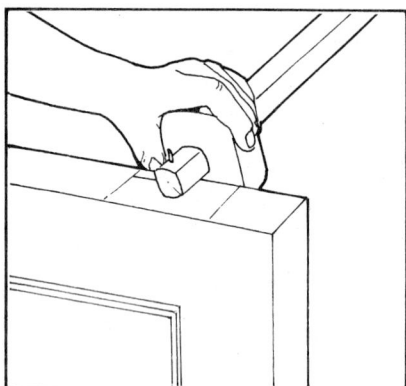

4. Set a marking gauge to the width of the door less the width of the hinge plate and score a deep line from the front (opening) edge of the door.

Handy hint: Door hinge screws may be difficult to remove if they have been in position for a long time. First make sure the slot in the head is absolutely clean, then use a screwdriver that fits the slot exactly. You can get more leverage on a screwdriver by clamping a self-locking wrench onto the shank. Failing this, heat the screwdriver by plunging the blade into boiling water, fit it quickly in the screwhead and hold it there for about 1 minute. The heat will transfer to the screw, which will expand in the wood and should then unscrew easily.

5. Use a 1 in (25 mm) chisel to cut out the hinge recess. Take care not to go below the depth of the hinge plate thickness.

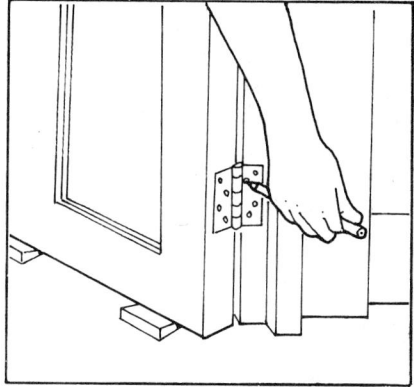

7. Stand the door on two wedges against the door frame and use the wedges to adjust the height. Fit the hinges into the frame recesses and mark the holes.

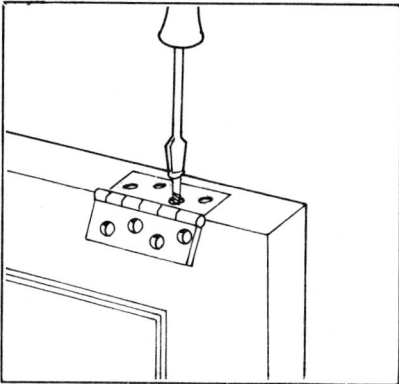

6. Place the hinges in their recesses and fix with one screw through a central hole.

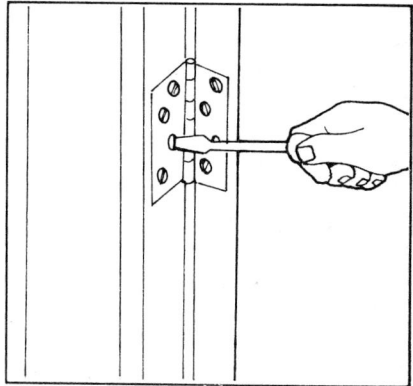

8. With the wedges still in position, screw the hinge to the frame and fit the remaining screws in the door edge.

Draughtproofing a door

You will need: sealing strip; scissors; bradawl; lightweight hammer; pin punch

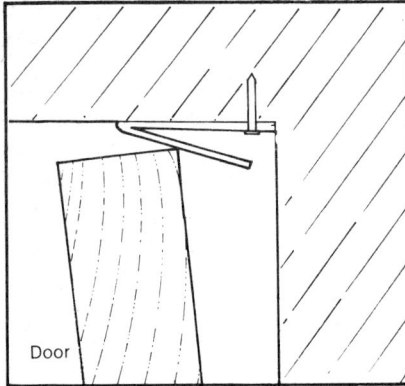

1. A draught excluder consisting of a V-shaped metal strip makes an effective seal on interior or exterior doors.

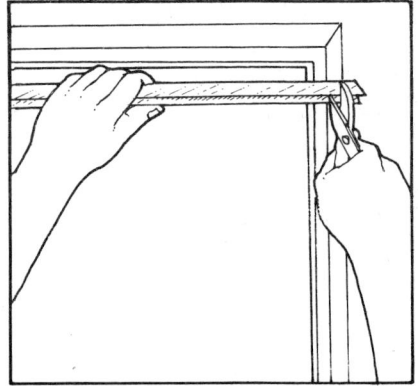

3. Place the strip against the frame and trim its ends so that it fits just inside the frame uprights.

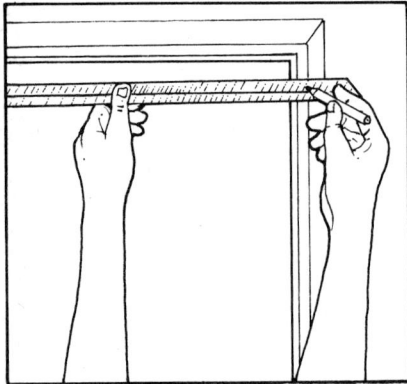

2. Start at the top of the door frame by measuring and cutting a length of seal which is slightly longer than the frame width.

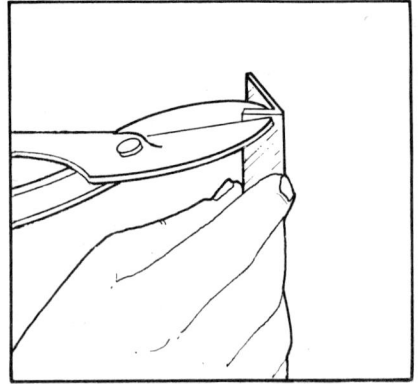

4. Cut the short side of the strip at an angle of 45° at both ends.

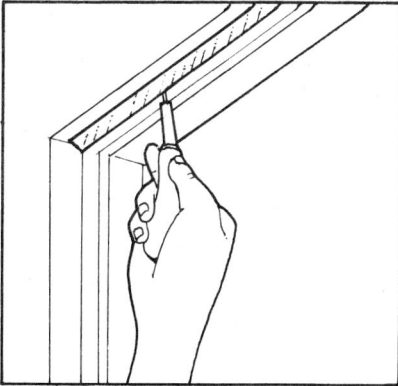

5. Hold the strip under the top frame with its V facing away from the door. Make holes with a bradawl and nail the strip to the frame.

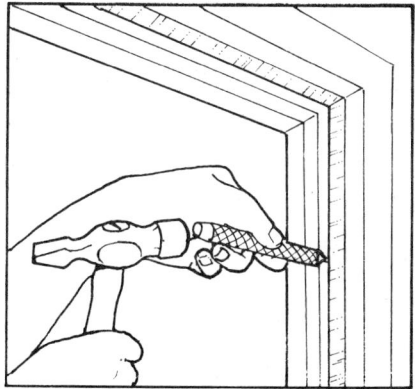

7. Nail the strips to the frame with panel pins placed about every 3 in (75 mm).

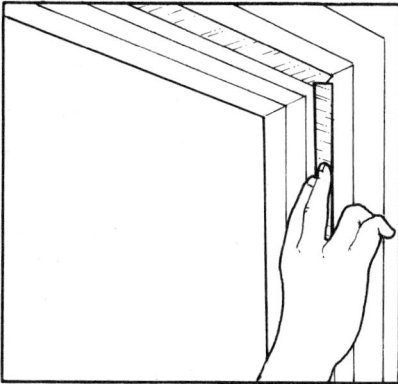

6. Cut and fit the side strips, with their ends cut to butt with the top strip.

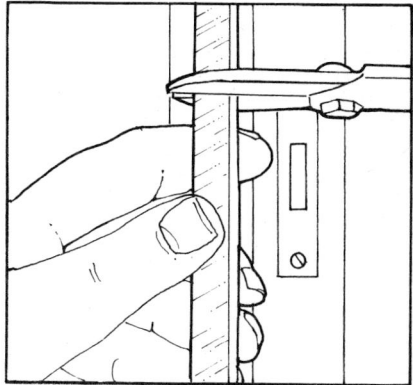

8. At a lock or latch, cut the strip just above it. *(continued)*

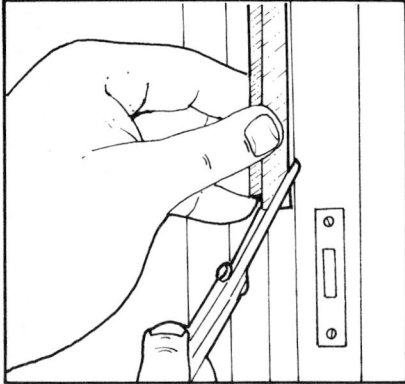

9. Bring the strip to a point by snipping through both sides at an angle.

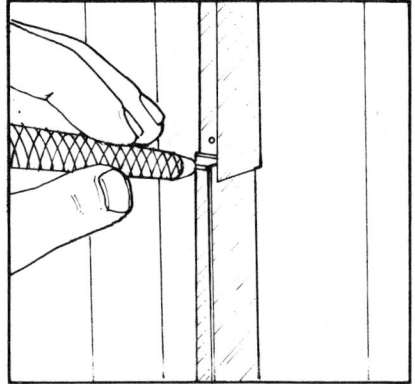

11. To make a join in the strip, overlap the two sections by about $\frac{1}{4}$ in (6 mm).

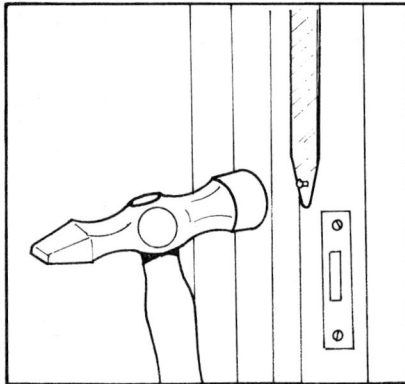

10. Nail the pointed end to the frame, going through both thicknesses of the strip.

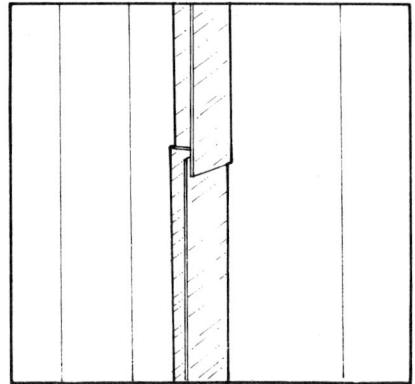

12. Interlock the two pieces and nail through both thicknesses of the long sides of the strips.

Fitting a mortise lock

You will need: screwdriver; hand-drill and $\frac{3}{8}$ in (10 mm) bit; $\frac{1}{2}$ in (13 mm) chisel; hammer; bradawl; padsaw

Handy hint: Where exterior doors are fitted with surface-mounted locks, however, it is a worthwhile investment to replace them with mortise locks, which fit into the door frame and cannot be prised off by an intruder.

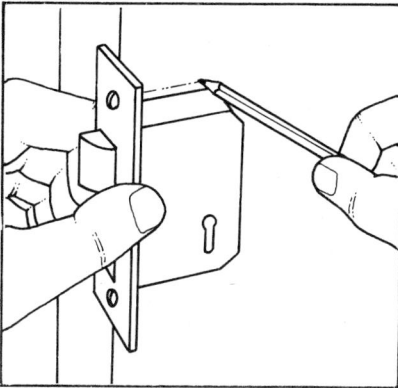

1. A mortise lock fits inside the door framework, so accurate marking and cutting is essential. Start by holding the lock against the door and mark its outline.

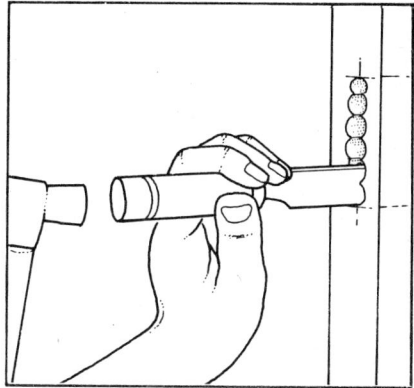

3. Chisel out the recess, taking out the ridges left by the drill, until the lock will fit snugly in the door.

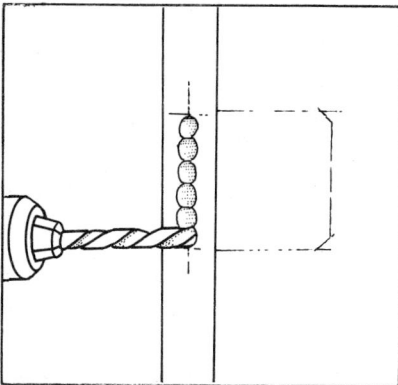

2. Mark a line down the centre of the door edge. Pencil in the height of the lock body. Drill holes along the centre line, to the depth of the lock.

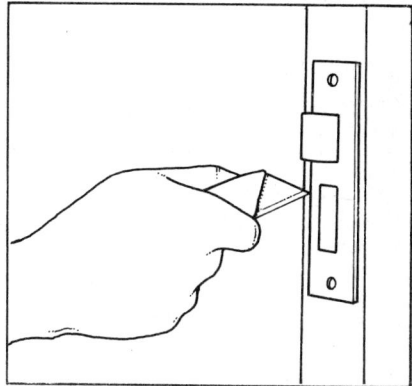

4. With the lock in the recess, mark around the face plate with a trimming knife. *(continued)*

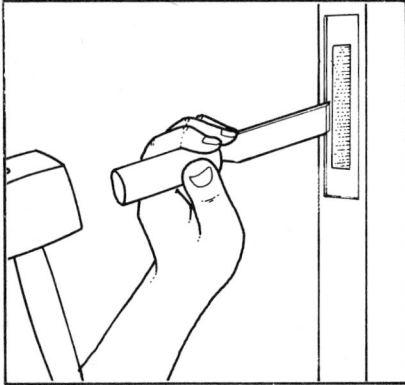

5. Remove the lock and chisel out the recess for the face plate, inside the marked outline.

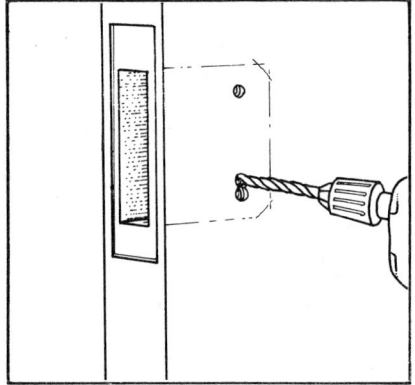

7. Drill the holes to the required diameter. Draw in the bottom part of the keyhole.

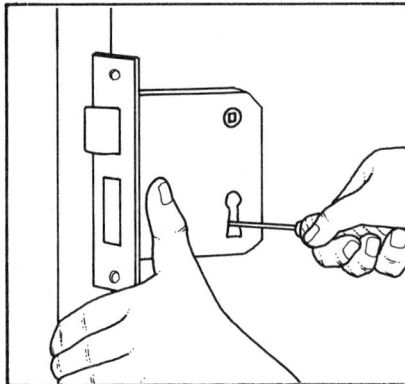

6. Hold the lock against the outside of the door again, lining up with the previously marked outline, and mark the key and spindle holes with a bradawl.

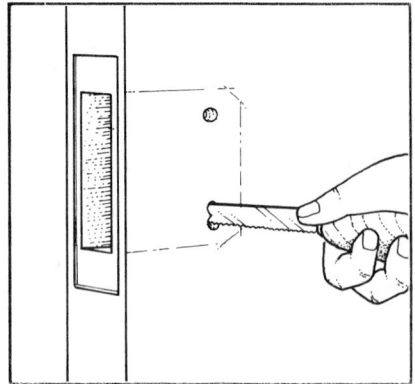

8. Use a small padsaw to cut out the keyhole shape. Work from both sides of the door alternately to ensure matching shapes.

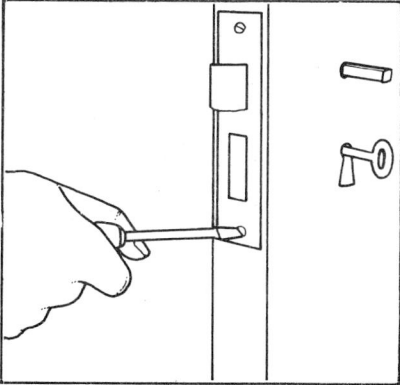

9. Put the lock back into the recess and locate it by inserting the spindle and key. Screw the face plate to the door.

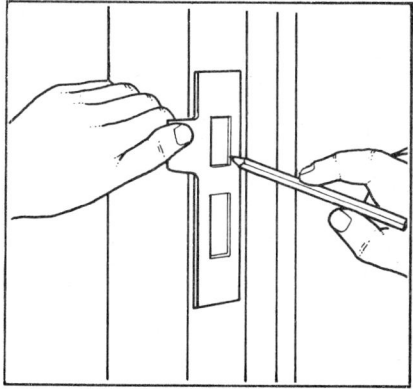

11. Hold the striker plate against the door frame, in line with the bolt and latch marks, and mark inside the cut-outs.

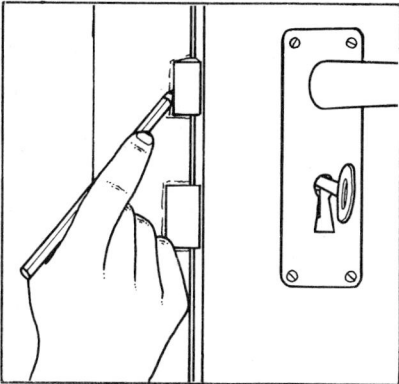

10. Fit the door levers and lever plates. Turn the key so that the bolt protrudes and mark the outlines of the bolt and latch on the door frame.

12. With a $\frac{1}{2}$ in (13 mm) chisel, cut out recesses for the latch and bolt. Start the fixing holes with a bradawl and screw the plate to the frame.

Fitting new hinges

You will need: screwdriver; panel saw; plane; hammer; chisel; bradawl

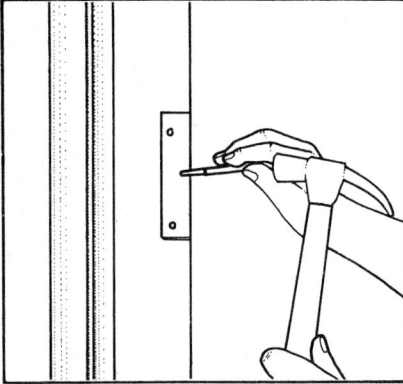

1. If the new hinges are larger than the old ones, or of a different type, fill the screw holes in the door and frame with small dowel pegs.

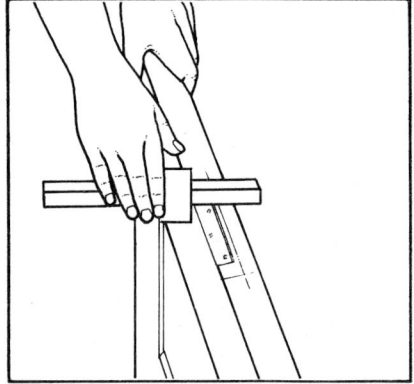

3. Set a marking gauge to the width of the hinge plate and score a deep line in the door edge. Score also the end marks.

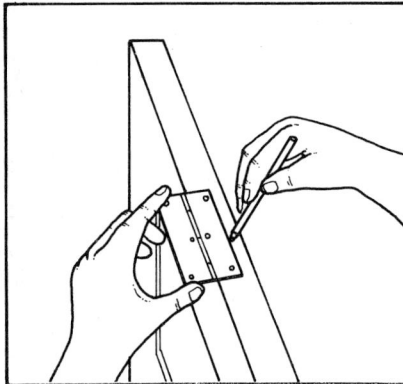

2. Hold the new hinge plate against the door, covering the old position, and mark the outlines with a pencil.

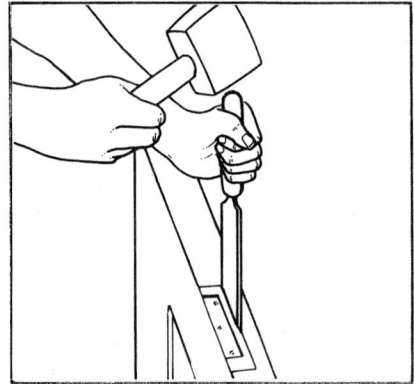

4. Chisel out the recess, working just inside the scored line, to the depth of the hinge thickness. Then lightly chisel along the score lines so that the hinge fits snugly.

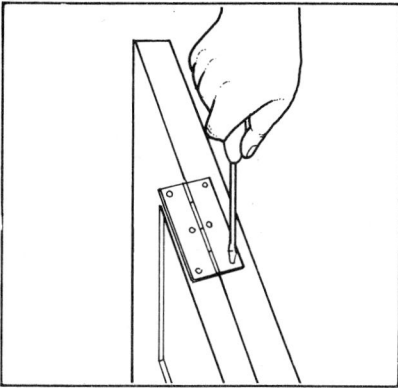

5. Fit the hinge plate into the recess and screw on the hinge plate. Repeat 1 to 5 for the other hinge.

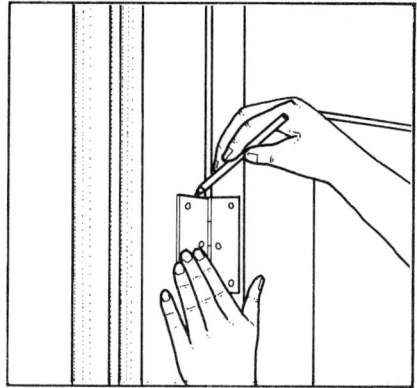

7. Hold the hinge plates against the frame and mark the outlines with a pencil. Remove the door and chisel out the recesses.

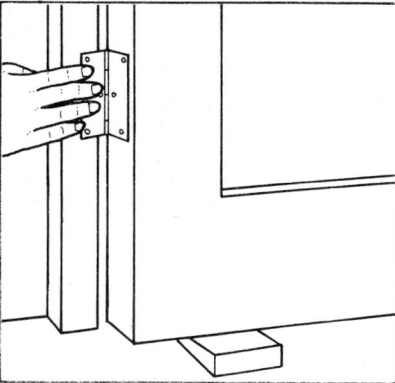

6. Slide wedges under the door, in the open position, and adjust the height to correspond with the old hinge positions in the door frame.

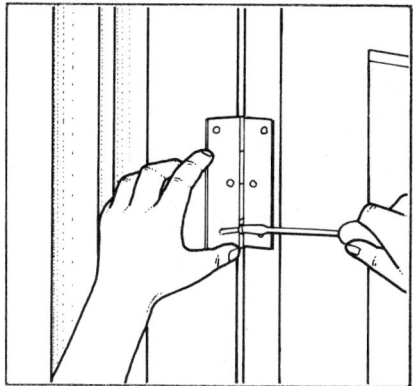

8. Position the door again, as before, and fit the hinges. Tighten the screws fully before removing the wedges under the door.

Painting a panelled door

Replacing a sill

You will need: rule; plane; hammer; chisel; panel saw

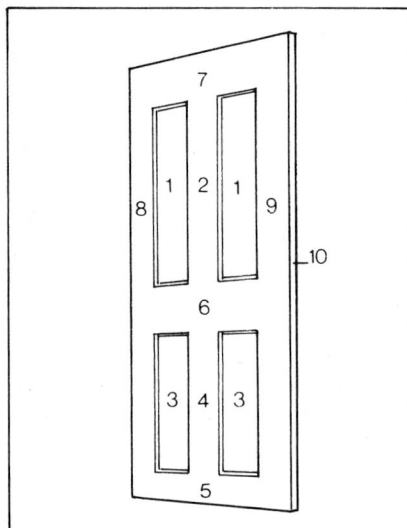

1. A worn or damaged timber sill can be replaced with a piece of hardwood cut and shaped to fit.

The numbered illustration shows the best sequence for obtaining a professional finish. Start by painting the door frame, with the door open. Lay newspaper under the door and hold it firm with a V-shaped wedge.

Paint with long, even strokes, along the length of each section; ie, up and down on panels and vertical frames, crosswise on top, bottom and middle rails. Overlap the joins, but do not overbrush especially if you are using a non-drip paint.

Leave the door wedged open until the paint is thoroughly dry. Drying time will depend on room temperature and the type of paint.

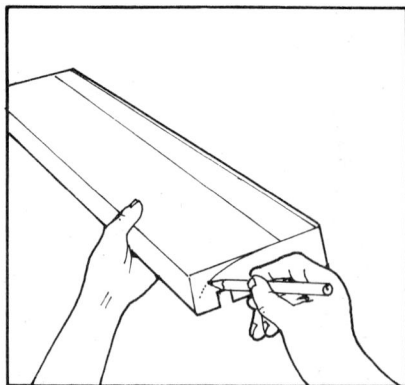

2. Cut the timber to length. With a plough plane cut a drip groove along the underside, about $\frac{1}{2}$ in (13 mm) from the front edge. Then mark the outlines for the sloping front.

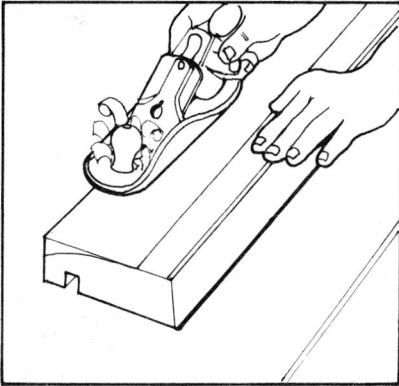

3. Plane evenly along the front edge, down to the slope outlines. Finish off with a rasp or shaping tool to get a smooth, rounded edge.

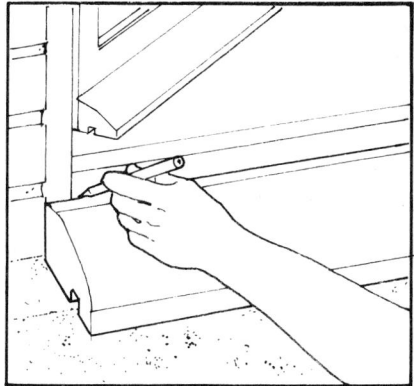

5. Offer up the new sill to the door frame and mark the positions of the frame on the sill.

4. Remove the old sill with a wood chisel. If the frame is jointed to the sill, cut through the join with a panel saw.

6. Cut recesses in the sill to the depth of the frame. Use a block of wood to protect the new sill and hammer it into position. Apply two coats of wood preservative.

Drains and gutters

The drainage system in a house serves two purposes – to dispose of waste water from sinks and the bath and to take away the used water from the WC. In prewar houses two main downpipes are used, one for each function. This is known as the two-stack system. It is easily recognizable by the two large-diameter pipes outside the houses. The soil pipe extends above the roof eaves and its bottom end goes into the ground to connect with the main drainage system. The waste pipe from the WC comes out through the wall and feeds into the soil pipe.

The pipe carrying water from the sinks starts just below the level of the bathroom and has a hopper at its head. This is a wide, funnel-shaped opening into which the waste pipes from the bath and bathroom basin feed. At its bottom end the down pipe feeds into an open gully, as does the waste pipe from the kitchen sink. The waste from a plumbed-in washing machine and/or dishwasher also goes into this gully.

The main problem with the two-stack system is that it is prone to blockage in the hopper and in the gully, usually through a build-up of fallen leaves or by waste or human hair washed down the sink.

A cover cut to shape from a piece of wood or metal will give protection against fallen leaves, but both gully and hopper should often be cleared by hand to prevent overflowing.

Modern houses use only one downpipe – the single-stack system. The pipe extends above the eaves and goes into the ground, as does the soil pipe on a two-stack system, but waste water is also fed into the pipe. There is no open gully and no hopper head. Waste pipes into a single-stack are very carefully angled so that they do not cause siphonage of soiled water, which could be drawn up and overflow into a sink, basin or bath.

Close to your house there is a manhole cover which gives access to the main drainage system. This should always be kept clear in case a blockage occurs between the points where waste leaves the house and enters the main drain. Such blockages can be cleared by 'rodding'. A series of flexible rods are screwed together and pushed along the underground drainpipe. The first section has a corkscrew head and twisting the rod picks up the material causing the blockage.

You may be able to hire rods from a hire shop, but usually clearing a blocked drain is an emergency operation. You should contact either the sanitation department of your local authority or a specialist firm that deals with drain clearance.

Blockages are the householder's responsibility up to the point where the drain enters the main sewer, so easy access to the inspection chamber at all times is important.

How drains work

Two-stack system. Most houses built before the 1950s have this system, which employs one stack-pipe for the waste water and one for lavatories.

Single-stack system. A single stack-pipe serves all the drainage requirements. The stack-pipe is usually within the house, with only the vent pipe protruding above the roof eaves.

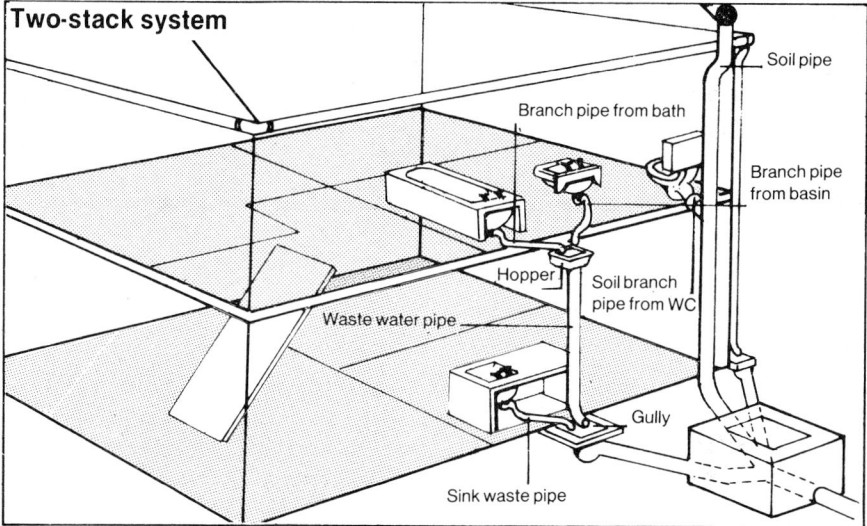

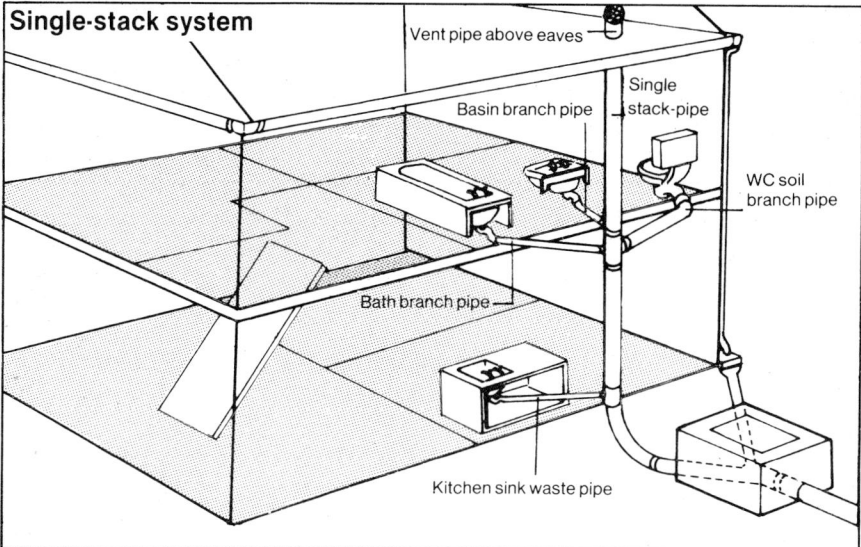

Two-stack system

Soil pipe

Branch pipe from bath

Branch pipe from basin

Hopper

Soil branch pipe from WC

Waste water pipe

Gully

Sink waste pipe

Single-stack system

Vent pipe above eaves

Single stack-pipe

Basin branch pipe

WC soil branch pipe

Bath branch pipe

Kitchen sink waste pipe

Clearing a blocked drain

You will need: flexible rods

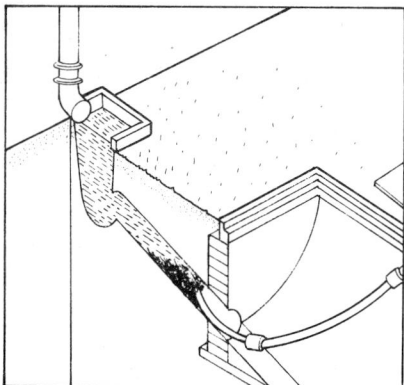

1. Use flexible rods and attachments, which can be hired. Lift the inspection cover; assemble the rods with a corkscrew head at one end. Push the rods into the drain.

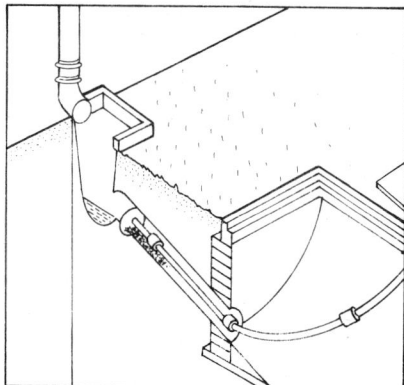

3. Push the plunger along the drain as far as it will go. Pull the rods back to remove the loose material in the pipe.

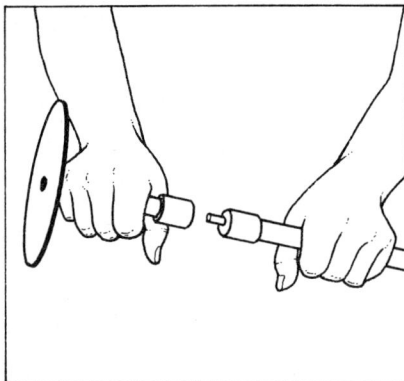

2. Twist the rods clockwise, pushing at the same time. The corkscrew will loosen the blocking material. Withdraw the rods and fit a plunger head.

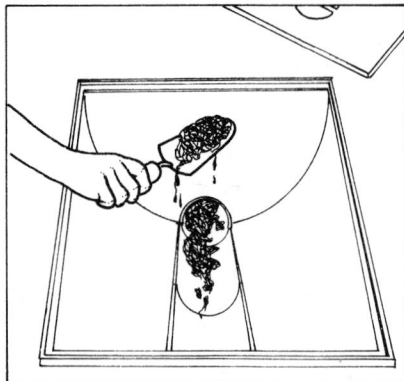

4. Scoop out the rubbish from the channel. Insert a hosepipe into the gully end and flush out the drain with clean water.

Fitting plastic gutters and downpipes

You will need: plastic guttering and brackets; solvent weld cement; 1 in (25 mm) No 8 countersunk screws; screwdriver; hacksaw; spirit level; flexible steel rule

Gutters and downpipes

Rainwater drainage from the roof is carried by gutters mounted on boards – called fascia boards – and downpipes placed at intervals which lead either to the main drainage system or to a soakaway. On older houses, all the gutters and downpipes were made of cast-iron which corrodes badly if not fully protected by a good coat of weatherproof paint. The downpipes are particularly vulnerable because of their closeness to the wall.

Most modern houses have plastic gutters and downpipes, and these are a worthwhile and easy-to-fit replacement once cast-iron fitments get beyond maintenance or repair. When replacing guttering it is important to remember that there must be a fall, or slope, towards the downpipe. This should be at least 1 in (25 mm) in every 10 ft (305 cm). Gutters and downpipes should be maintained regularly. On cast-iron systems inspect and paint if necessary every spring. Use a mirror to look for holes behind the downpipes. Clear the guttering of leaves and debris with a stiff brush and scoop it out – **do not brush it into the downpipe** as this may cause a blockage that will be difficult to clear.

If possible, use scaffolding when working on gutters. It is safer than using a ladder and makes the work easier. If you use a ladder, take care not to risk a fall by overstretching.

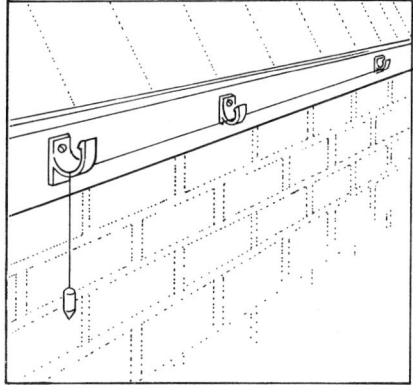

1. Remove old guttering and fit plastic brackets at 2 ft (61 cm) intervals. Use a plumbline to measure the slope, which should be 1 in (25 mm) per 10 ft (305 cm) of guttering.

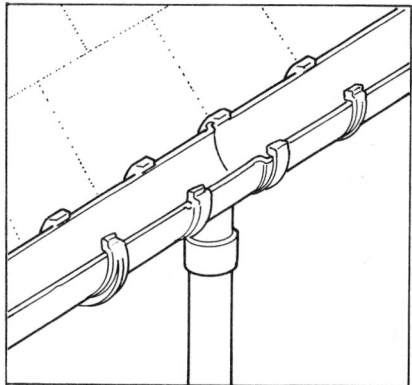

2. Fit extra brackets where there is a downpipe. One on either side of the join. *(continued)*

53

Drains and gutters

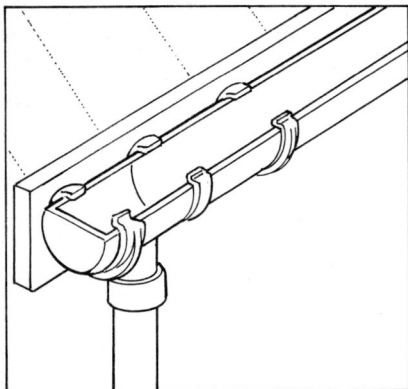

3. At the end of the guttering fit a stop-end, which should also be supported with its own bracket.

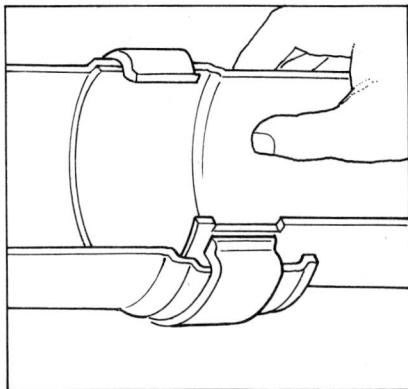

5. Slide the next section of gutter into position, so that its back notch is under the clip.

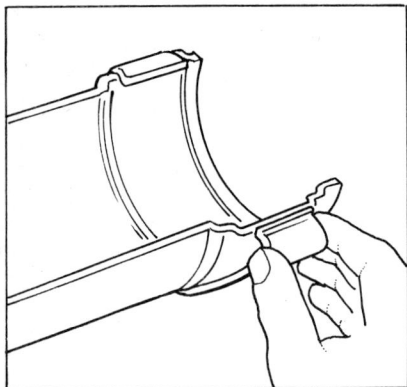

4. To make a joint, fasten a union clip round the socket end of the guttering and clip it into one of the notches.

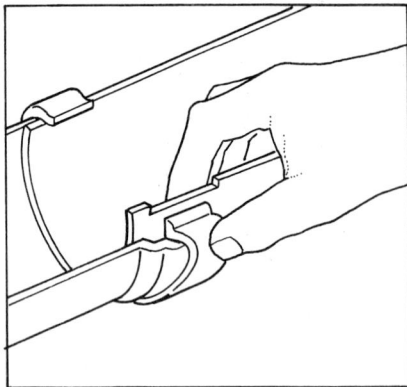

6. Pull the front edge of the gutter down so that it snaps under the front edge of the clip.

54

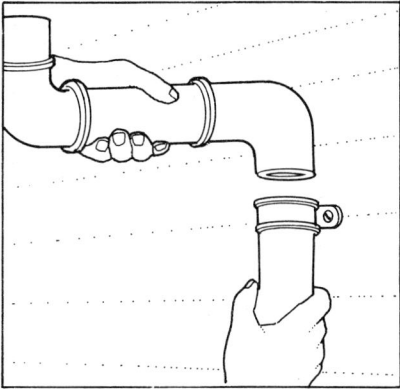

7. Where required, fit a downpipe. If the pipe is not directly underneath the gutter, fit a swan-neck and push its ends over the gutter outlet into the downpipe.

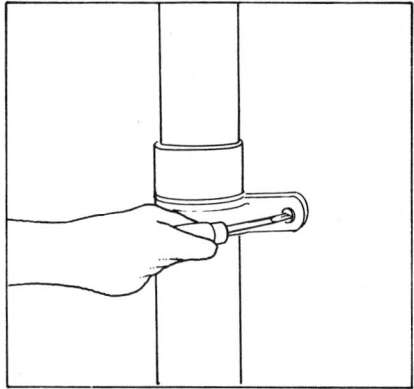

9. Screw the brackets to the wall, using wooden plugs or proprietary wall plugs and $1\frac{1}{2}$ in (37 mm) long screws. Do not tighten the screws yet.

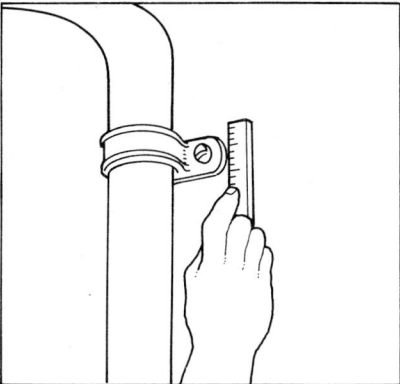

8. Line up the downpipe bracket so the holes coincide with a mortar joint. If necessary cut the bottom end of the swan-neck to raise the bracket position.

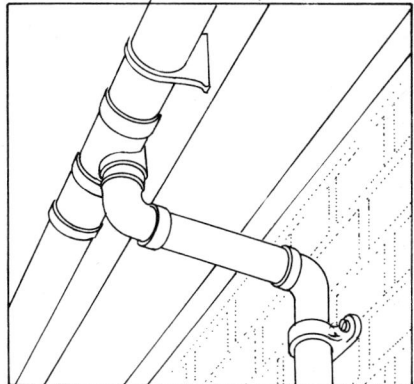

10. When all the brackets are fitted (there should be one at every join) check that the pipe and swan-neck are aligned and tighten the screws.

Fixing a loose downpipe

You will need: wood plugs; hacksaw;
claw hammer; masonry drill bit and power drill;
galvanized screws or nails

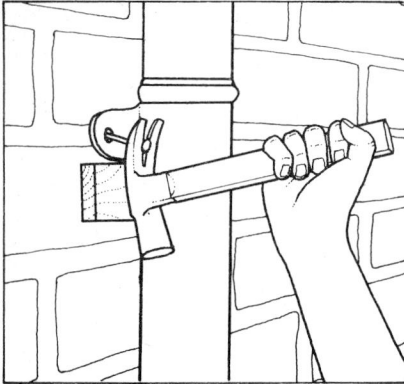

1. If a downpipe bracket has worked loose, first lever out the nails with a claw hammer. Use a piece of wood behind the pipe to give the hammer leverage.

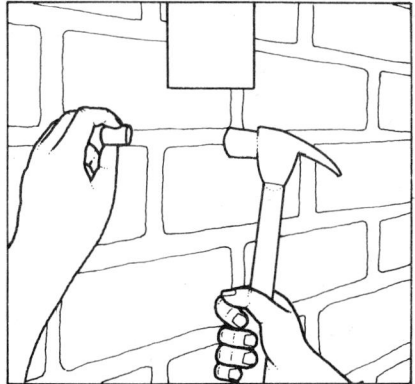

3. Make two tapered plugs from softwood dowelling and hammer them into the holes.

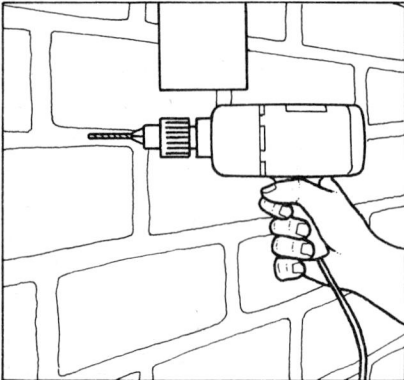

2. Remove the bracket and pipe. Enlarge the fixing holes to about $\frac{1}{2}$ in (13 mm) diameter and 2 in (50 mm) deep.

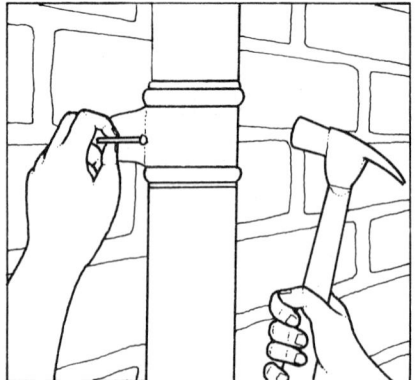

4. Drive the plugs home until they are flush with the wall, or cut off protruding ends with a coping saw. Refit the pipe and bracket using 2 in (50 mm) clout nails.

Repairing a joint in a cast-iron gutter

You will need: galvanized bolt and nut; paintbrush bitumen paint; screwdriver; putty knife; spanner; bitumen paint; mastic

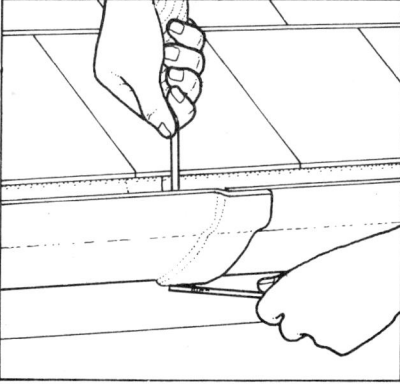

1. A single bolt holds the two sections together firmly. Hold the nut with a spanner or self-locking grips and undo the screw with a screwdriver.

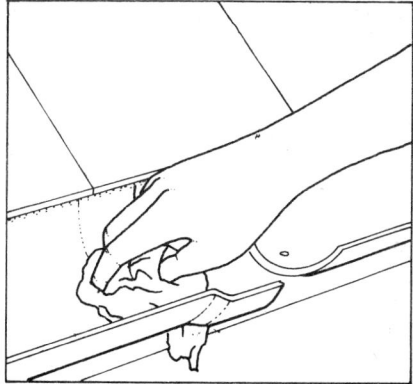

3. Rejoin the two sections, making sure that the sealant completely fills the gap between them.

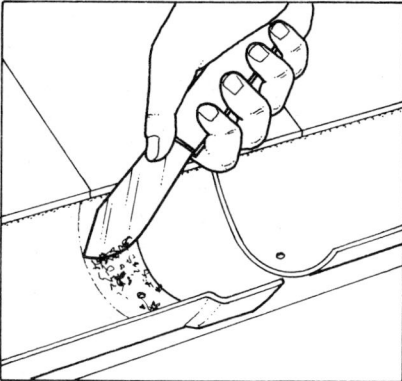

2. Scrape out the old putty used to seal the joint and replace it with a proprietary mastic sealant.

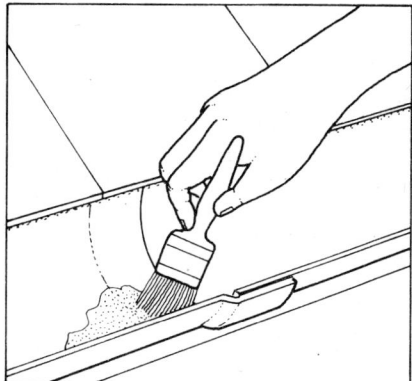

4. Line up the two holes and fit a new screw and nut. Paint inside and outside the gutter with black bituminous paint.

Electricity

Electricity is supplied to a house by a pair of wires coming from the supply generated at the power station. Inside the house there is a sealed fusebox and a meter which records the amount of current consumed. **These should not be tampered with by the householder**.

The house may be wired in one of several ways, depending on the age of the installation, and each installation usually consists of four circuits — two for power and two for lighting.

In modern houses the power circuit starts at a fusebox, which is accessible to the householder, and runs around the house in a continuous loop and back to the fusebox. This is called the ring-main system and there are usually two separate rings, one for each floor of the house. At intervals along the ring there are socket outlets, the power points found in most rooms in the house except the bathroom. Each point has three socket holes designed to take flat-pin plugs and is rated at 13 amps.

Because it has to supply appliances that consume a heavy current, the power wiring is rated higher than the lighting circuit. Its wires are thicker and each ring is protected by a 30 amp fuse in the fusebox. It is important to know which fuse protects which ring so that you can replace a blown fuse quickly.

Appliances designed to plug in to the power circuit should always be fitted with a fused plug, and with a fuse of the correct rating — 3, 5, 10 and 13 amp being the most common. Always check the fuse rating of an appliance before fitting a plug or replacing its fuse. The rating may be marked on the appliance. **If in doubt consult a dealer**.

Some typical ratings are:

13 amp: Electric kettle; 3 kW fire; vacuum cleaner; washing machine.
5 amp; colour TV.
3 amp: Electric blanket; extractor fan; power tools; radio; record player; black and white TV.

Never connect to the lighting circuit an appliance intended to be plugged into the power circuit — the wires will overheat and could easily start a fire (see pp 70-71).

The lighting circuit has only a 5 amp fuse in the fusebox, and again there are usually separate circuits for each floor of the house. The lighting circuit in a modern house is called the loop-in system. Cables run from the fusebox to a ceiling rose which has four terminals; the live, neutral and earth leads each go to a separate terminal and a lead from the live terminal goes to the light switch, from the other side of which a lead runs back to the fourth terminal.

The twin wires in the flex to the lampholder are connected to the live and neutral terminals in the ceiling rose. The cables for the next rose in the chain are taken from the live, neutral and earth terminals, and so on until the final fitting is reached.

Houses built prewar had two different systems for power and lighting circuits, and if your house has either of these it is long overdue for rewiring. The power circuit was known as the radial system, in which cables radiated from the fusebox to each socket outlet. The outlets had round sockets and the round-pin plugs were not fused. This type of layout is easy to identify, by the number of fuses in the box and by the round-pin sockets.

The lighting circuit had a junction box layout, and in fact this method continued until the 1960s. Two wires, one live, one neutral, run from the fusebox to junction boxes mounted on the ceiling joists. A lead from the live terminal in the junction box goes to the light switch, and a lead from the other side of the switch returns to the live terminal. There are two terminals in the ceiling rose, connected by cables to the live and neutral terminals in the junction box, to which the lampholder twin flex is wired. This system is easily identified by the junction boxes on the ceiling joists.

One reason why a house with the old type of circuits should be rewired is that the cables were rubber insulated. In time the rubber perishes and the insulation breaks down. Modern wiring is insulated by PVC sheathing

which can easily be identified by its colour – grey – and flat shape. Fuses in the older circuits consisted of a length of bare wire connected to terminals in a porcelain holder. Modern fuses are of the cartridge type which clip into the fuseholder.

Major repairs or alterations to an electricity circuit should always be entrusted to a qualified electrician. But there are some jobs which can be tackled safely by the householder; for example replacing a broken socket outlet, switch or ceiling rose or fitting new twin flex.

Before attempting such work make sure that the supply is turned off.

Some appliances can be repaired by the handyman, and fitting a plug is a simple task providing certain rules are followed. There is a colour coding for flexible cables which is standard throughout Europe and in most parts of the world. The live wire is coloured brown, the neutral wire blue and the earth wire yellow and green. Old type flexible cable was coloured red for live, black for neutral and green for earth. If you have an appliance with wires to the old coding the cable should be replaced.

When replacing flexible cable, make sure it is the correct rating for the appliance; 10 amps for loads of up to 2400 watts; 15 amps for up to 3000 watts and 25 amps for up to 6000 watts.

How a house is wired

Radial circuit In many prewar and early postwar houses the power circuit consists of cables radiating from the fusebox to each socket.

Ring mains circuit The more modern ring main has a continuous circuit serving all sockets. There is usually a separate circuit for each floor.

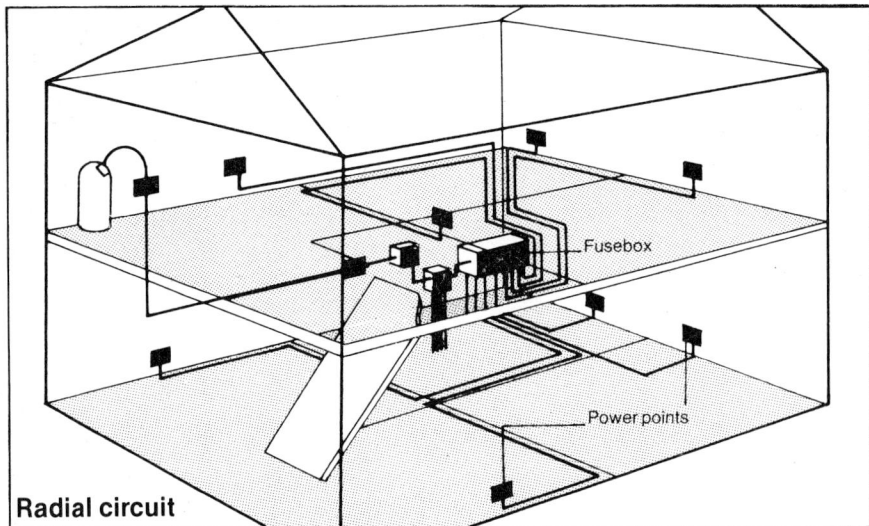

Fusebox

Power points

Radial circuit

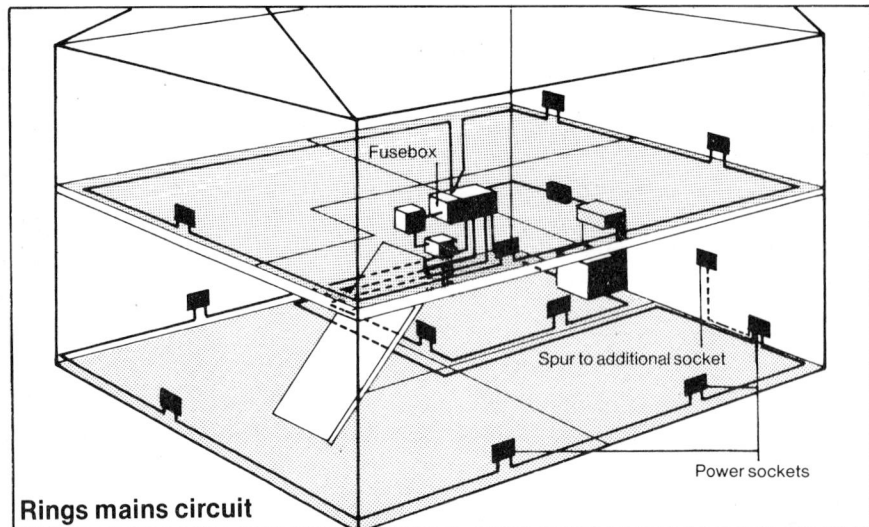

Fusebox

Spur to additional socket

Power sockets

Rings mains circuit

Junction box wiring In older houses the lighting circuit has junction boxes fitted to the joists. Each junction box serves one light fitting.

Loop-in wiring Modern houses have a continuous circuit for each floor and the light fittings are 'looped in' to it.

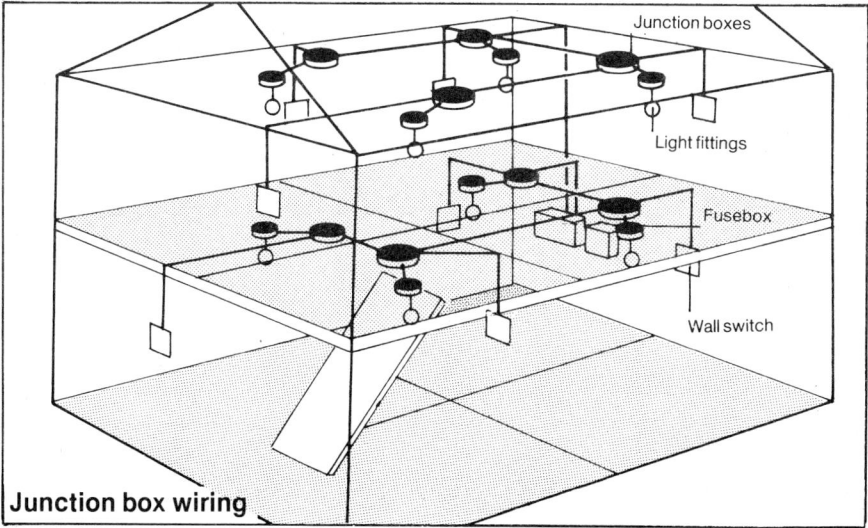

Junction boxes

Light fittings

Fusebox

Wall switch

Junction box wiring

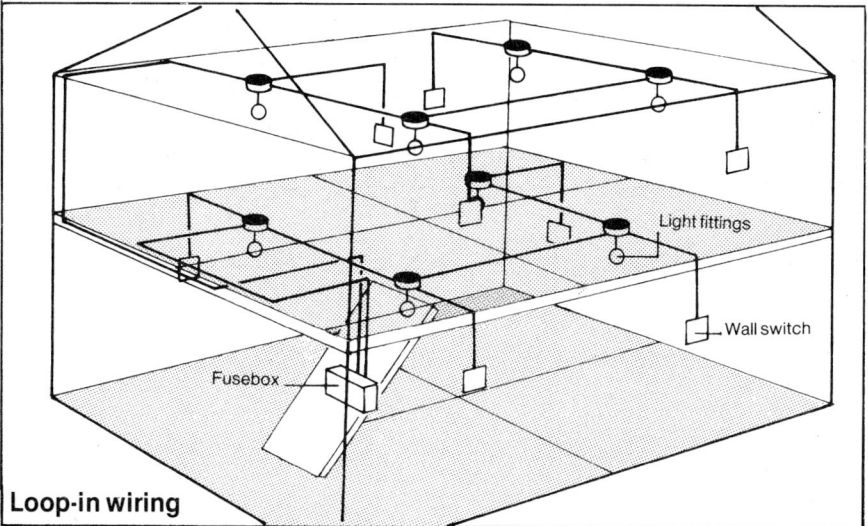

Light fittings

Wall switch

Fusebox

Loop·in wiring

A fusebox and two types of fuse

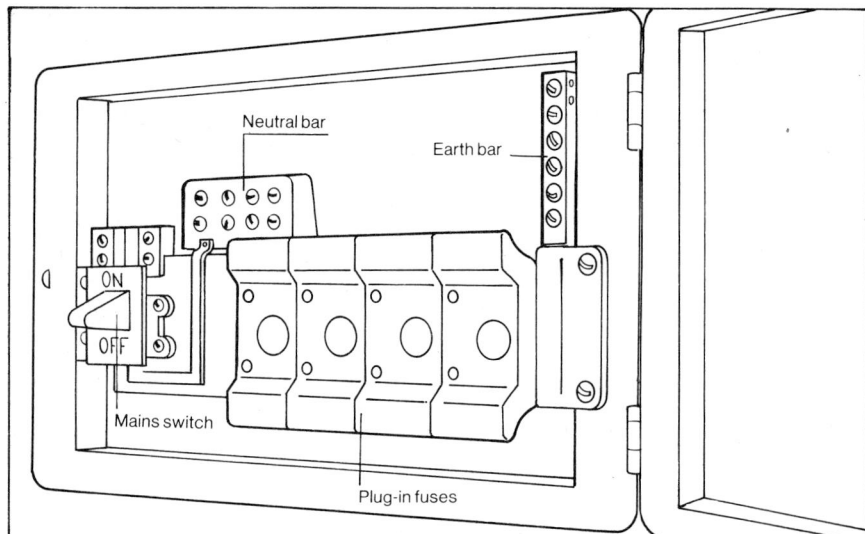

Neutral bar

Earth bar

ON

OFF

Mains switch

Plug-in fuses

A typical fusebox for ring main and loop-in wiring In a modern fusebox there will probably be at least four fuses, as shown – two for the lighting circuits and two for the power circuits. There may be additional fuses for an electric cooker or an extension to the house. All the neutral wires are taken to a terminal bar and the earth wires are taken to a similar bar. The mains switch cuts off both lighting and power supplies.

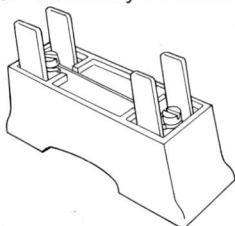

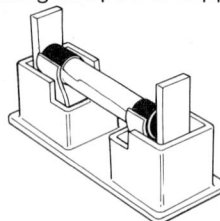

1. In this type a thin wire is connected between terminals attached to the fuse plug pins. If the circuit is overloaded the wire melts and breaks the circuit.

2. A cartridge fuse clips into the fuse holder and can be quickly replaced. Unlike fuse wire, it is not always possible to see if it has 'blown'.

Changing a wire fuse

You will need: small screwdriver; fuse wire

Changing a cartridge fuse

You will need: small screwdriver; cartridge fuse

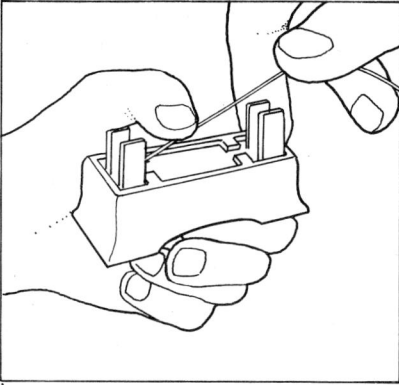

1. Switch off the power supply.
Remove the fuse from the holder in the fusebox and disconnect the ends of the fused wire.

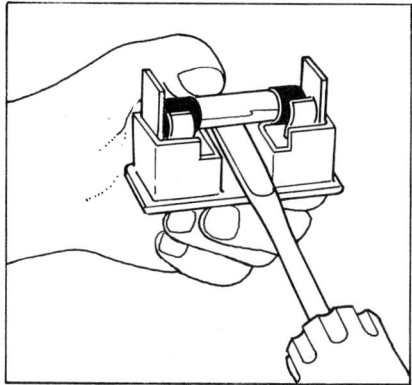

1. Switch off the power supply.
Remove the fuse from the fusebox and lever out the blown fuse with a small screwdriver.

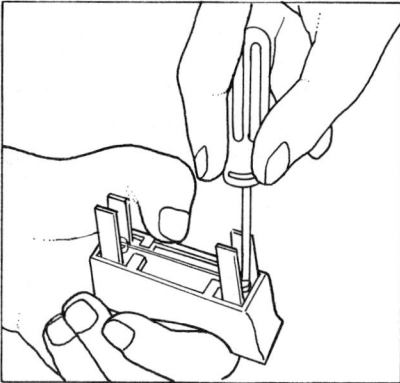

2. Choose a length of fuse wire of the correct rating and lay it across the fuse bridge. Insert the ends into the terminals. Tighten the screws.

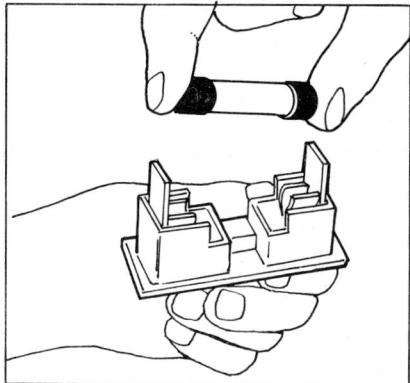

2. Use a cartridge fuse of the correct rating, marked on the fuse body. Press the cartridge into the clips, so that the metal caps are in contact with the clips.

Fitting a fluorescent light

You will need: small screwdriver; toggle screws; three-core flex

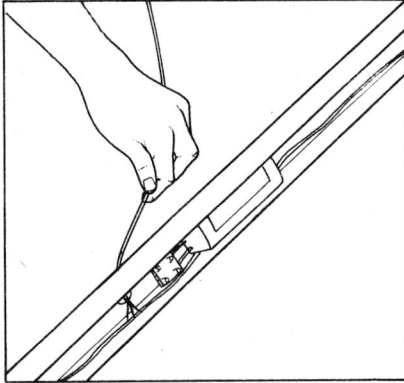

1. Remove the cover on the light fitting. Insert a three-core flex (6 amp rating) through the hole in the top of the box. **Ensure there is a rubber grommet in the hole to prevent the flex chafing.**

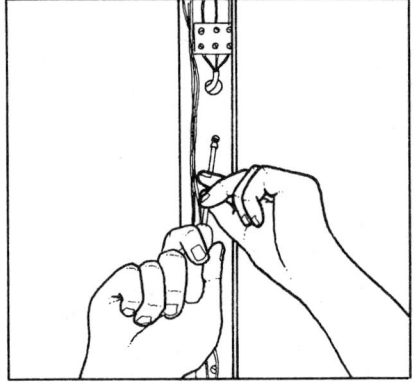

3. Mark off the fixing holes and screw the fitting direct to the ceiling. Try to screw into a joist, or use toggle screws (see p 213).

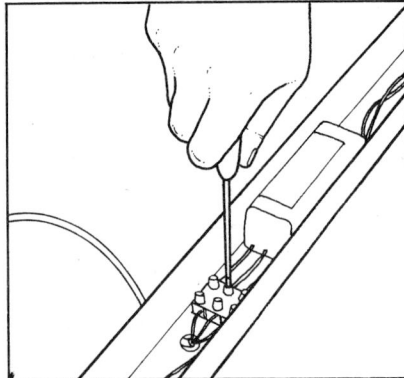

2. Connect the flex to the terminal connector – brown to live, blue to neutral, green/yellow to earth.

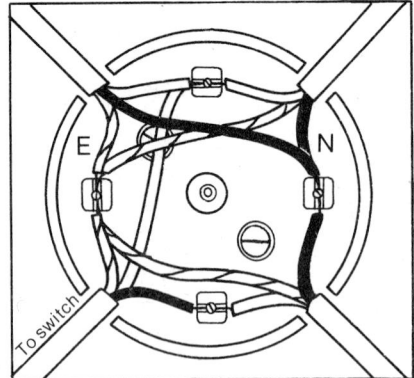

4. The light can be wired direct to a ceiling rose. Otherwise fit a 4-way junction box in the wiring above the ceiling and wire in the light as shown.

Replacing a switch

You will need: small screwdriver; switch

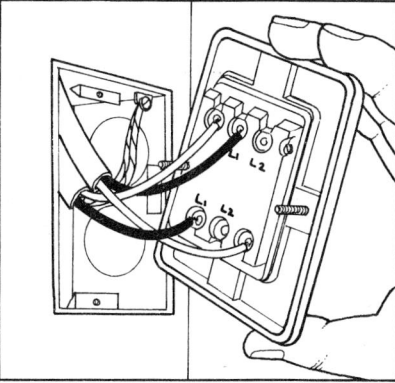

1. Unscrew the switch plate and pull it away from the matrix box. If it is a double switch, note carefully where the wires go.

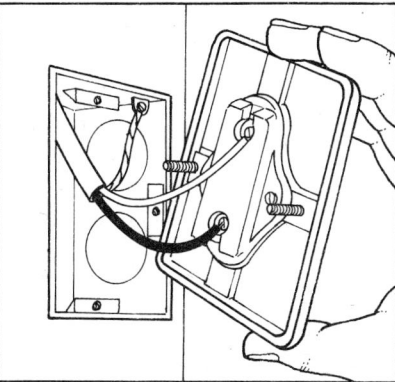

2. On a single switch the red and black wires are connected to the terminals. The earth wire is connected to the metal matrix box.

Replacing a socket

You will need: small screwdriver; socket

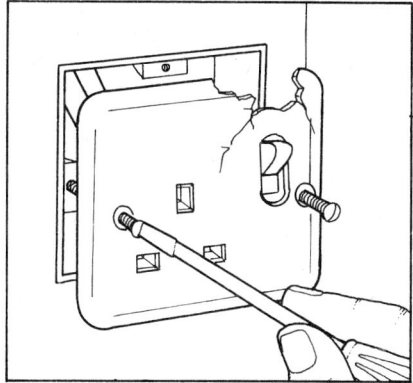

1. **Switch off the power supply.** Undo the two screws holding the socket plate to the matrix box.

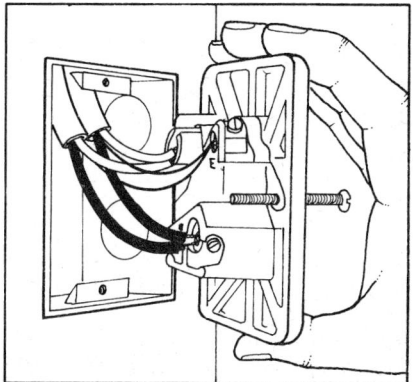

2. Note the positions of the wires – red to the L terminal, black to N and green to E. Unscrew the terminals and wire the new socket in the same way.

Replacing a plug

You will need: small screwdriver; plug

Replacing a light fitting

You will need: small screwdriver; lampholder

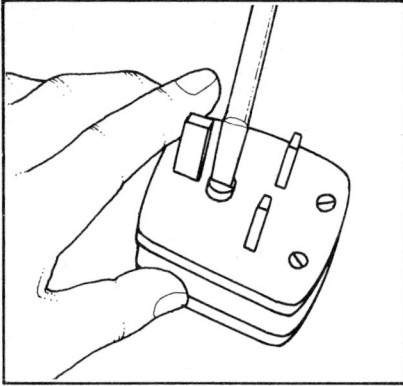

1. Loosen the two small screws holding the cable clamp and remove the large screw holding the cover to the plug body.

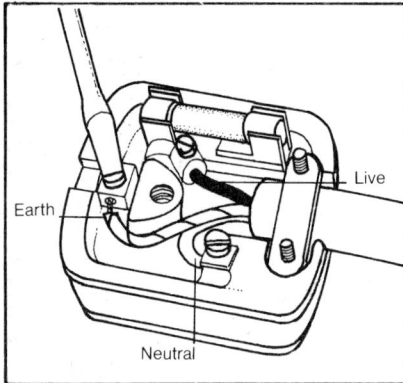

1. Unscrew the cap covering the terminals. Slide the cap along the wire and disconnect the two wires with a small screwdriver.

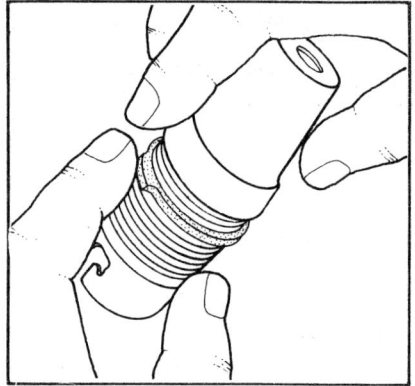

2. Disconnect the wires and remove the plug. Rewire the new plug – brown to the live terminal, blue to neutral and green/yellow to earth.

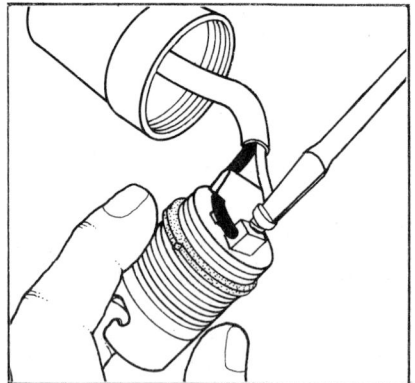

2. When fitting the new holder, remember to slide the cap onto the wire first. Attach the wires to the terminals – each wire can go on either terminal.

Replacing a ceiling rose

You will need: small screwdriver; ceiling rose

Replacing a light flex

You will need: small screwdriver; flex

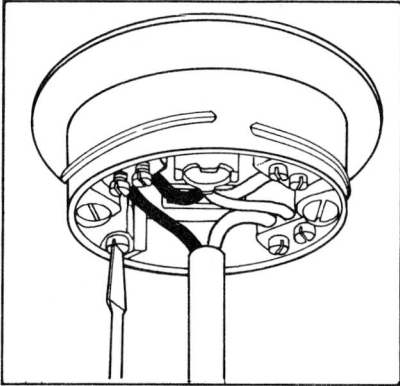

1. Switch off the supply at the mains. Unscrew the rose cap; disconnect the wires noting their positions. Remove the screws holding the rose to the ceiling.

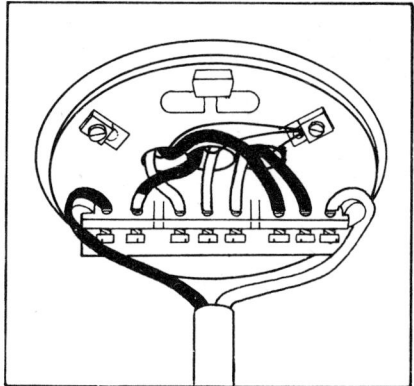

1. In loop-in wiring, note the terminals to which the old flex is wired and fit the new one to the same terminals.

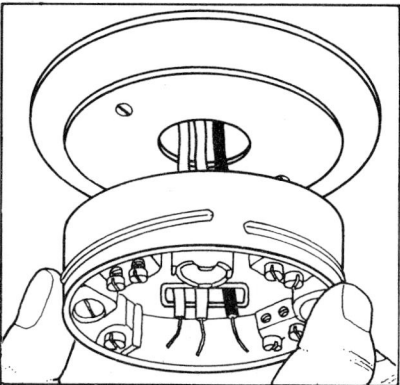

2. Feed the wires through the new rose and screw it to the ceiling. Refit the wires to the terminals.

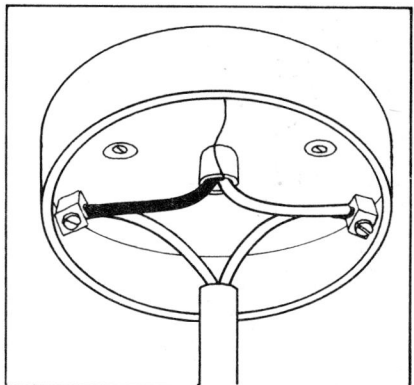

2. There are only two terminals in a junction box wiring rose. When fitting new flex, ensure that the feed wire and flex wire are inside the terminal.

Changing a kettle element

You will need: small screwdriver; complete kettle element

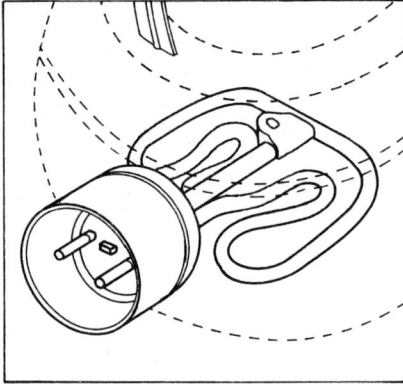

1. The element assembly in an electric kettle consists of the element, a rubber washer and fibre washer and a screw-on shroud.

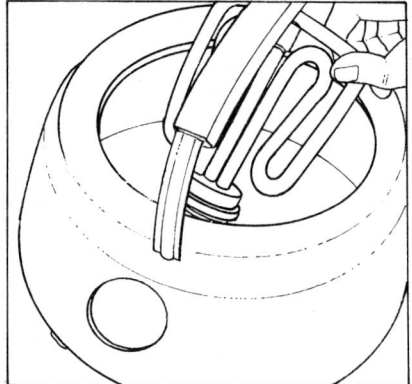

3. Remove the fibre washer under the shroud. A new washer, and the rubber washer inside the kettle, will be supplied with the new element. Remove the old element.

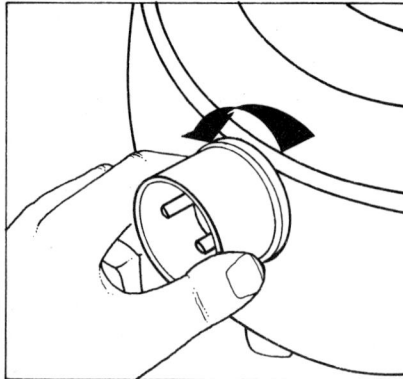

2. First unscrew the shroud. You may need to hold the element inside the kettle with your other hand.

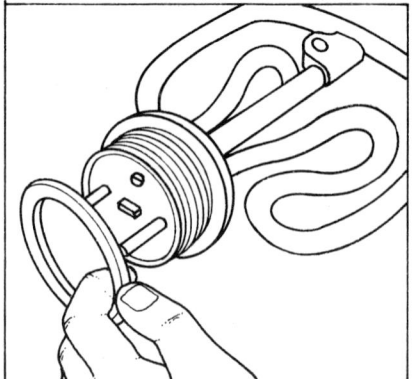

4. Fit the new rubber washer over the element threads. Insert the element in the kettle, fit the fibre washer and screw on the shroud.

Replacing a fire element

You will need: small screwdriver; fire element

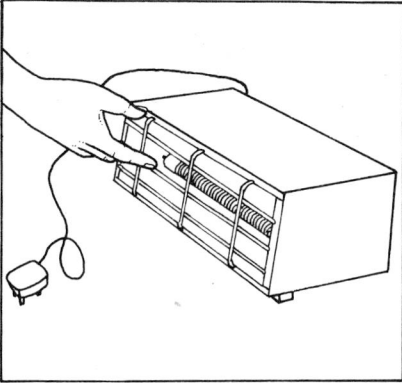

1. To replace a wire element, first remove the guard which may be held by screws or may be a snap-in fit.

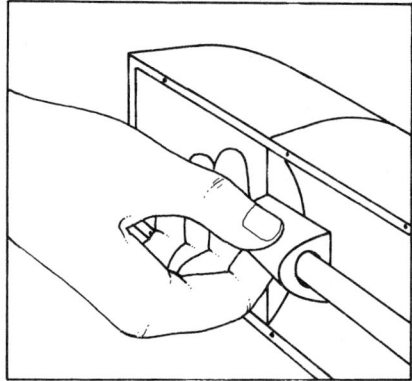

3. On a fire with a glass-enclosed element, remove the guard and slide back the sleeves covering the element terminals.

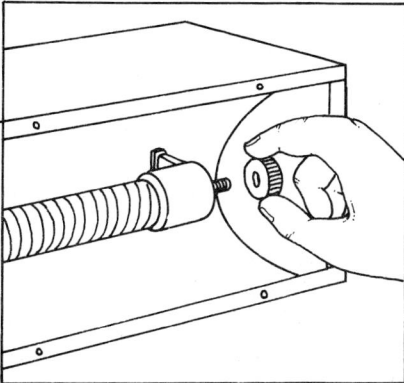

2. Unscrew the end terminals, pull out the element from its support brackets and fit the new element. Screw on the terminals finger-tight.

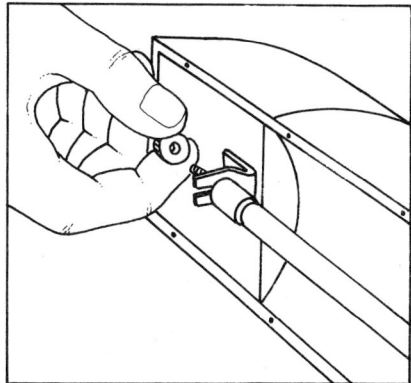

4. Unscrew the terminal nuts, lift off the element and fit the new one.

Electricity

Safety with electricity

Electricity is a clean and efficient way of supplying heat and lighting, but if it is neglected or not treated with respect it can become a killer. If electrical wiring is allowed to deteriorate it can cause a fire. **Bodily contact with exposed live wires can result in electrocution**.

In most houses the major part of the wiring circuit is out of view, buried behind plaster or running below floorboards, and if these wires overheat they can start a fire in the main structure of the house. There are two main causes of wiring overheating — breakdown of the cable insulation leading to a short-circuit between bare wires, and overloading of the circuit. A properly installed circuit using PVC insulated wiring will eliminate the first risk. If your house is wired with rubber insulated wiring have the circuit checked by the electricity board, but be prepared to have the house rewired as soon as possible.

Even PVC insulation will melt and break down if it is overheated, and this can be caused by a short circuit coupled with inadequate fuse protection. **Never fit a fuse of a higher rating than recommended in any appliance or in the main fusebox**. If a short circuit occurs and the fuse fails to blow, the wiring itself becomes the weak link in the circuit and will overheat. If a fuse blows constantly, find the cause. Some circuits have circuit breakers instead of fuses — never reset a constantly tripping circuit breaker without first tracing the fault.

Apart from the main house wiring, however, there are leads and flexes to appliances which should be regularly inspected and replaced where necessary. Light flexes, for example, are often overlooked — and these often not only carry current but the weight of a lampshade as well!

The old rubber-and-fabric covered twisted flex is a major hazard — the rubber perishes and the weight of the lamp and shade pull the twisted wires together. Replace twisted flex using twin core PVC-sheathed cable of 3 amp rating.

If you want to run cable along a skirting board or across a door frame, use insulated clips not metal staples. **Never run flex under a carpet** — continual treading on the carpet will fray the flex covering.

Appliances such as electric fires and blankets should be checked regularly, particularly blankets. Changing the element on an electric fire is simple enough, but **never try to mend an electric blanket element**. Electric blankets should be used as the manufacturer intended, that is as an overlay or underlay, and should be switched off before getting into bed unless it is fitted with a voltage-reducing transformer.

Remove an electric blanket during the summer months and fold it carefully so as not to damage the elements.

Electric shocks will result if an appliance is not properly earthed. Every modern plug has an earth pin, the one at the end of the plug, which serves a dual purpose – it pushes open shutters covering the live and neutral sockets and connects with the socket earth pin. Thus the appliance body is connected directly to the house earth. If a break occurs in the earth wire, or if it is not soundly connected, a fault in the appliance many render it 'live'.

The danger of electrocution is increased where there is water – an excellent conductor of electricity. **Power sockets should never be installed in a bathroom and electrical appliances should never be touched with wet hands.**

There is one room in the house, however, where not only is water ever-present but more appliances are usually found than any other room in the house – the kitchen. Manufacturers of such devices as electric kettles, washing machines and dishwashers are required to meet high standards of safety where water and electricity are in such close proximity. In the UK all electrical equipment should carry the British Electrical Approvals Board's label.

Extra care should be taken, in using any electrical appliance in the kitchen. Do not fill an electric kettle while it is plugged in to a socket, and always unplug it when pouring. Make sure that the lead to a kettle or coffee-maker cannot trail across a cooker ring. If an electric iron is used in the kitchen, avoid letting its lead trail across a damp floor.

If an electrical fire does start in your house, switch off the current at the main switch immediately before trying to tackle the fire. Get everyone out of the house and send for the fire brigade. Once the power is switched off you can use water to douse a fire started by an electrical fault, but it is a good idea to have a fire extinguisher handy. The powder-filled type are best for dealing with most fires and should be of at least 2 lb (1 kg) capacity. Aerosol extinguishers have a very short range and small capacity; they are suitable only for dealing with a very small outbreak.

When tackling a fire never allow your escape route to be cut off, and the moment it gets out of hand abandon your efforts and leave it to the experts.

Floors

There are two types of floor in a house; suspended timber floors and concrete or composite floors. In modern houses the ground floor is often concrete, though suspended floors are still used, but most older houses have suspended floors both upstairs and down.

Floorboards are usually made of softwood, tongued and grooved or butt jointed, though flooring grade chipboard has superseded timber in many new buildings. The boards are nailed to joists, and on ground floors these are supported by sleeper walls built below floor level. The walls are constructed like a honeycomb which allows air to ventilate under the floor. Adequate ventilation is essential to prevent dry rot and air bricks are set into the house walls below the floor. **These should never be covered in order to stop draughts**; a draughty floor can be cured by filling the cracks between the boards with papier maché or strips of wood.

In modern houses the ground floor joists stop short of the end and side walls by about $1\frac{1}{2}$ in (37 mm), but in houses with solid walls the joists were set into the walls.

In upstairs floors the joists are supported at their ends by metal hangers embedded in the brickwork. The partition walls, (the walls that divide the house into rooms) provide additional support and the joists may also be braced by struts nailed between them.

Most of the problems likely to occur with timber floors involve the floorboards — in time they tend to work loose and simply require refixing, but badly worn or split boards should be replaced.

Lifting a butt-jointed floorboard is done by levering under the board with a bolster chisel and then prising the board up with a claw hammer. To lift a tongued and grooved board, however, the tongue must be cut through with a padsaw. On an upstairs floor particularly there may be an electricity cable running beneath the board — part of the downstairs lighting circuit — so as a precaution the power should be switched off until the board has been removed. If more than one tongued and grooved board is to be lifted it is necessary only to cut through one tongue, the remaining boards can then be lifted with a bolster and claw hammer.

Concrete floors are laid on a bed of hardcore with an intervening damp-proof membrane. A thin screed of concrete forms the base for the floor covering which may be tiles, or wood blocks or simply a coating of smoothing compound.

If a concrete floor is uneven or cracked it can be repaired with cement filling mixed with a PVA adhesive (see pp 184-185). When a large area of floor is uneven it can be resurfaced with smoothing compound from a builders' merchant.

How wooden floors are constructed

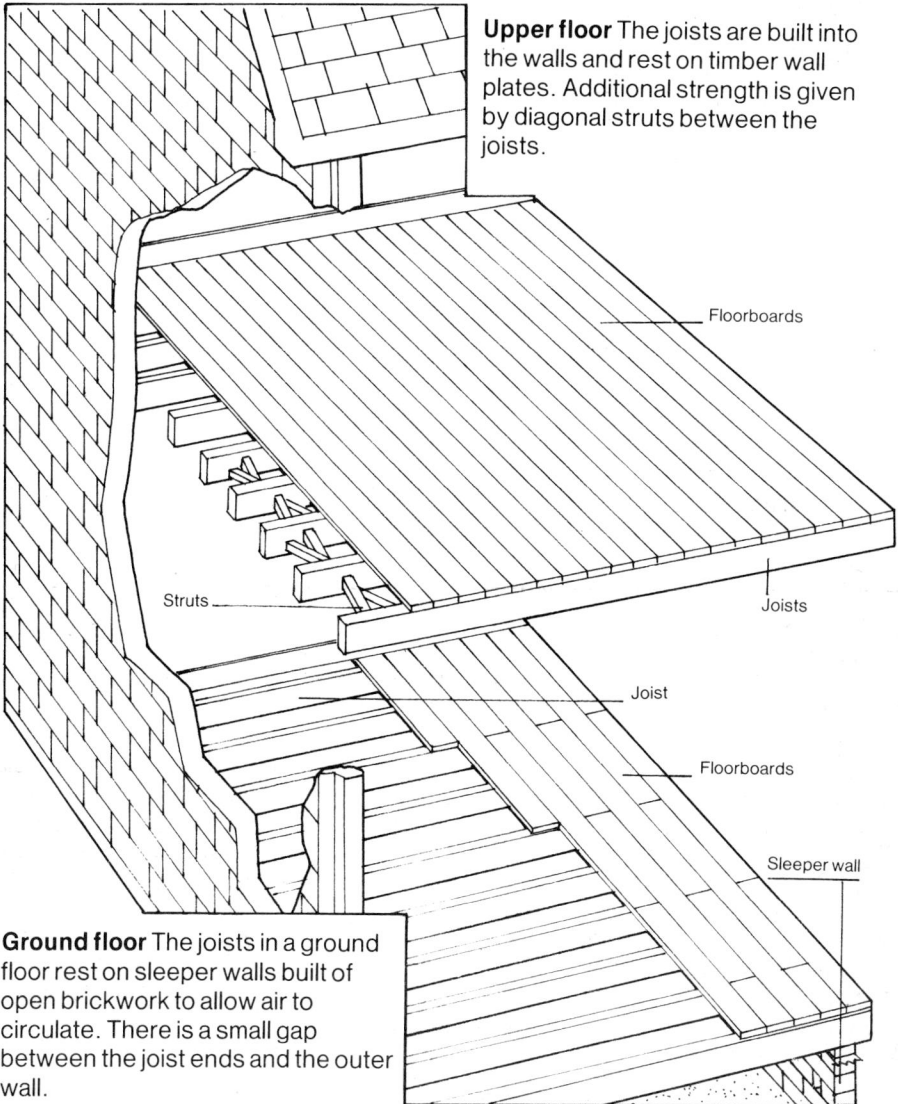

Upper floor The joists are built into the walls and rest on timber wall plates. Additional strength is given by diagonal struts between the joists.

Floorboards

Struts

Joists

Joist

Floorboards

Sleeper wall

Ground floor The joists in a ground floor rest on sleeper walls built of open brickwork to allow air to circulate. There is a small gap between the joist ends and the outer wall.

Floors

Fixing a loose floorboard

You will need: hammer; punch; floor brads

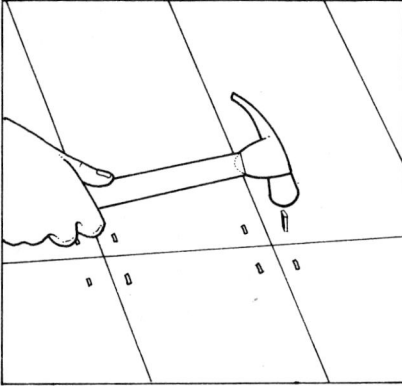

1. Drive in extra flooring brads close to the old ones and in line with them.

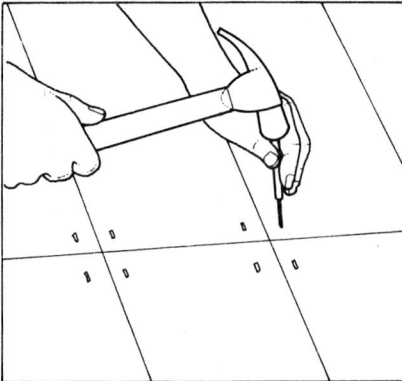

2. Sink the brad heads below the surface of the floorboard with a nail punch.

Removing a floorboard

You will need: bolster chisel; claw hammer; padsaw; boards; floor brads; combination square; saw; 1 in (25 mm) wood chisel

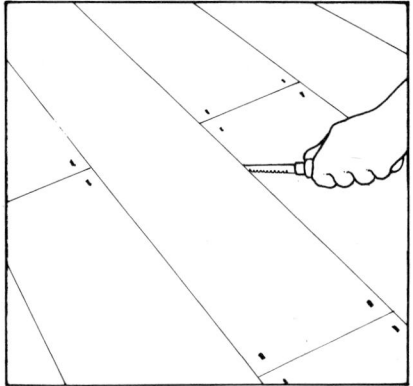

1. If the floorboards are tongued and grooved, (i.e, each board has a strip, or tongue, which slots into the adjacent board) cut through the tongue with a padsaw.

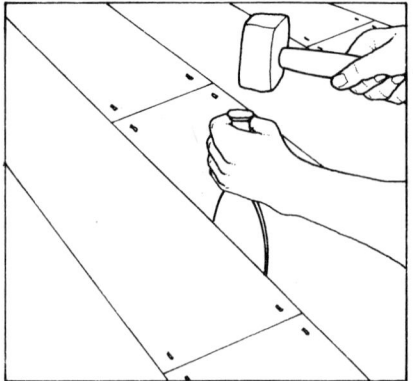

2. Slide a bolster chisel between the boards, near the end of the board to be removed, and drive it well down.

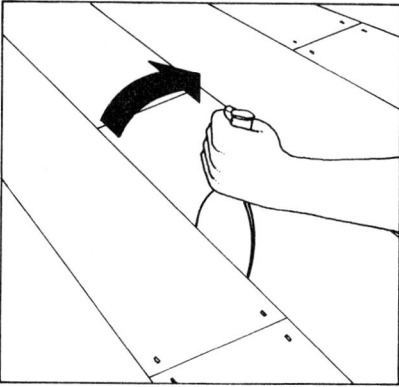

3. Lever the chisel outwards until the nails in the board are loosened.

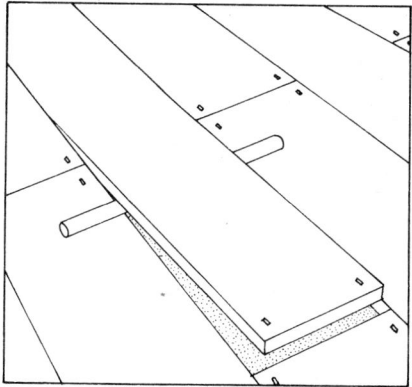

5. Pull the board upwards and progressively push the rod further along.

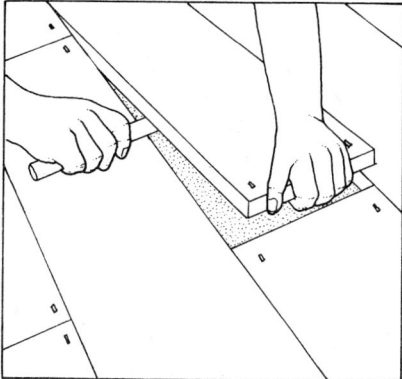

4. Pull up the end of the board when the nails are free and slip a rod underneath.

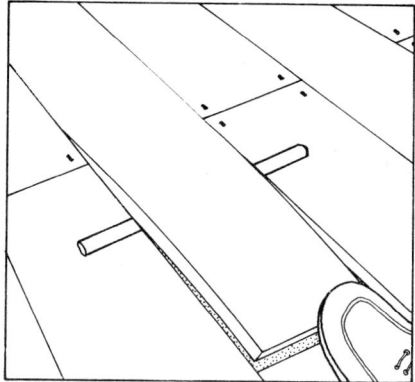

6. Press down on the board with your foot to spring the nails at the next joist. Keep moving the rod and treading the board until it is free.

Filling gaps with papier mache

You will need: scraper; brush; bucket; paper; wallpaper adhesive; sandpaper

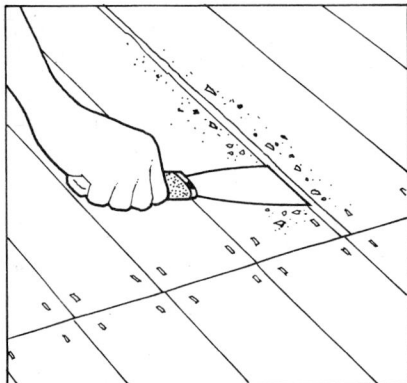

1. Small gaps between floorboards can be filled with a compound of paper and wallpaper adhesive. First clean out the cracks with a scraper and brush.

3. Let the mixture cool, then add cellulose wallpaper adhesive and mix to a thick consistency.

2. Tear up paper into scraps (use soft white paper for the best results) and pour in boiling water. Mash the paper to a thick paste.

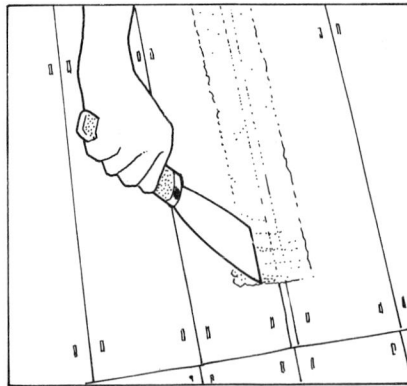

4. Use a scraper or stripping knife to ram the mixture into the crack, working across the gap. Leave to set and then rub down with glasspaper.

76

Filling gaps with wood strips

You will need: hammer; punch; hand saw; hand-drill; floor brads; pencil

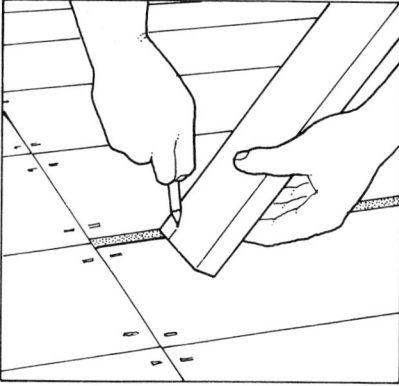

1. Gaps of $\frac{1}{8}$ in (3 mm) or more can be filled with wood strips. Use a piece of softwood the same thickness as the floorboards and mark on it the width of the gap.

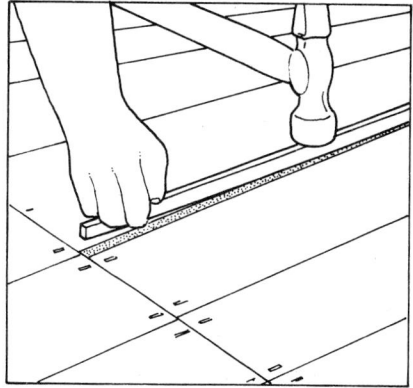

3. Press the tapered edge of the strip into the gap. Tap it home with a hammer.

2. Cut the strip to the length of the gap and taper one edge with a plane or shaping tool.

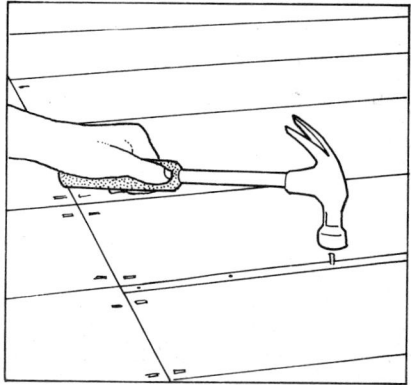

4. Pin the strip to joists using small panel pins. On narrow strips, say less than $\frac{1}{4}$ in (6 mm), drill a small hole for the pin or the wood may split.

Covering a floor with hardboard

You will need: hammer; punch; scraper; pincers; hand saw; coping saw; combination square; sheets of hardboard; floor brads

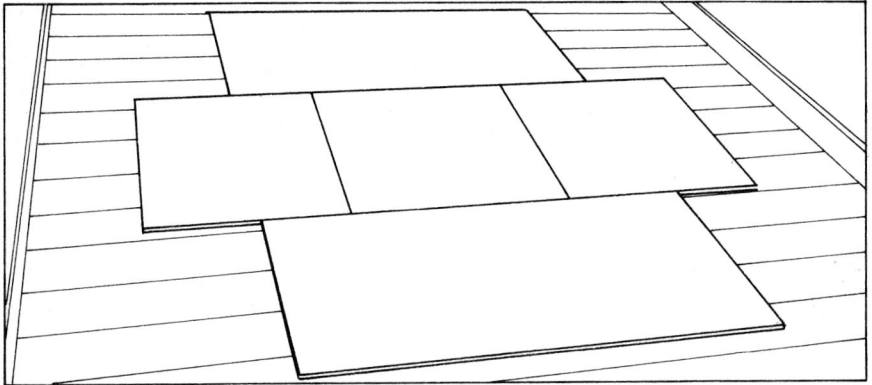

An uneven floor, caused by warped or worn floorboards, makes it impossible to obtain a level surface for floor coverings, especially tiles. The floor can be levelled by covering it with hardboard sheets (laid rough side up for tiles).

Prepare the floor first by punching in any protruding nail heads and plane or sand any boards that have raised edges. If necessary, replace any boards that are badly worn (see p 74).

Use tempered hardboard, which is available in sheets 8 ft × 4 ft (240 cm × 120 cm). Prepare the sheets 24 hours before laying by wetting the rough side with about 1 pint of water. Then lay the sheets back to back on a flat surface. When the sheets are dry, cut some of them into two pieces so that the joints between the panels will be staggered.

Use hardboard panel pins for securing the boards, and for extra adhesion apply spots of contact adhesive (see pp 184-185) to the undersides of the boards and to the corresponding area on the floorboards.

Sweep the floor thoroughly (to remove all dust and grit) before laying the boards, and afterwards before laying the floor covering.

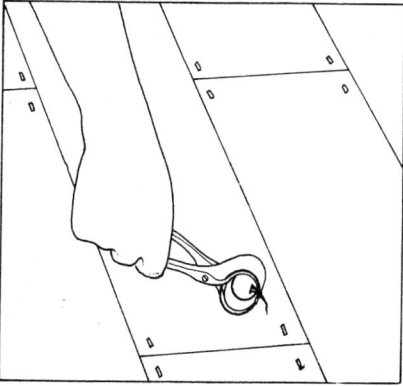

1. First get rid of any tacks or nails in the floorboards. Level off any irregularities with a plane or shaping tool.

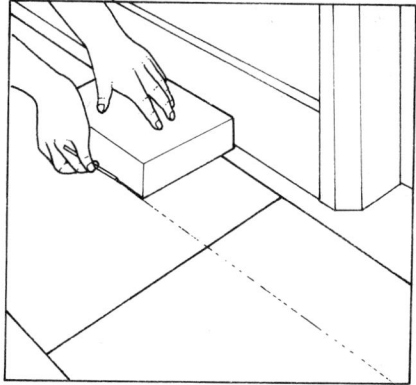

2. Lay the first sheet in the centre of the floor. Hammer in nails at 4 in (100 mm) intervals all over the board. Work evenly across to avoid warping.

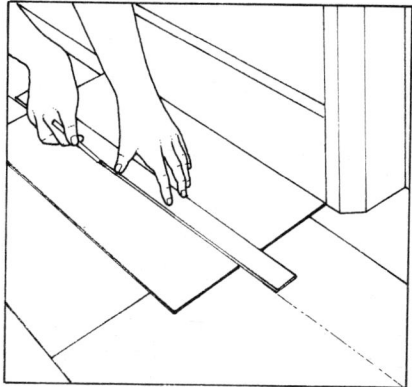

3. At the skirting, place a piece of hardboard against it, overlapping the last board. Using a wood block as a guide, mark a line coinciding with the skirting.

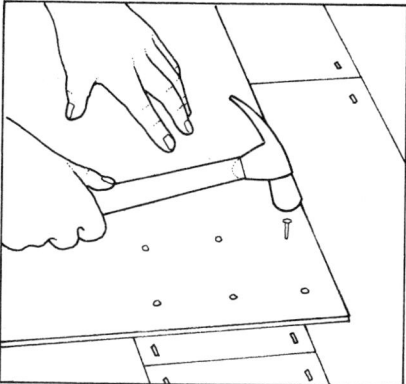

4. Cut down the line with a trimming knife. Lay the board against the skirting and cut the board flush with the last-laid board.

Replacing a skirting board section

You will need: hammer; hand saw or jigsaw; punch; bolster chisel; skirting board; masonry nails

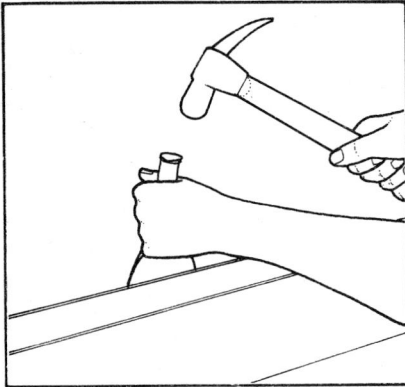

1. Use a bolster chisel and hammer to prise away the damaged area of skirting board.

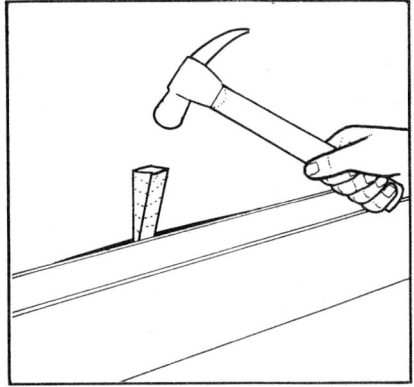

3. Make a wedge, about 2 in (50 mm) wide at its thick end, and drive it into the gap.

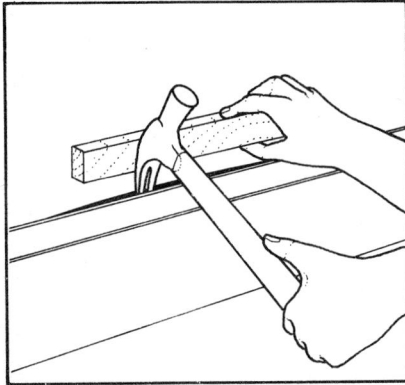

2. When there is a sufficient gap, use a claw hammer and a block of wood to detach the board from the wall.

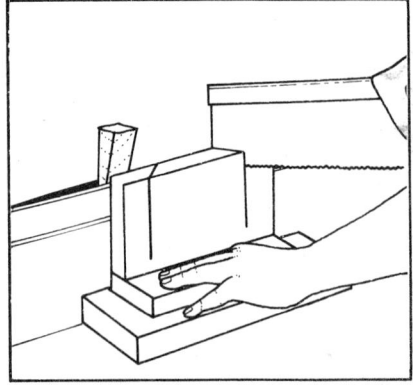

4. Mark off the section to be removed and use a mitre board and tenon saw to cut out the section.

80

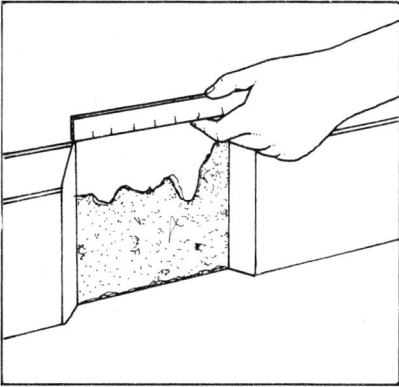

5. Remove the wedge. Measure across the width of the gap in the skirting board at the widest points.

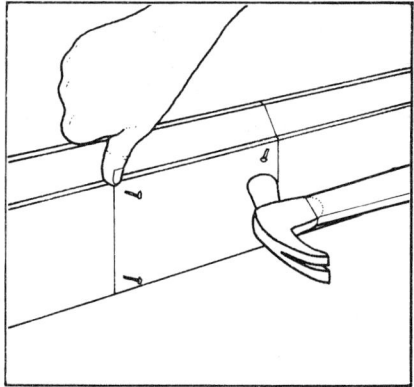

7. Fit the new section into the skirting board. Hammer in nails at an angle to make sure that they pass through both faces of the mitred ends.

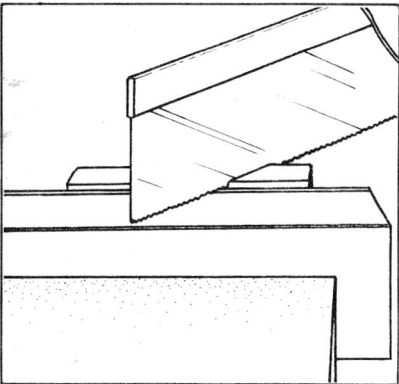

6. Make a new section of skirting board from softwood, mitring the ends.

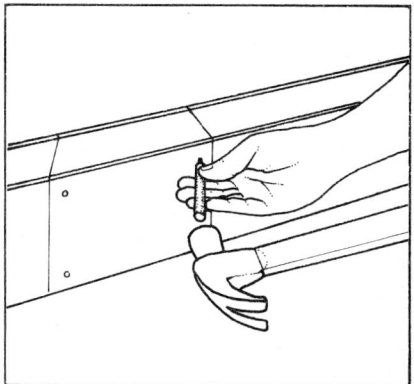

8. Sink the nail heads below the surface using a nail punch. Fill the holes with wood filler, sand down and paint.

Repairing a concrete floor

You will need: trowel; cement; PVA compounds

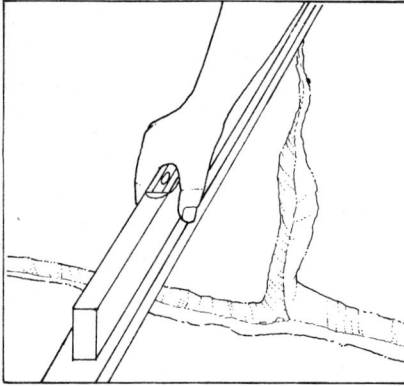

1. Before dealing with cracks in a solid floor, check the level to see if the floor has sunk around the area of the crack.

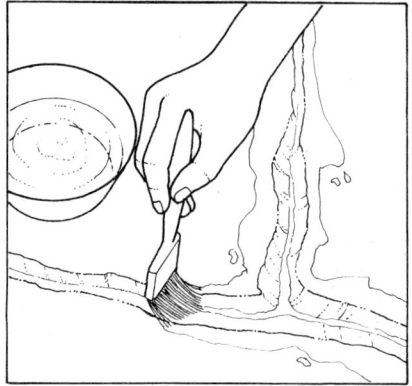

3. When the crack is clean, apply PVA bonding agent with an old paint brush.

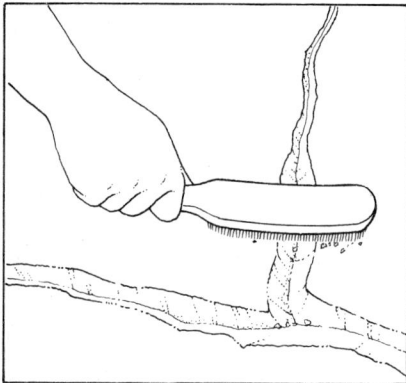

2. If the floor has sunk it can be levelled with a self-levelling compound . First brush out the crack thoroughly, ready for filling.

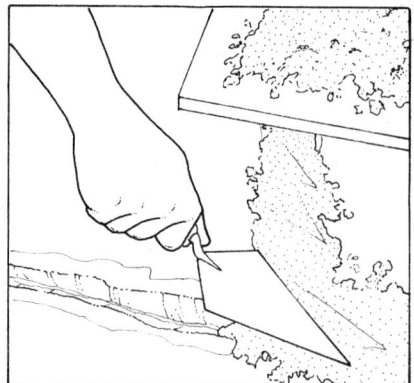

4. Make a mortar mix (see pp 188-189) and fill the crack while the bonding agent is still wet. Level off with a trowel.

Resurfacing an uneven floor

You will need: smoothing compound; trowel; bucket; stiff broom

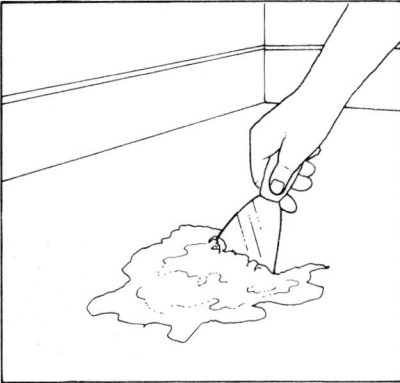

1. The floor must be perfectly clean and smooth. Scrape off any protrusions and sweep the floor thoroughly.

3. Obtain a bag of rapid hardening, self-levelling powder from a hardware or DIY shop. Mix 3 parts powder to 1 part clean water.

2. Dampen an absorbent floor (such as concrete) with water. Use neoprene primer on a composite floor.

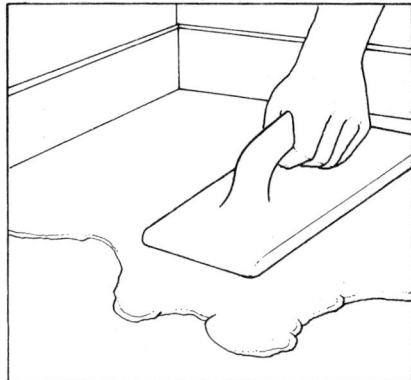

4. Use the compound within 30 minutes of mixing. Pour it on to the floor and spread quickly. Work into the floor, then leave it to find its own level.

Foundations

The construction of house foundations are strictly controlled by building regulations, which lay down the depths, widths, thicknesses and reinforcements as well as the quality of the materials.

All houses 'settle' when they are new, and the natural settlement may go on for up to five years. It is apparent mostly in hairline cracks in the interior plasterwork, which though annoying are nothing to worry about. If new cracks appear or old cracks continue to widen after five years, however, you should notify **in writing** the National House Building Council (in the UK) whose ten-year guarantee covers major structural faults.

Although postwar standards are high, it was not always so. The infamous 'jerry-built houses' often had poor foundations built on unsuitable subsoils, and had walls of inferior bricks and mortar. Settlement in these houses led to wide cracks appearing in the outside walls and at corners of windows and doorways. Uneven settlement, where one part of the foundations sinks lower than the rest, causes vertical cracks and leaning in the walls.

Sometimes settlement occurs due entirely to the nature of the subsoil and the siting of the house. For example, a sandy subsoil may shift sideways if the house is built on a slope, resulting in uneven settlement of the foundations.

Another cause of settlement is the presence of large trees near the house. Their roots may extend under the foundations and draw moisture from the soil, especially during a long period of drought. Any large trees within 40 ft (12 m) should be cut down if they are believed to be the cause of settlement — even small trees within 20 ft (6 m) can undermine foundations built on clay.

Before you take such drastic action, however, you must notify the local authority of your fears and intentions.

Continuing settlement can usually be cured only by first shoring up the house and then underpinning the foundations. Sometimes a leaning wall can be supported by a buttress, or with steel tie rods taken right through the house at floor or ceiling level, but more often a badly affected wall must be demolished and rebuilt after underpinning the foundations.

Such work is, of course, beyond the scope of the handyman. Before sending for a builder, **make sure that settlement is continuing**. Cracks with a weathered appearance will have ceased to spread, but if the ends of the cracks are a bright brick-red then movement is still taking place. Another way of checking is to fill the cracks with cement (see p 161), and if settlement is still taking place the cemented joints will soon open up again.

How trees can cause settlement

A tree growing too close to a house may draw moisture from the soil, causing the foundations to sink, or settle. Often the first sign of settlement is cracking of the outer walls at weak points such as around windows and doors.

Gardens

Whether you are a keen gardener or not, fences, gates and paths should be kept in good order. Fences and gates are frontiers of privacy, and well made paths to the front and back doors are essential for preventing mud and dirt being brought into the house. Furthermore, you may be responsible in law for the upkeep of certain boundary fences.

Wooden fencing will last longer if it is treated regularly with a preservative such as creosote, or painted with a good, weather-resisting paint. Examine posts for rot and repair or replace them before the damage becomes serious. Fix loose posts as soon as possible — the next high wind may bring down a whole section of fencing

Check paths every spring, especially after a hard winter when frost and snow may have cracked concrete or asphalt. Cracks and holes can be filled with either ready-mixed cement or macadam obtainable from a builders' merchant. At the same time repair crumbling edges.

If you have a garden shed the most likely repair needed will be re-roofing. Use a heavy grade roofing felt and coat it with bitumen paint every two or three years.

Greenhouse frames, whether wood or metal, will need painting regularly. And, of course, broken glass panels may need replacing from time to time. If possible, buy horticultural glass which is cheaper than household glass and have it cut to size by the glazier.

There are three main types of wooden fencing. Perhaps the most common is the feather-edged board fence in which upright boards are nailed to cross members, called arris rails. The boards are wedge shaped, or feather-edged, and overlap each other. The arris rails should be securely fixed into the upright posts to give rigid support to the boards.

Another type of fencing has interwoven slats of thin wood. The slats are woven in panels 6 ft (1.8 m) wide which are nailed to the inside of 3 in × 3 in (75 mm × 75 mm) posts. A similar type of fencing panel has overlapping slats.

Replacement slats for both overlapping and interwoven fence panels are difficult to obtain, unless you can salvage them from another panel. So keeping this type of fencing in good shape is important.

Gateposts should be examined regularly in the same way as fence posts, and repaired or replaced accordingly. Often the main problem is a badly shutting gate due to wear or looseness of the hinges. Loose hinges are often caused by corrosion of the fixing screws; fitting new screws will solve the problem but first fill the screw holes with wooden plugs.

Mending a broken fence rail

You will need: handsaw; screwdriver; galvanized screws; galvanized bracket or brackets

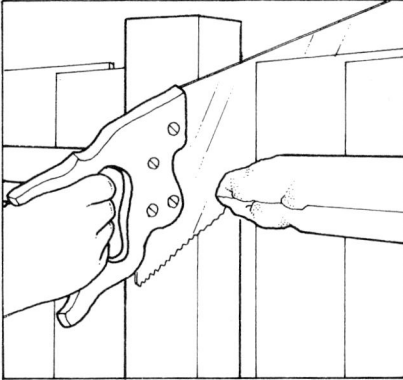

1. If a fence rail has broken at the post, remove the end board and cut the rail as close to the post as possible.

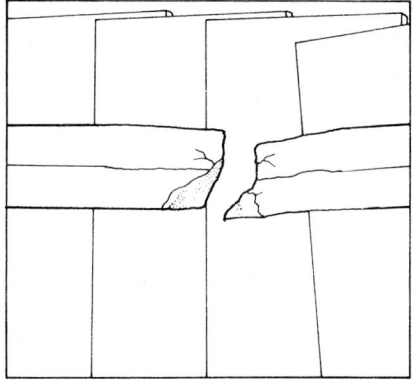

3. A break in the centre of a rail can be repaired with a steel bridging bracket.

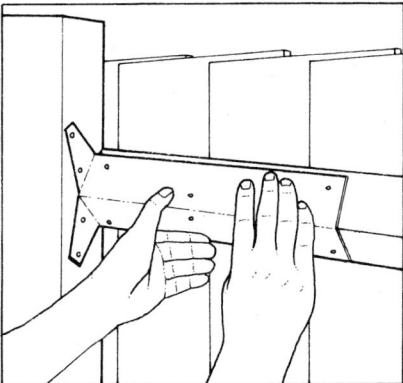

2. Purchase a galvanized steel joining bracket from a hardware merchant or garden centre. Attach the bracket to the rail and post using galvanized screws.

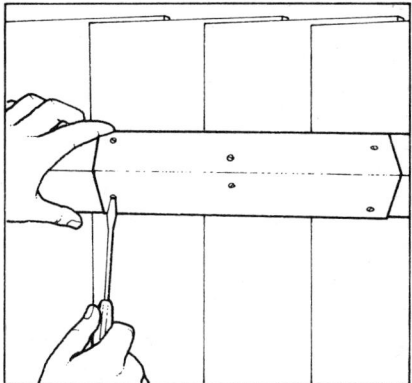

4. Align the two broken sections and place the bracket centrally over the break. Attach the bracket with galvanized screws.

Replacing a fence post

You will need: handsaw; spade; spirit level; battens; nails; galvanized brackets; galvanized screws; hardcore; concrete; paint

1. Support the fence with battens nailed to the arris rails on each side of the post and not more than 2 ft (61 cm) from it.

3. Fit the new post. Fill the hole with hardcore followed by concrete. Check that the post is vertical and aligned with the fence before the concrete sets.

2. Remove a fence board on each side of the post. Cut through the arris rails close to the post. Dig out the old post.

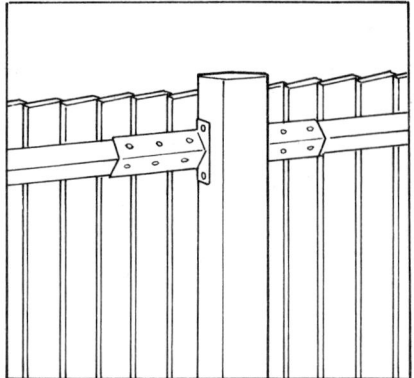

4. Attach the arris rails to the new post with metal brackets. Use galvanized screws and paint the brackets to prevent rusting. Refit the fence boards.

Supporting a loose post

You will need: pick axe; bolster chisel; hand drill and bit; spanner; spirit level; spur; coach screws; hardcore; concrete

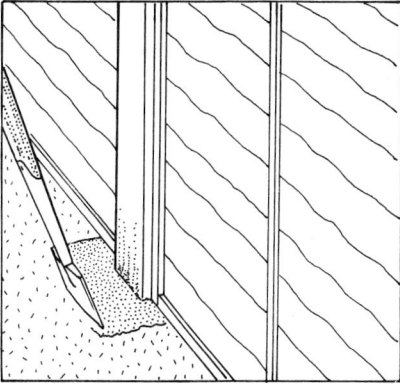

1. If the post is set in concrete, break this up with a pick axe or bolster chisel to a depth of about 2 ft (61 cm). Clear the hole around the post.

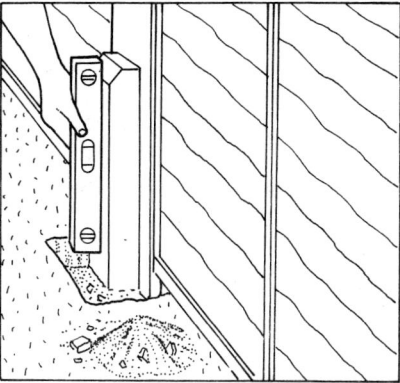

3. Fill the hole with hardcore and concrete, making sure that it surrounds both the post and spur.

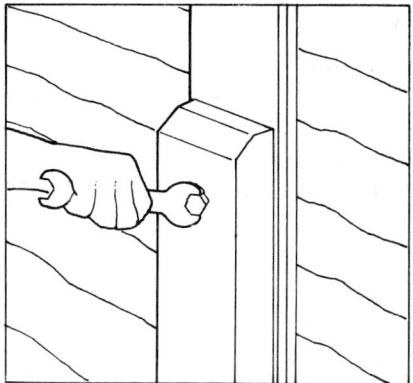

2. Make a supporting spur from hardwood, or buy a ready-made concrete spur, and set it in the hole. Use a spirit level to see that it is upright.

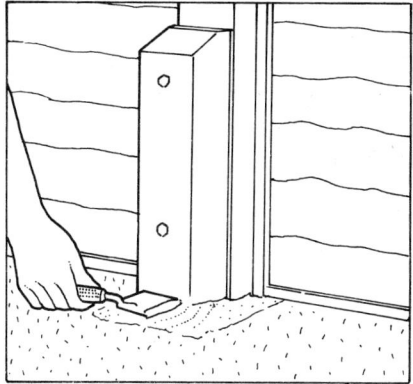

4. When the concrete has set, drill holes through the spur – if it is of wood (concrete spurs have holes already made) and fit coach screws. Tighten screws with a spanner.

Fitting new fence boards

You will need: hammer; saw; nail punch; spirit level; guage; nails; wood blocks

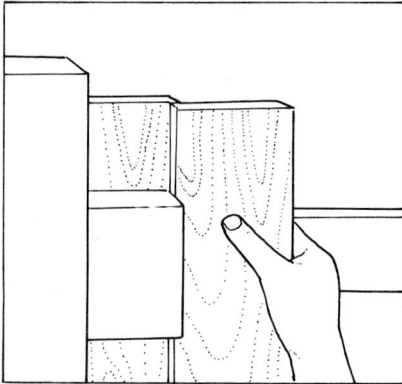

1. To ensure an even overlap of each board, make a gauge $\frac{1}{2}$ in (13 mm) shorter than the board width. Nail the first board against the post.

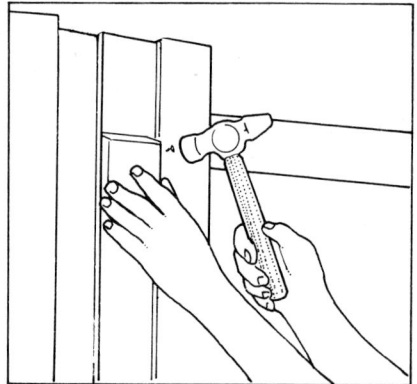

3. Fix the boards with the thick edge overlapping the thin edge of the previous board.

2. Use the gauge to position the second board at top and bottom and nail through the overlapping sections into the rail.

4. If renewing only part of a fence, punch in the nails of the existing board, slide the new board underneath and renail through both thicknesses.

5. At every other board, check with a spirit level top and bottom to see that the boards are upright.

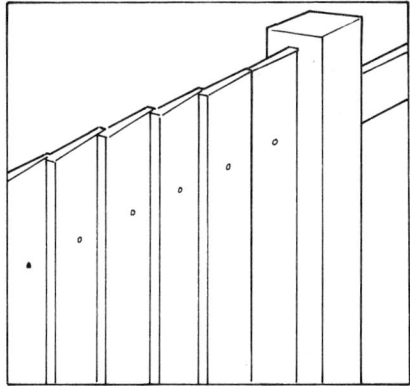

7. If the gap between the last but one board and post is very small, cut a strip from the thick edge of the last board.

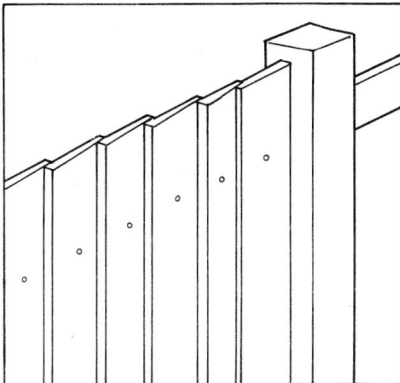

6. At the fence post fit the last board with its thick edge against the post.

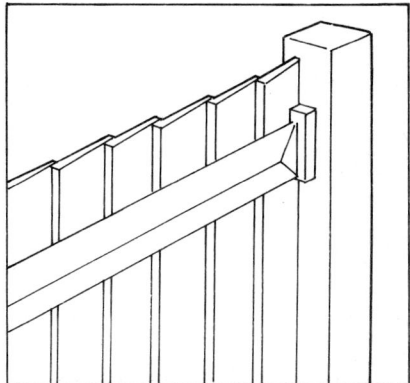

8. Check that the rail is a tight fit in the post. If it is not, support it in four wood blocks screwed to the post before fitting the last board.

Maintaining gates

You will need: screwdriver; screws; brace or bracelets as required

Handy hint: A gate latch that will not rust and never needs oiling can be made from dressmaker's Velcro. This material has tiny hooks that grip corresponding loops in the facing material. Attach one piece of Velcro to the gate and the corresponding piece to the post so that the two are in contact when the gate is closed.

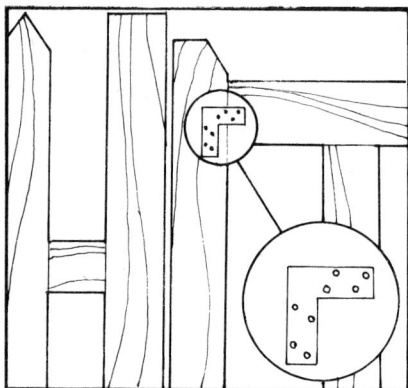

1. A flat corner brace can be used to strengthen a gate where the joint between an upright rail and cross-rail has weakened for any reason.

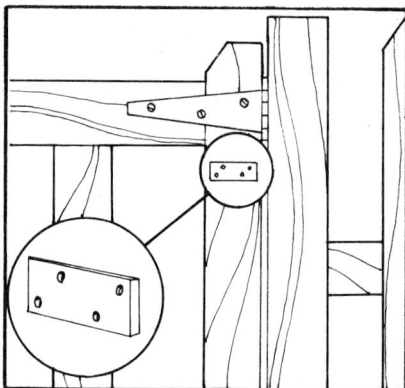

3. Use a straight brace for a minor repair to a gate frame, such as a split in the timber.

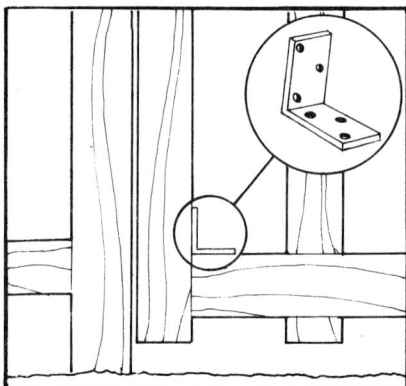

2. Where there is no diagonal brace, a right-angle bracket makes a neater repair than a flat brace.

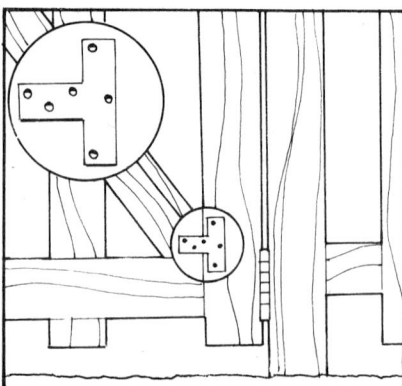

4. Use a T bracket to strengthen a joint between the frame and a diagonal brace.

Fitting a new gatepost

You will need: screwdriver; spirit level; pencil; battens; hinges; wedges; countersunk screws; wood filler plugs; concrete

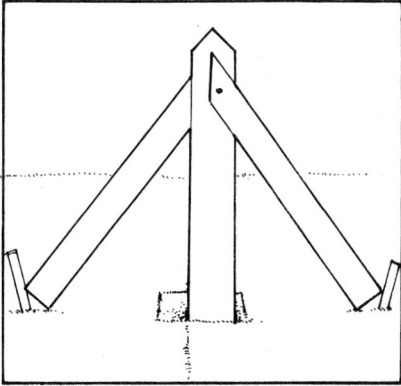

1. Remove the gate and any fencing attached to the old post. Set the new post in concrete to a depth of about 18 in (45.5 cm). Support the post with battens.

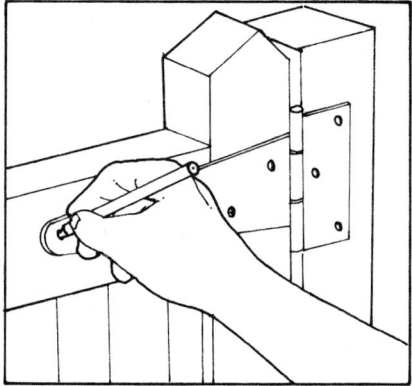

3. Position the gate against the post, line up the hinges and mark the fixing holes on the post. Fill the old holes in the gate.

2. Before refitting the gate, make sure that the post is upright.

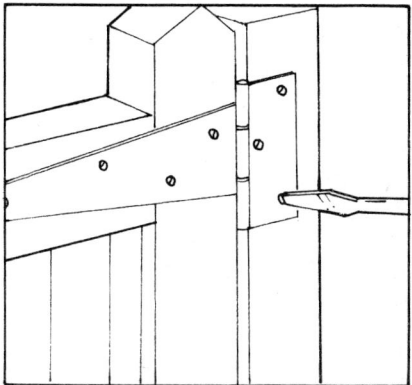

4. Attach the hinges to the gate, then use wedges under the gate to align the hinge plate holes with the hole marks on the post. Secure with countersunk screws.

Repairing a concrete path

You will need: bolster chisel; club hammer; trowel; wire brush; PVA bonding agent; cement

Handy hint: A concrete or paved path can be made attractive by 'painting' it with cement colouring mixed with water. When the finish is dry, treat it with a clear damp-proofing compound to prevent the colour being washed out by rain.

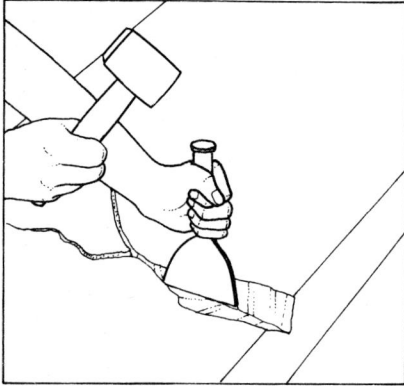

1. To make a strong repair, first open up the crack into a V using a bolster chisel and club hammer.

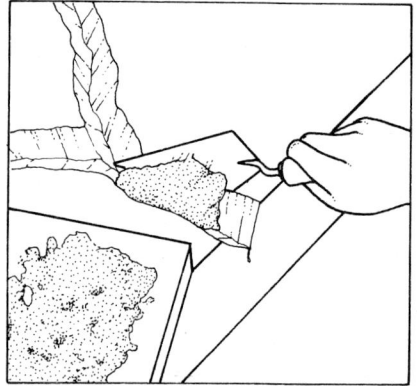

3. Mix the cement (see pp 188-189) and add PVA bonding agent. Pack the cement into the crack.

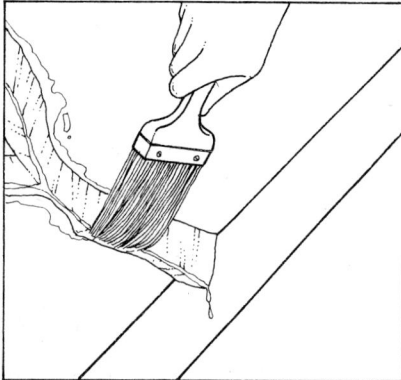

2. Brush out the crack with a wire brush. Then apply PVA bonding agent with an old paintbrush.

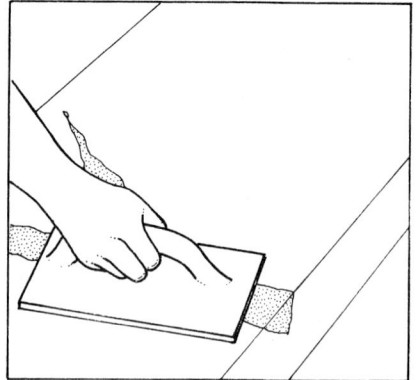

4. Press the cement well into the crack and level off with a trowel or ·steel float.

Repairing a crumbling path edge

You will need: bolster chisel; club hammer; shovel; trowel; stakes; timber former; concrete

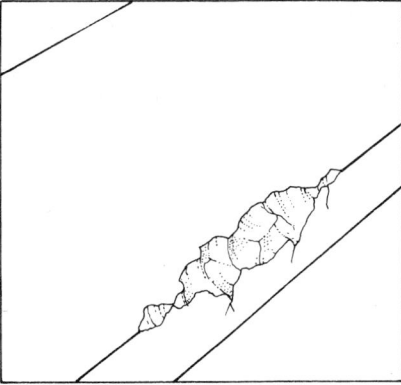

1. A damaged edge, such as above, should be repaired as soon as possible to prevent the complete break-up of the path.

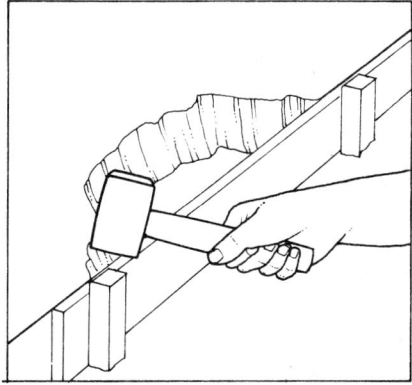

3. Make a timber former and fit it against the path edge. Drive in stakes to hold the former in place.

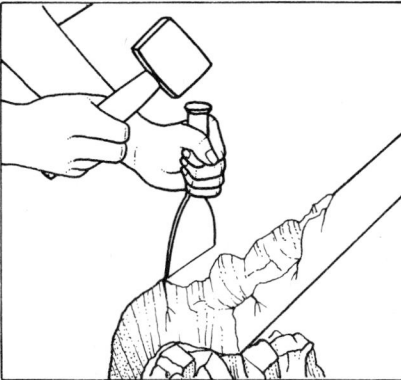

2. Use a hammer and bolster chisel to chip away loose concrete. Work back and along until you reach the solid concrete.

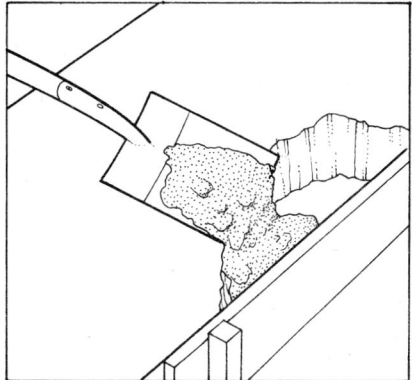

4. Mix the concrete (see pp 186-187) and shovel it into the space behind the former. *(continued)*

Repairing a gravel path

You will need: spade, rake; gravel

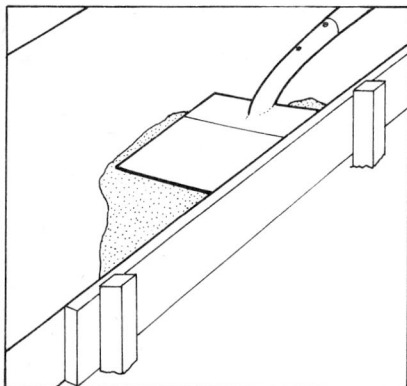

5. Level off the concrete with the back of the shovel. Pat it down to make sure the gap is completely filled.

1. Sometimes hollows occur in gravel paths and the gravel layer becomes thin. Enlarge the hollow by digging out enough material to leave a solid base.

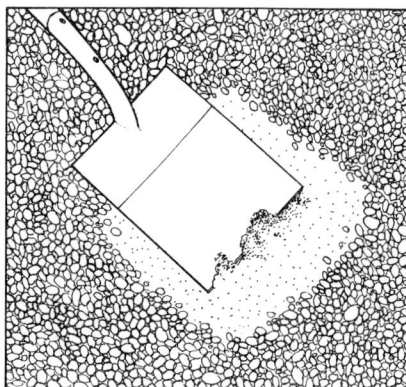

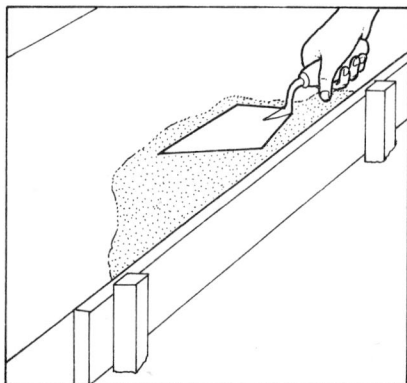

6. Finish off with a trowel, levelling the concrete to the top of the former. Leave the former in place for at least one week.

2. Obtain fresh gravel, as near as possible in colour and grade to the old, and fill the hollow. Rake over the gravel to blend it with the surrounding material.

Repairing an asphalt path

You will need: bolster chisel; club hammer; former; punner; ready-mix tarmac

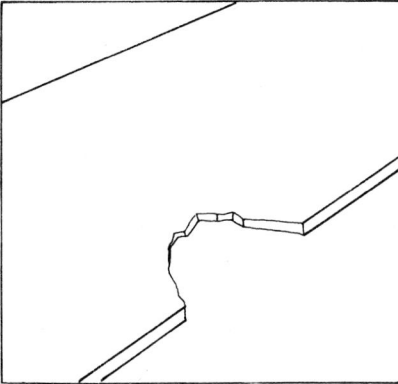

1. Asphalt is a hard-wearing surface, but it tends to become brittle with age and may break away, as above.

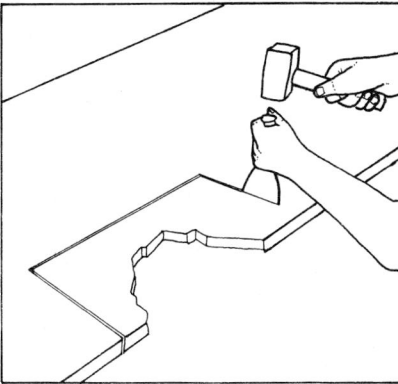

3. Make up a ready-mix tarmac, which must be warmed prior to application. Fit a former board along the edge and then pour in the mix.

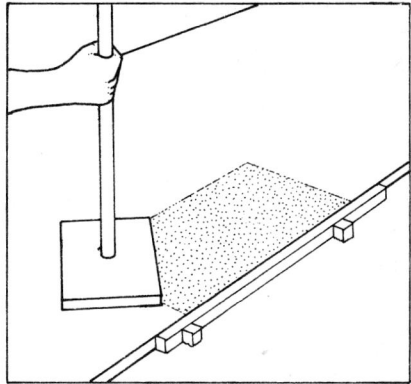

2. First cut back the worn edge, well back from the damaged area and in straight lines.

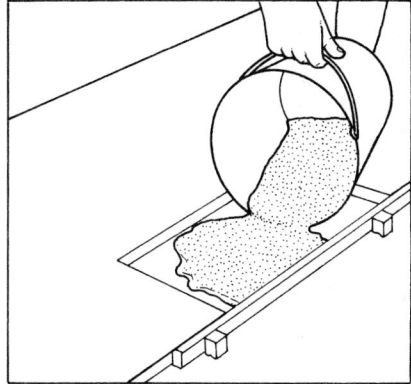

4. Compress the tarmac with a punner. This you can make by using a piece of blockboard 6 in (150 mm) square nailed to a broom handle.

Gardens

Recovering a shed roof with felt

You will need: hammer; screwdriver; trimming knife; battens; countersunk screws; clout nails; roofing felt

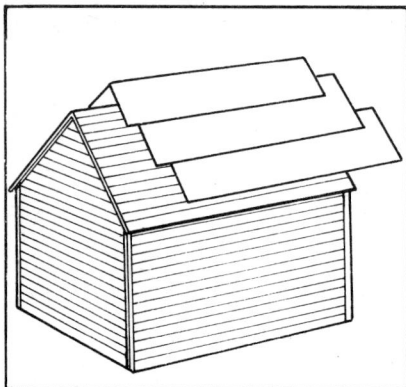

1. Cut five strips of felt, allowing for an overlap of about 3 in (75 mm). Make the ridge strip 12 in (304 mm) wide.

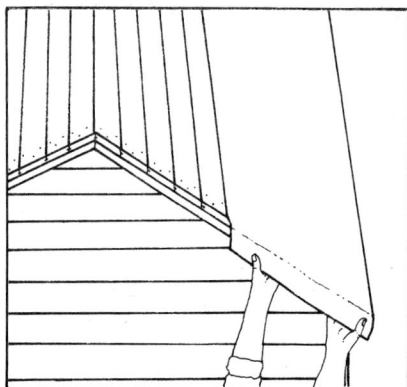

3. Start with the lower strip. Lay it to overhang the eaves by 1 in.

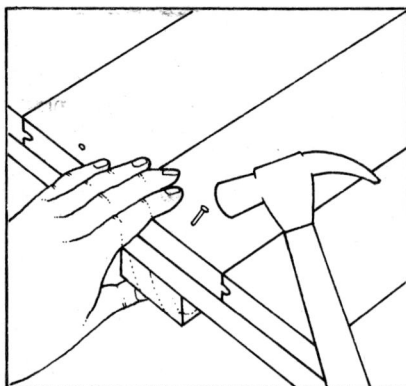

2. Cut 1 in × 1 in (25 mm × 25 mm) battens and nail them to the undersides of the eaves; use a block of wood for support while nailing.

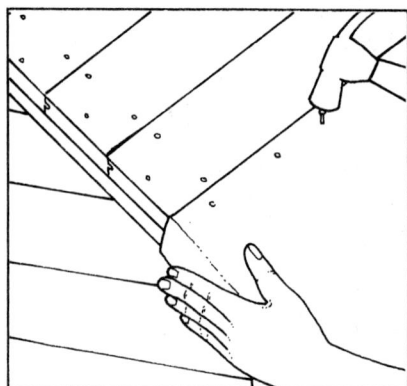

4. Secure the top edge of the strip with galvanized clout nails placed about 6 in (150 mm) apart.

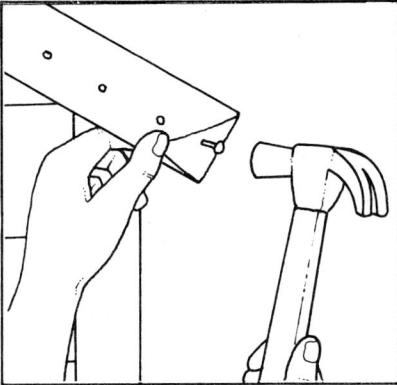

5. Nail the overhang to the battens. Make a double fold at corners and nail through both thicknesses.

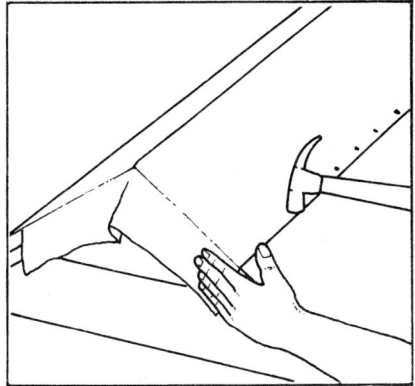

7. Lay the lower and upper sheets on the other side of the roof. Then fit the ridge strip so that it overlaps by an equal amount on both sides.

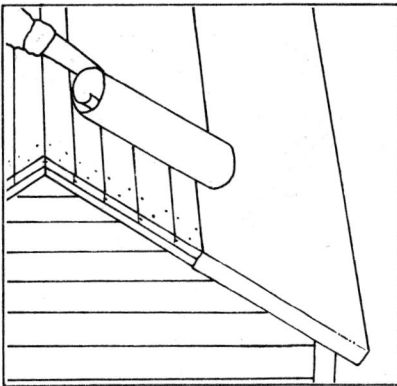

6. Lay the second strip with its top edge not more than 3 in from the ridge.

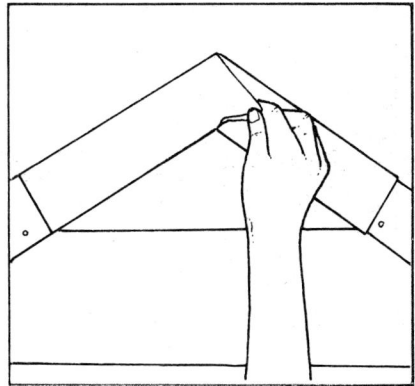

8. Make a fold in the ridge strip overlap and nail it to the roof ends.

Replacing glass in a greenhouse

You will need: small hammer; stripping knife;
putty knife; glazing putty; panel pins; glass

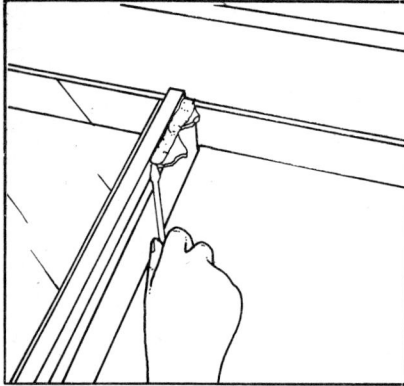

1. Panes in a timber-framed
greenhouse are held in with putty.
Remove the broken glass, scrape
out all the old putty and remove the
fixing pins in the glazing bars.

3. The new pane should overlap the
pane below it by about 2 in (50 mm).
Lay the glass on the putty and press
firmly into place.

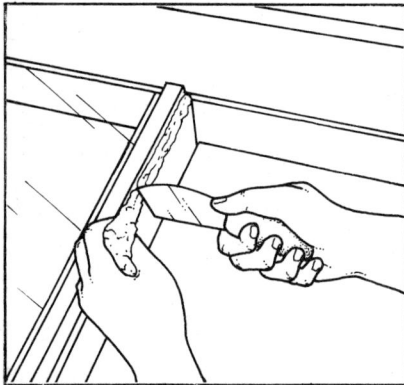

2. Make sure the frame is dry before
applying fresh putty — it will not stick
to damp wood. Use a putty knife to
press it well home.

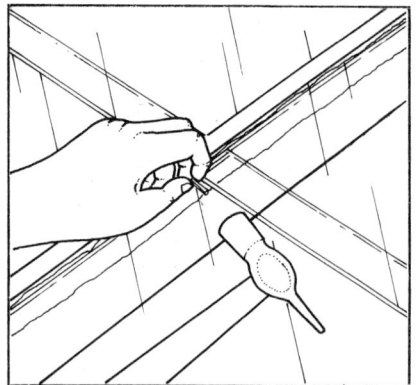

4. Fix pins below the pane on each
side to prevent it slipping. Slide the
hammer along the glass to avoid
breaking it.

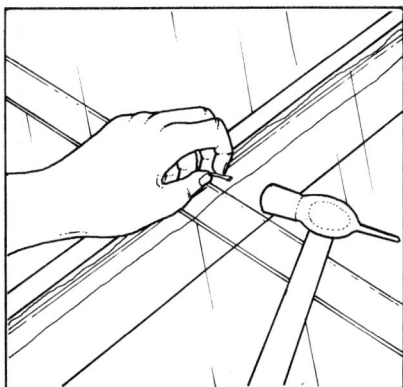

5. Fix pins above the overlap to hold the glass in firm contact with the putty.

7. Remove excess putty on the outside with a stripping knife held flat against the glass.

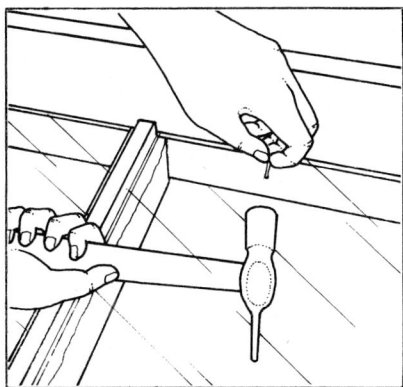

6. Hammer in pins around the three sides of the glazing bars at about 6 in (150 mm) intervals.

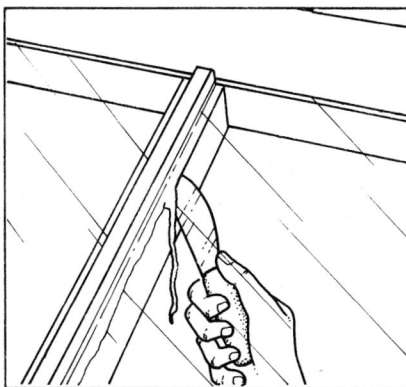

8. Inside the greenhouse, trim off the excess putty with the stripping knife blade held flat against the glazing bar.

Plumbing

Like electricity, the domestic water supply comes into the house at one point and is then directed to various parts. The point of entry is a main pipe, called the riser, which is usually situated under or near the kitchen sink. A stopcock on the riser can be turned off in an emergency, or if the house is to be left unoccupied for some time, and access to it should be kept clear.

After the stopcock the pipe goes up into the roof space and supplies the cold-water storage cistern. In most modern plumbing systems a pipe from the riser also supplies the kitchen sink tap, and this is the only tapped supply of fresh water in the house. In many older systems all the cold water taps — kitchen, bath and bathroom wash-basin — are taken from the fresh water supply.

The storage cistern may be galvanized iron or plastic. It contains a ball valve which controls the level of the water and an overflow pipe to prevent flooding should the ball valve fail. Water from the cistern is fed to the hot-water cylinder, bathroom taps and the lavatory cistern.

The hot-water cylinder is a copper tank which may be on the ground floor or upstairs, and is often incorporated into an airing cupboard. It may be heated from a separate boiler, sometimes as part of a central heating system, or by an immersion heater (see pp 16-17).

The cold water supply is taken to the bottom of the cylinder and the hot water leaves through a pipe rising vertically from the cylinder's domed top. This pipe is vented over the cold-water storage cistern, and the hot water supply to the taps is taken from a T junction just after the supply leaves the cylinder.

The system employs the U tube principle, in which water finds its own level, and therefore the pressure at the hot water taps is dependent on the height of the cold-water storage cistern. In a two-storey house with an upstairs bathroom the pressure at the bathroom taps will be lower than the pressure at the kitchen sink hot tap. For this reason, shower units that fit over bathroom taps are often ineffective because the shower head is usually only a foot or so below the level of the cistern.

Modern plumbing systems employ copper or plastic piping, both of which are easy to maintain by the handyman. Lead or iron piping used in older systems requires the skills of a qualified plumber, though temporary repairs can be carried out by the householder. Lead or iron piping can be replaced by copper, but only as a continuous run — it is not practical to try to join copper to lead.

While it is both easy and cheap to carry out your own repairs, this is as much as you are allowed to do. **Any alterations to a plumbing system require permission from the local authority.**

The indirect plumbing system

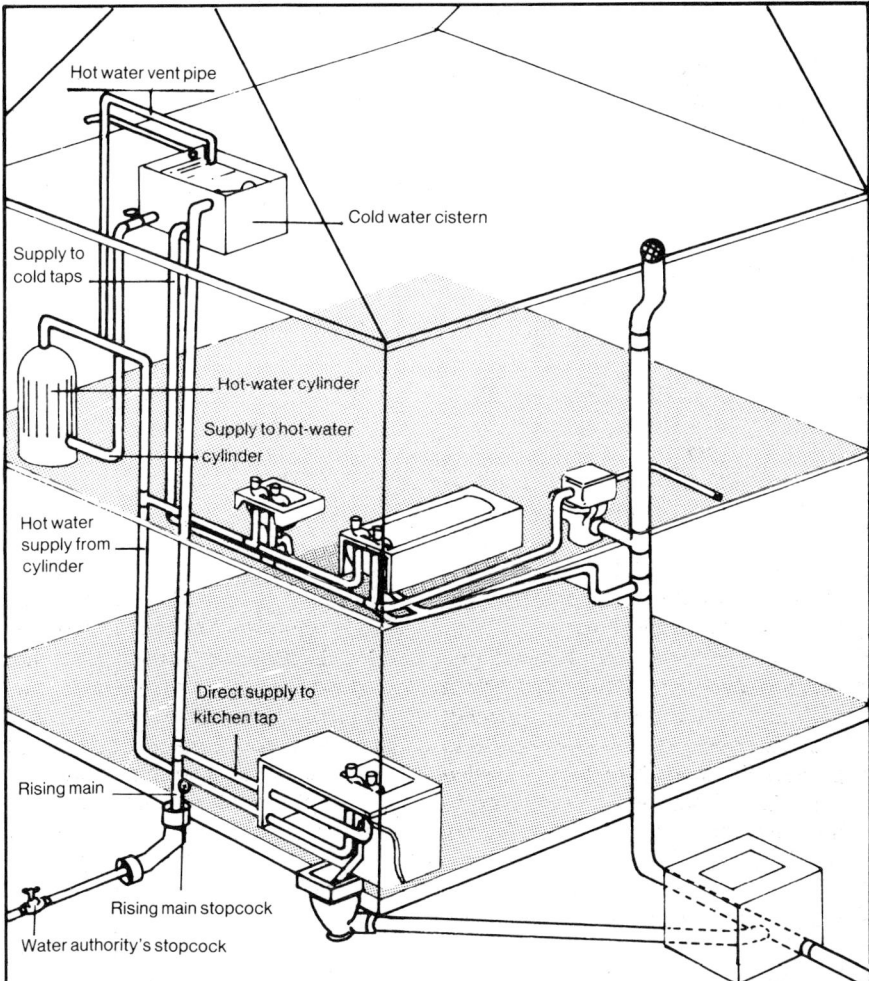

Hot water vent pipe

Cold water cistern

Supply to cold taps

Hot-water cylinder

Supply to hot-water cylinder

Hot water supply from cylinder

Direct supply to kitchen tap

Rising main

Rising main stopcock

Water authority's stopcock

In modern houses, mains water is fed to a cistern in the roof from where it is distributed to serve cold taps and the hot water system. The only direct supply of mains water is to the kitchen tap.

103

What to do in an emergency

What to do in an emergency
In the case of serious flooding, cut off the water supply at the stopcock in the rising main. If there is a stop-cock on the outlet from the cold-water storage cistern, turn that off too or jam a cork into the outlet pipe inside the cistern. Fully open all the cold taps in the house and flush the WC cistern several times to drain off the water in the pipes. **If water is coming through a ceiling, turn off the electricity at the fusebox.**

Look for the source of the leak, and if it is a burst pipe or joint, wrap rags around it to stem the flow and place a bowl or bucket underneath. As soon as the leak stops, repair the pipe or joint, or send for a plumber. You can carry out an emergency repair with a length of impregnated tape available from a hardware merchant. It is advisable to have a roll of this tape in your tool kit.

A less serious emergency such as an overflowing cistern can be dealt with by tying up the arm of the ball valve. This should stop water entering the cistern, but if it does not then turn off the water at the rising main and replace the valve or its washer. If the valve is not faulty, bend the ball float arm down so that the cistern ceases to fill when the water level is just below the overflow outlet. If, despite this, the water level continues to rise then the ball float is leaking and must be replaced.

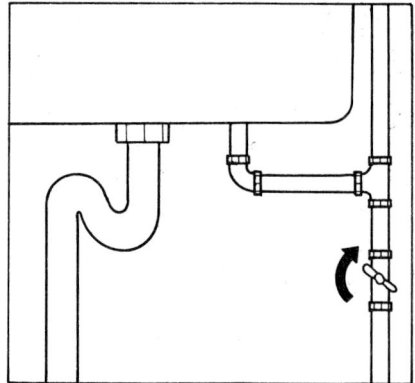

1. Whenever flooding occurs, whether caused by burst pipes or an overflow, turn off the stopcock on the rising main, which is usually under or near the kitchen sink.

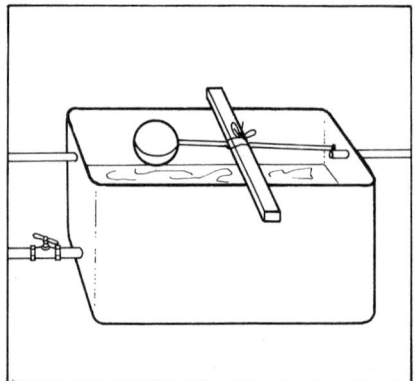

2. If the leak is in a pipe supplied by the storage tank, tie up the ball float arm. You can then open the rising main to use the kitchen tap.

Handy hint: To make repairs to the plumbing easier, especially in an emergency, identify pipes as hot or cold. At convenient points, and particularly where two or more pipes run together, paint on a band of colour — red for hot, blue for cold

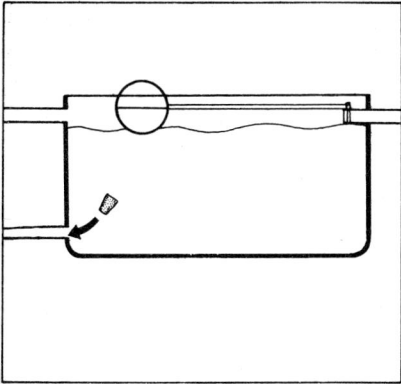

3. Next turn off the water from the storage tank in the loft. There may be a stopcock in the outlet pipe, close to the tank. Otherwise, plug the outlet with a cork.

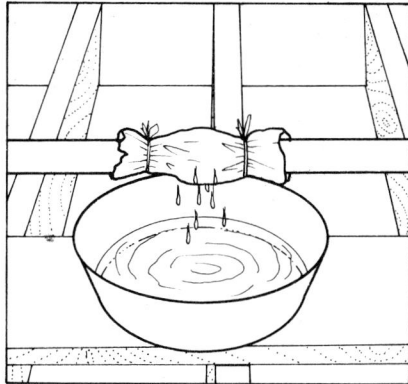

5. If a pipe burst occurs, turn off the supply and place a bowl under the leak. Wrap the pipe with rags to stem the leak until water ceases to flow.

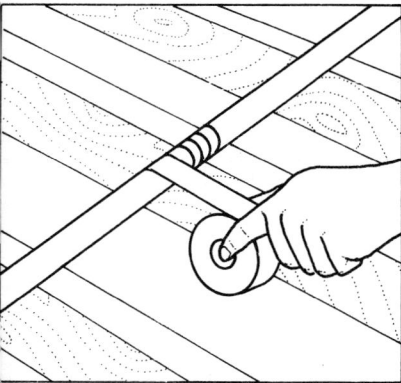

4. A split pipe can be temporarily repaired with an impregnated tape available from hardware merchants. Turn on the supply at reduced pressure until properly repaired.

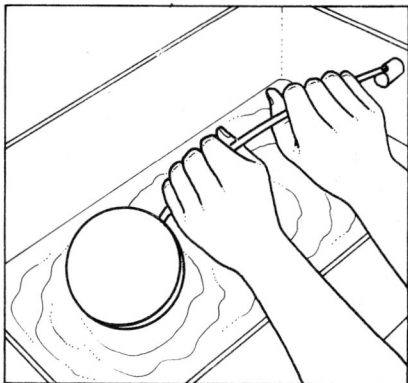

6. Fit a new washer to ball valve or bend ball valve arm to lower water level.

Frozen pipes – prevention and cure

You will need: hair dryer or fan heater; rags; bowl; impregnated tape

Dealing with frozen pipes
The best way to deal with frozen pipes is to prevent it happening. Many older houses have water pipes running along outside walls, and almost all houses have pipes and a cold-water cistern in the roof space. If you insulate your loft, remember that the water pipes are above the insulation and must be lagged. Lengths of foam plastic lagging are available from hardware merchants and DIY shops, or you can use strips of felt held in place by string binding. Insulate the storage cistern with slabs of polystyrene or a glass-fibre blanket. Lag all pipes running under the ground floor or outside the house.

If water in a pipe freezes it may burst the pipe or a joint. To locate the frozen pipe, work back from the tap which has ceased to flow and look for signs of the ice protruding from a split or around a join. **Do not attempt to thaw the pipe until you have cut off the water supply and are ready to repair the burst**.

If there is no sign of a burst, thaw the pipe by playing hot air on to it from a hair dryer or fan heater. **Do not use a naked flame**. If the pipe to the kitchen tap is frozen you may be able to clear it by removing the top half of the tap and pouring hot water down the pipe, but be ready to turn off the rising main stopcock as soon as water begins to flow. Reassemble the tap and turn on the rising main.

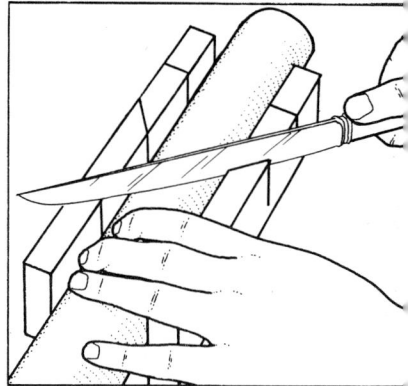

1. Effective lagging of pipes can be done with tubular foam plastic. Use a mitre box to cut the insulation at an angle to allow for bends in the pipe.

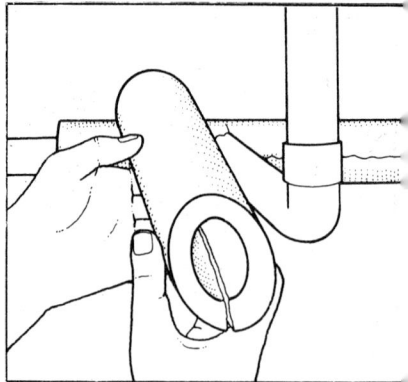

2. Slit open one side of the insulation and place it around the pipe. Make sure that angled joints are a good fit.

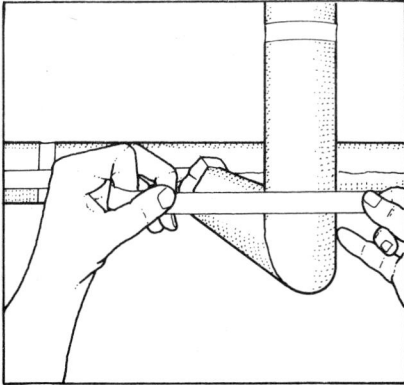

3. Secure the insulation with adhesive tape. Fit the tape close to angles and joins, and any other points where the insulation may tend to come away.

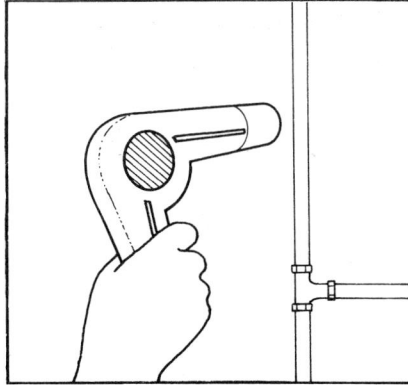

5. To thaw out frozen pipes, turn off the water supply at the rising main and apply heat from a hair dryer or fan heater.

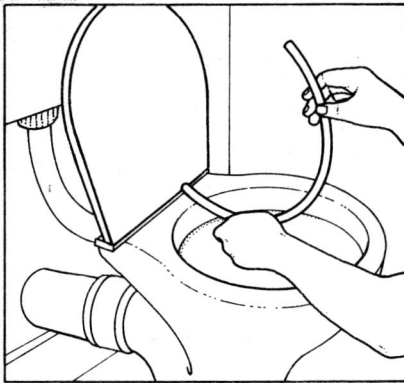

4. A length of rubber hose, with one end blocked, will prevent frost damage in a WC. Slip the hose into the trap; as the water freezes it absorbs expansion.

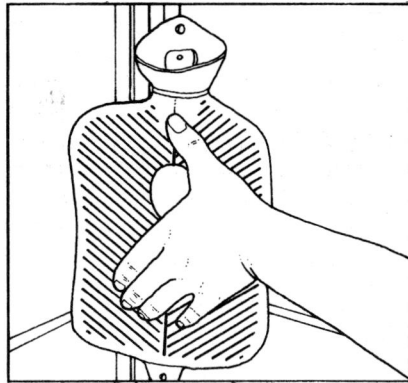

6. Where using a hair dryer is impracticable, or impossible, tie a hot-water bottle against the pipes.

Plumbing

Repairing a lead pipe

You will need: ball-pein hammer; epoxy resin; glass-fibre sheet

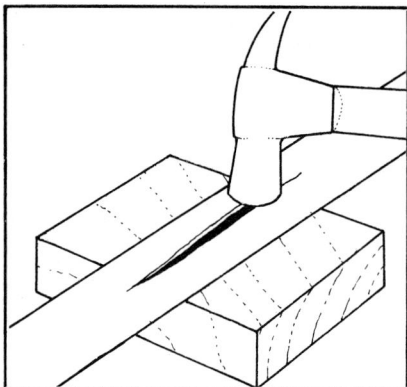

1. If a lead pipe splits as a result of freezing, first turn off the water at the rising main. Hammer along the edges of the split to close the gap.

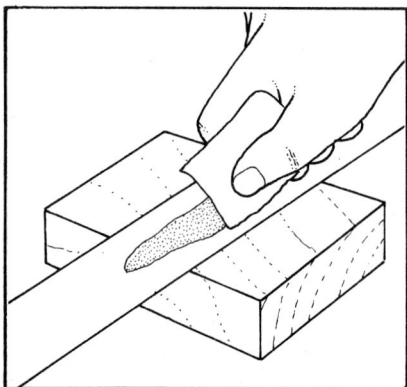

2. Cover the split with epoxy resin and allow it to set before turning on the water. **Do not use full pressure until a permanent repair has been made**.

Curing a leaky cistern

You will need: wire brush; epoxy resin

This is a temporary repair; get your cistern replaced as soon as possible.

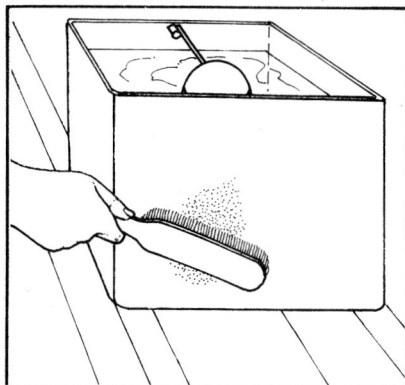

1. If a galvanized iron cistern corrodes and starts to leak, first drain off the cistern to below the level of the leak. Wire-brush over the corroded area.

2. Remove all loose rust and treat the area with a rust inhibitor. Mix a two-part epoxy resin and spread it evenly over the crack.

Types of joint used in plumbing

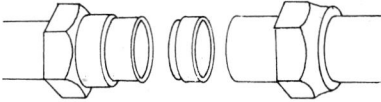

A manipulative compression joint used in plastic or metal pipes. Special tools are needed to shape the pipe ends.

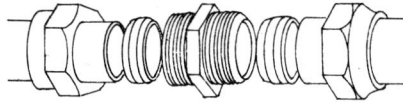

A non-manipulative joint is easy to make, requiring only spanners to thread the two halves together.

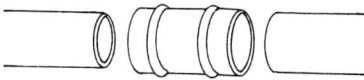

A capillary joint consists of a metal sleeve containing a ring of solder which flows when heated to seal the joint.

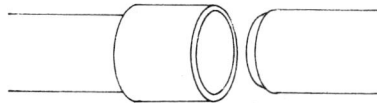

Plastic pipes can be joined using a solvent-welded joint. A special solvent coated on the pipe ends fuses them together.

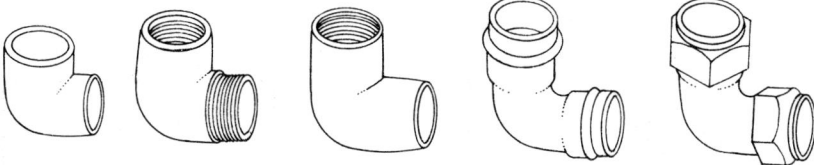

Elbow and bend joints are for making a 90° or 45° bend between two pipes.

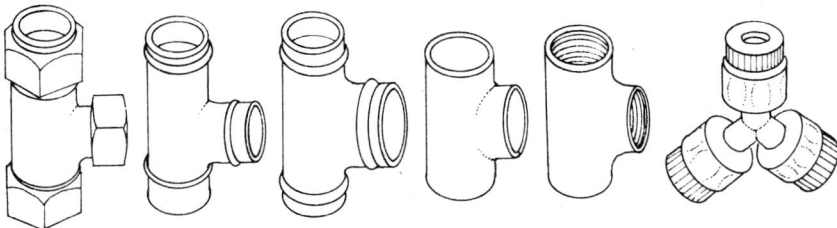

T joints or three-way joints are used to join three pipes and can also include one reduction joint.

Mending a capillary joint

You will need: blowtorch; multi-core solder; wire wool

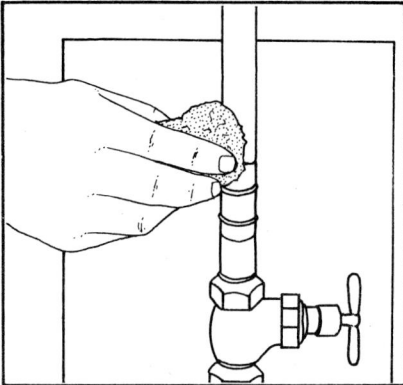

1. Turn off the water and drain the pipe. Clean the joint with wire wool.

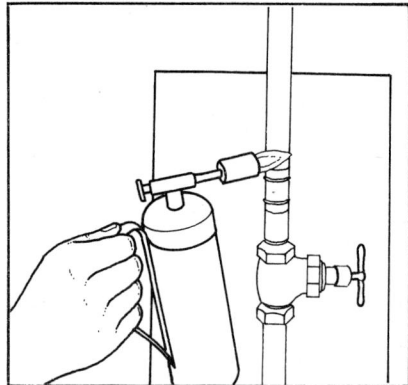

3. Heat the pipe until the solder in the joint begins to flow.

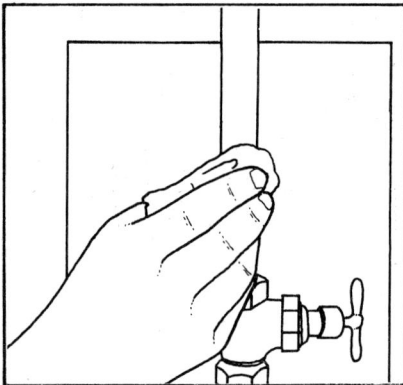

2. Place a non-flammable shield behind the pipe, such as asbestos or glass-fibre sheet. Wipe the joint with flux.

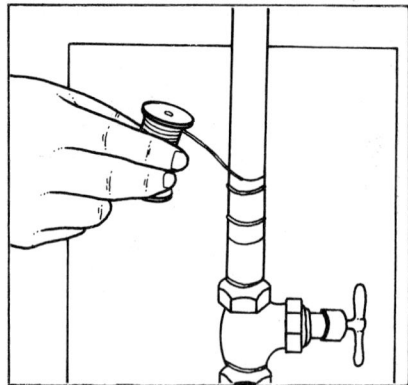

4. Run solder around the heated joint until there is an unbroken ring around the joint end. Allow the joint to cool naturally.

Mending a compression joint

You will need: adjustable spanner; ptfe tape

Clearing an air lock

You will need: screwdriver; length of garden hose; hose clips

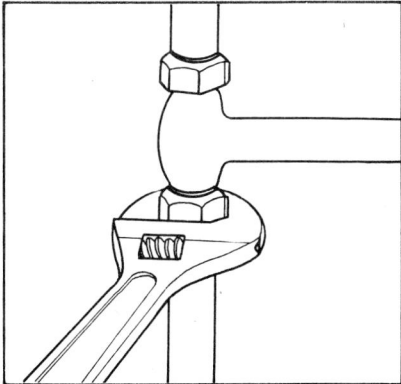

1. Drain the pipe and undo the nut with an adjustable spanner.

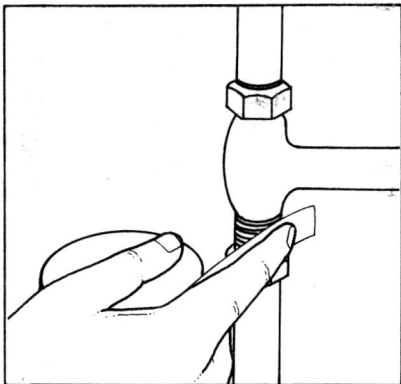

1. An air lock in the plumbing system will prevent water flowing from the kitchen hot tap. First attach one end of a piece of hose to the cold tap.

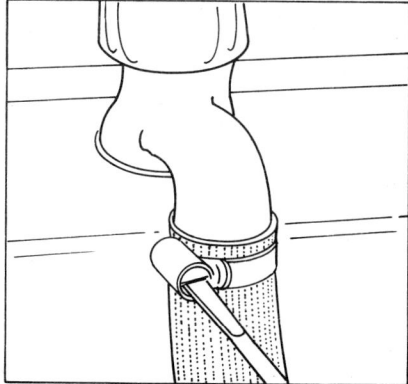

2. Wrap the threads with ptfe tape or smear with boss white. Tighten the nut.

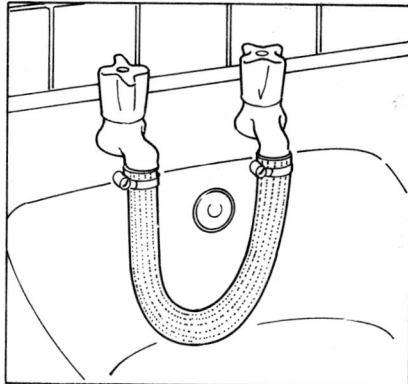

2. Attach the other end to the hot tap. Open both taps. Mains pressure water from the cold tap will eventually force the air out of the system.

Looking after taps

There are two types of tap commonly used in a domestic water supply — the capstan tap which has a central spindle and is turned on or off by a cross-head or pull-off knob, and the supatap which is controlled by turning the outer body of a nozzle.

Problems that may occur with a capstan tap are leaks at the gland nut or past the washer. Both faults are easy to cure, either by tightening the gland nut or replacing the washer respectively. If tightening a gland nut fails to stop a leak, remove the nut and pack the gland with knitting wool impregnated with petroleum jelly. Sometimes a washer leaks because its seat has corroded and become uneven; this can be cured by fitting a plastic insert.

Always have a supply of tap washers in your tool kit. There are two sizes, $\frac{1}{2}$ in (13 mm) for all kitchen and wash-basin taps and $\frac{3}{4}$ in (19 mm) for bath taps.

The gland nut on a supatap is at the top of the nozzle and should always be kept tight. A supatap washer can be replaced without turning off the water supply — a check valve in the tap automatically stops the flow when the nozzle is removed.

Keep all taps clean and polished to avoid corrosion. Apart from the unsightly appearance of corrosion build-up around joins it will make a tap difficult to dismantle for repairs.

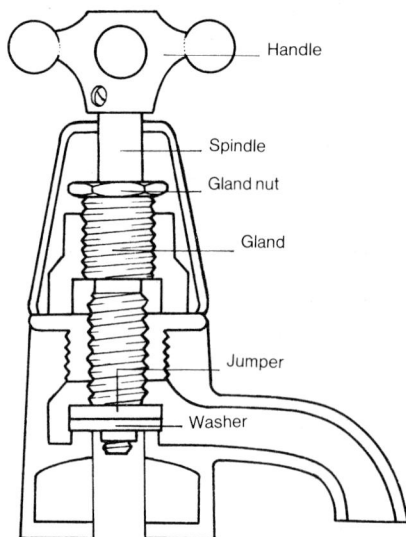

Pillar taps come in a variety of shapes but only two sizes — $\frac{1}{2}$ in (13 mm) for basins and sinks and $\frac{3}{4}$ in (19 mm) for baths. They all work on the same principle, when the tap handle is turned anti-clockwise a jumper with a washer at its base is lifted off its seat and allows water to flow.

Check valve

Jumper

Washer

Anti-splash device

Nozzle

Handle

Spindle

Gland nut

Gland

Jumper

Washer

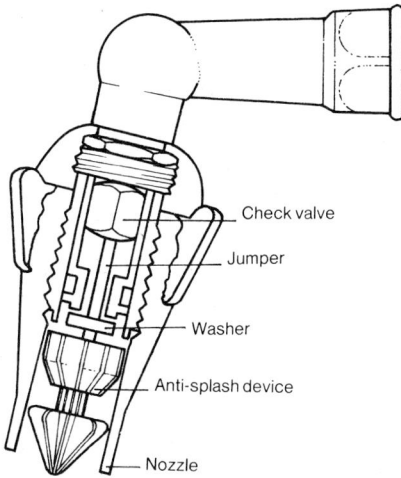

In a supatap the handle and nozzle are part of the same fitting and turn together. As the nozzle is screwed downwards, water flows past the washer and jumper and through an anti-splash device. Supataps also include an automatic check valve which cuts off the water when the tap is dismantled for repair or changing a washer.

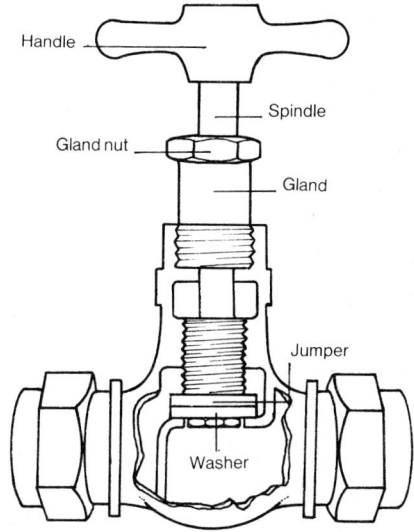

A stop valve is used to control the flow of water through pipework, such as the rising main, and works on the same principle as a pillar tap. Isolating stop valves, fitted in some low pressure pipelines, have an internal barrel with a hole through it which controls the flow.

Changing a pillar tap washer

You will need: adjustable spanner; pliers; washer

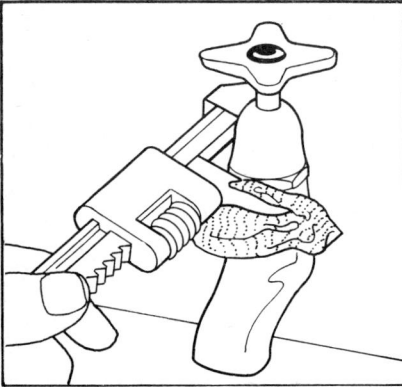

1. First turn off the water supply at the rising main. Unscrew the domed cap beneath the tap handle. If using self-locking grips, protect the chrome with a rag.

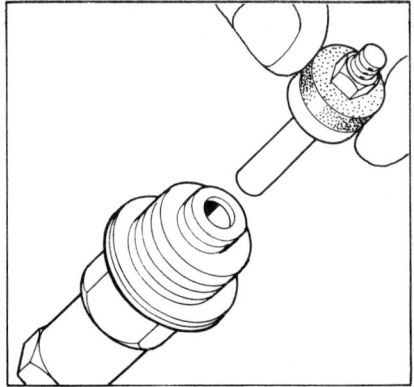

2. Open the tap fully. This should allow the cap to be lifted high enough to reveal the hexagon nut beneath. Unscrew the nut and remove the tap assembly.

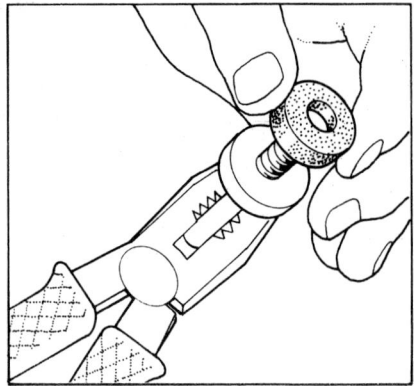

3. On a cold tap the jumper and washer are a loose fit in the tap; on a hot tap the jumper is fixed in the base.

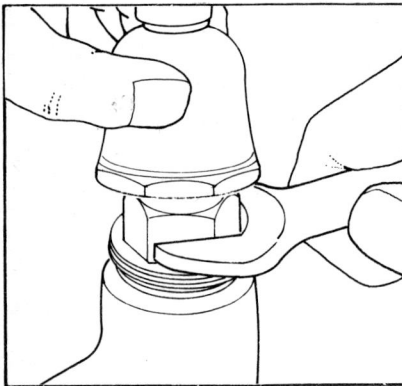

4. Hold the jumper with pliers, undo the small nut and replace the washer with one of the correct size — $\frac{1}{2}$ in (13 mm) for a basin tap, $\frac{3}{4}$ in (19 mm) for a bath.

Changing a supatap washer

You will need: adjustable spanner; washer

Handy hint: Shower units fitting over bathroom taps are often ineffective. This is because the shower head is usually placed only just above the level of the cistern. The result is a dribble rather than a shower and the solution is to have a booster pump fitted to the unit.

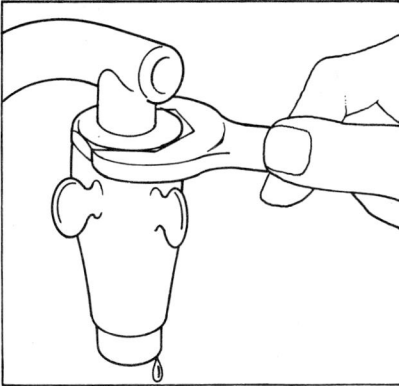

1. Supataps cut off the water automatically when dismantled. Open the tap slightly and undo the nut. When the nozzle is free the water will stop flowing.

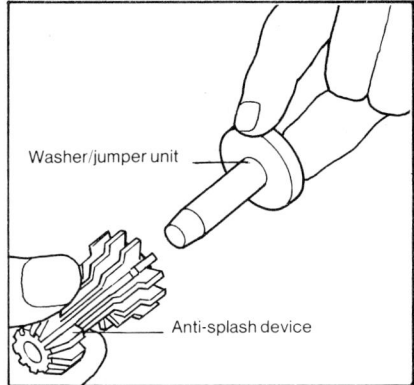

Washer/jumper unit

Anti-splash device

3. Fit a new washer/jumper unit and drop the anti-splash device back into the nozzle.

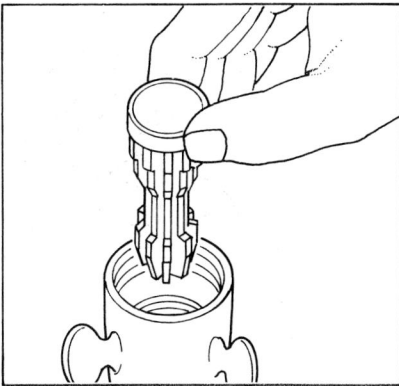

2. Tap the nozzle on a hard surface to free the anti-splash device and withdraw the combined washer and jumper unit.

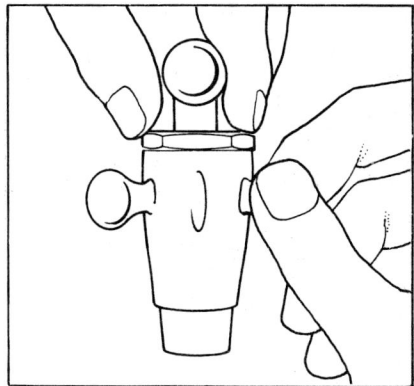

4. Screw the nozzle back on to the gland nut. Tighten the nut.

Curing a leaking gland in a pillar tap

You will need: adjustable spanner; knitting wool; petroleum jelly

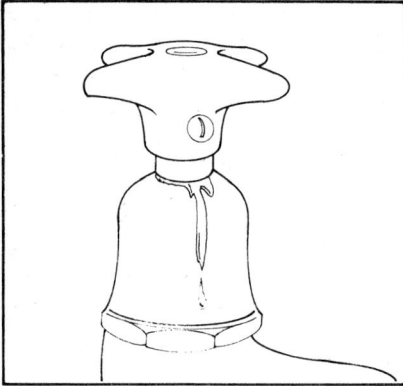

1. Water trickling over the top of the domed cover is a sure sign that the gland is leaking. It can either be tightened or replaced.

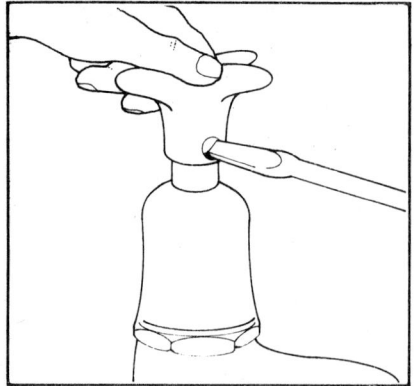

2. In this cross-section of a tap, the gland and its nut can be seen. Tightening the nut should compress the gland to improve the seal.

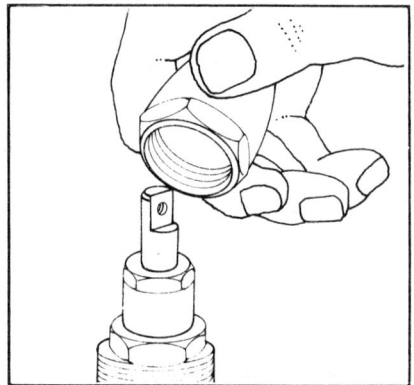

3. Remove the small screw in the handle. If the handle is a tight fit, tap it upwards gently to free it.

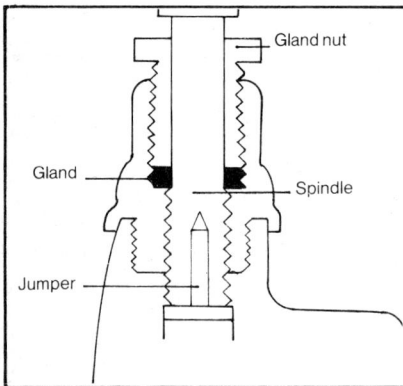

4. Unscrew and remove the domed cap. The gland nut is the smaller of the two hexagon nuts.

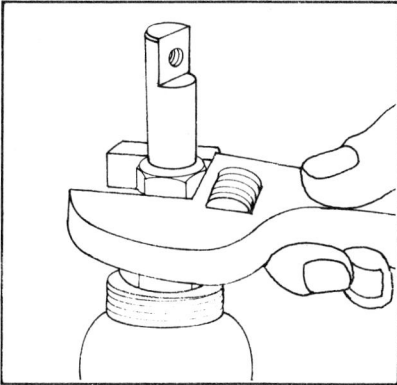

5. Tighten the nut about a quarter of a turn. Open the tap and check for a leak.

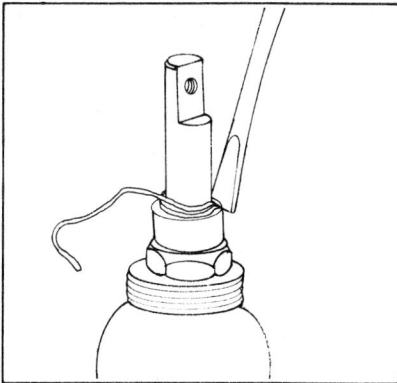

6. If the gland still leaks, remove the gland nut and dig out the old packing. Repack, with knitting wool smeared in petroleum jelly. Reassemble the tap.

Other problems, causes and cures
Water hammer. A violent knocking in the pipes when a tap is turned suddenly off is caused by a build-up of pressure in the system or a vibrating ball tap.

In a properly designed and laid-out system this should not happen, but it can sometimes be cured by fitting extra fixing brackets on long runs of pipe. Loose fitting brackets will also allow a pipe to rattle when pressure builds up. If water hammer is excessive and persistent, consult a plumber.

Insufficient flushing of a pan. This is another problem that may occur in old installations. Sometimes the joint between the pipe from the cistern and the pan is made of rag and putty, which eventually can block or partially block the pipe. The simplest cure is to remove the joint completely and replace it with a rubber push-on joint obtainable from a hardware shop.

Noisy cistern fill. In some modern lavatory cisterns the ball valve has a pipe which projects below the level of the water and so reduces the noise of water filling the cistern. If your system does not have this pipe obviously the noise will be increased. The noise can be eliminated by buying and installing a new ball tap with a soft plastic pipe, namely a Torbeck equilibrium ball valve, or equivalent.

Plumbing

Types of WC and how they work

There are two types of WC system used in domestic lavatories — the washdown and the siphonic. The washdown WC is the most widely used, it works when 2 gallons of water are released from a cistern to flush the pan. The cistern is filled via a ball valve which cuts off the supply when the ball, on the end of an arm attached to the valve, floats to a predetermined level.

The water is released when a plunger in the cistern is lifted. In a high-level suite the plunger is a cast-iron 'bell' which is raised by pulling a chain. In a low-level suite the plunger is a diaphragm inside an inverted U tube. When the diaphragm is lifted by depressing a lever it forces water over the top of the U bend into the flush pipe. This creates a vacuum in the pipe and atmospheric pressure forces the water in the cistern into the downpipe to the pan. On some slimline cisterns there is a button on top of the cistern instead of a lever.

In a siphonic system the cistern and its filling and emptying mechanisms are the same as in a washdown system. But siphonic action is used also in the pan itself. The pan has a trap that prevents the water flushing straight through and the pan fills completely; then the water transfers to a second section which causes a partial vacuum in the pan. Atmospheric pressure does the rest, forcing the water down the outlet.

Faults and cures

If a WC fails to flush it may be because there is insufficient water in the cistern. Check that the ball valve is functioning; water should flow through it freely when the arm is depressed. If not, replace the valve after turning off the water supply at the rising main. If water is flowing into the cistern but the valve is cutting off the supply before the cistern fills, bend up the ball float arm. Check to see that the water level does not rise above the overflow outlet.

In a high-level suite the plunger 'bell' is virtually foolproof, but in a low-level suite a perforated diaphragm will cause poor flushing. To replace the diaphragm, tie up the ball valve and empty the cistern. Disconnect the outlet pipe beneath the cistern and the plunger handle and shaft. Lift out the U tube and withdraw the plunger and diaphragm. Fit the new diaphragm.

After a cistern has been flushed it should refill within about 2 minutes. A slow fill may be caused by a corroded valve, which should either be dismantled and thoroughly cleaned, or replaced. When replacing a ball valve make sure to get the right type — a low pressure valve is used for a lavatory cistern, unless the cold water storage cistern is only a little way above the WC when a full-way valve is used. A high-pressure valve is used in the cold-water storage cistern.

A modern WC

Over the years, water closets have changed in style and design. Ceramics and plastics have replaced cast-iron for the cistern, levers or push-buttons have replaced the chain and more sophisticated mechanisms are used in place of the cast-iron 'bell'. But the basic principle remains the same – water stored in the cistern is released to flush the pan and take away the soil water to the main sewage system.

Wash-down system

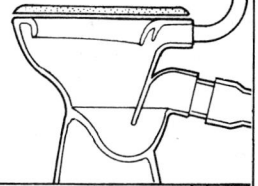

Siphonic system

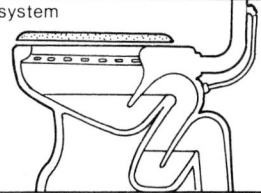

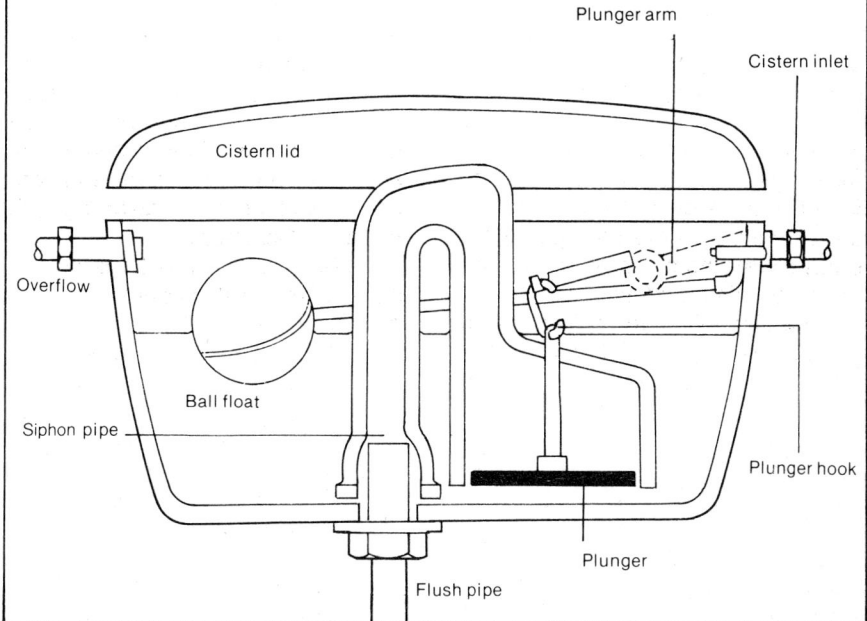

Plunger arm

Cistern inlet

Cistern lid

Overflow

Ball float

Siphon pipe

Plunger hook

Plunger

Flush pipe

Replacing a cracked WC

You will need: hammer; cold chisel; trowel; hacksaw; screwdriver; lavatory pan; cement; brass screws

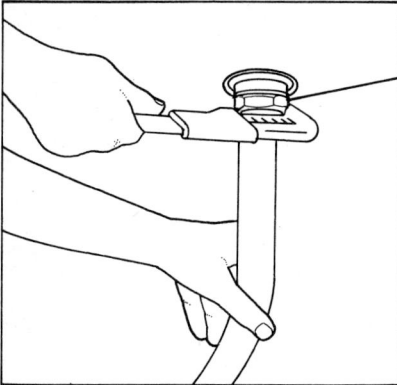

1. First turn off the water at the rising main. Flush the cistern out and mop it dry with rags. Loosen the flush pipe under the cistern.

3. Unbolt the screws holding the pan to the floor, or break the base of the pan with a cold chisel.

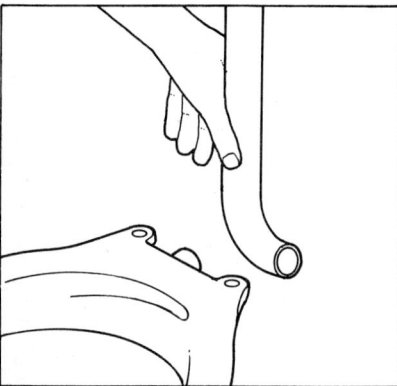

2. Have a bucket ready to catch any drips and pull the flush pipe out of the rubber joint behind the pan.

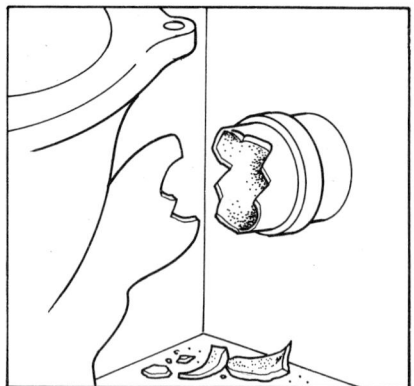

4. Break the soil outlet about halfway between the pan and the soil pipe joint.

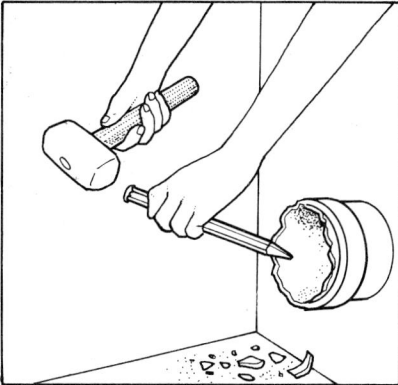

5. Chisel out the jointing compound and remains of the soil outlet. Take care not to damage the pipe.

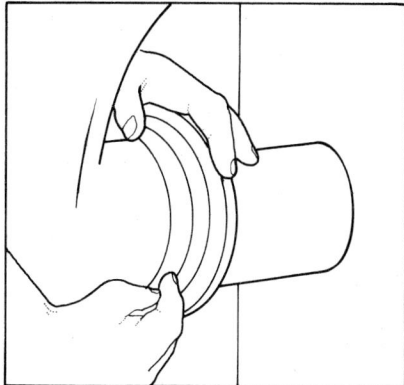

7. Fit a soil pipe gasket and push it into the joint until it meets the joint collar.

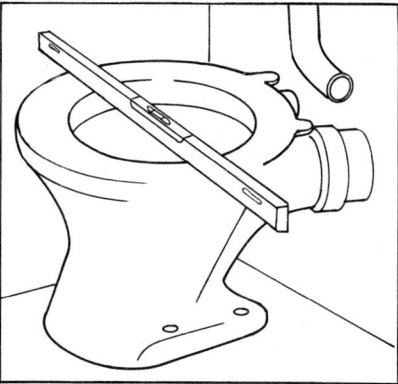

6. Fit the new pan in position. Check that it is level, and that the soil outlet fits centrally in the soil pipe joint.

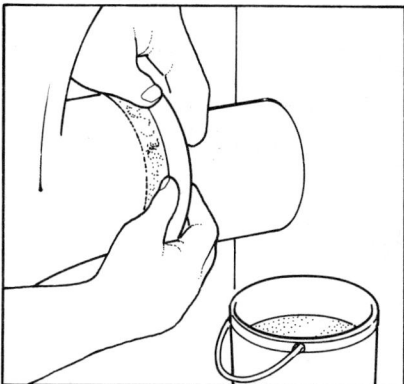

8. Fill the joint with a suitable waterproof compound, such as red lead putty. Smooth it off slightly proud of the joint and allow it to set.

(continued)

Replacing a washer in a cistern valve

You will need: screwdriver; pliers; washer

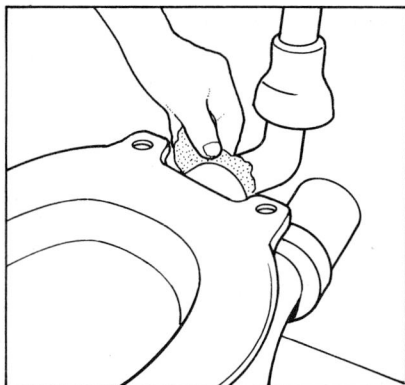

9. Fit a rubber or plastic connector on to the flush pipe. Smear the inside with a waterproof compound and slide the connector over the flush inlet on the pan.

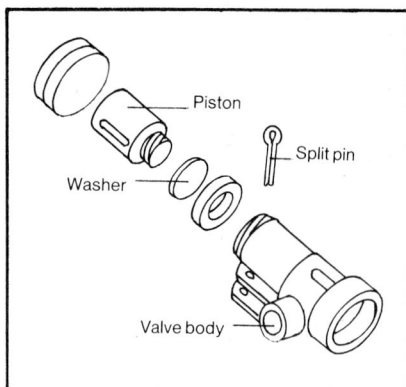

1. This exploded view shows component parts of a Portsmouth valve, which has a horizontal piston.

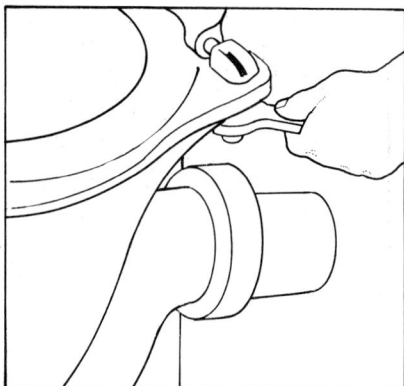

10. Fit the seat. Turn on the water at the rising main, let the cistern fill and then flush and check for leaks.

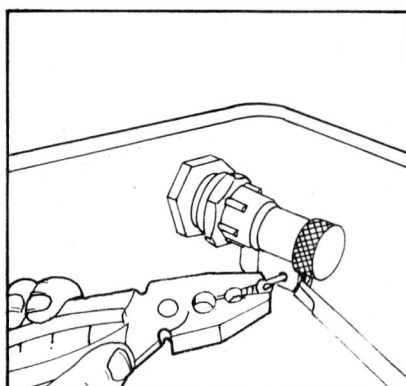

2. Turn off the water supply. Hold the ball float arm and extract the split pin holding it to the valve.

Changing the diaphragm in a low-level cistern

You will need: adjustable spanner; diaphragm valve

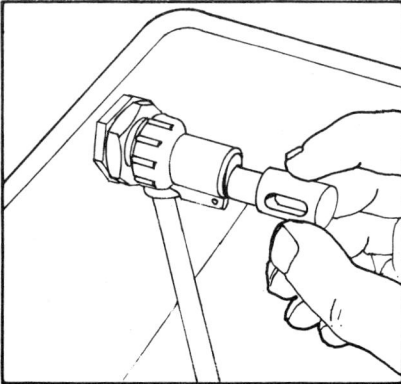

3. Pull out the piston, or lever it out with a small screwdriver pushed into the slot.

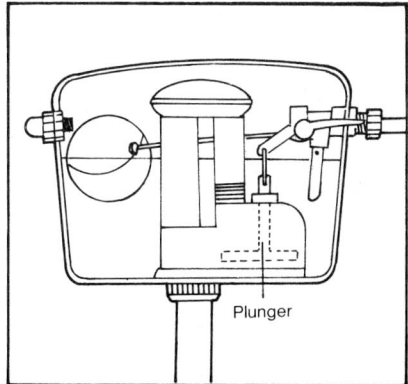

1. A perforated diaphragm may cause slow or bad flushing. Drain the cistern, disconnect the handle assembly, undo the outlet nut and remove siphon unit.

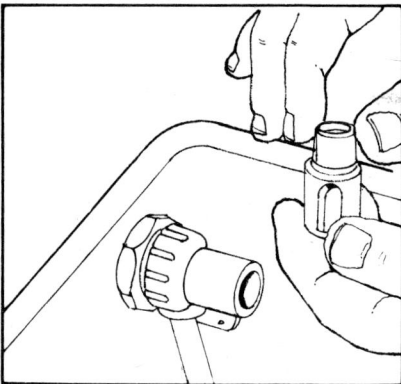

4. Unscrew the two parts of the piston and replace the washer in the cap. Make sure you lightly grease the piston before reassembling the valve.

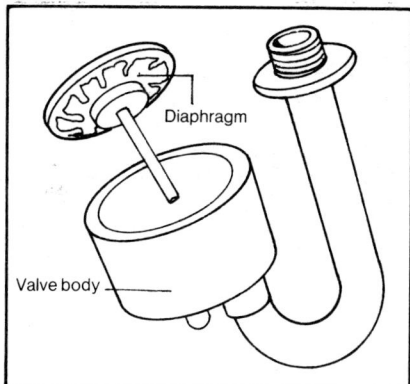

2. Remove the plunger; slide off the weight retaining the washer above the diaphragm. Make a new diaphragm from thick PVC sheet, or buy one.

Changing a ball valve

You will need: adjustable spanner; pliers; ball valve assembly

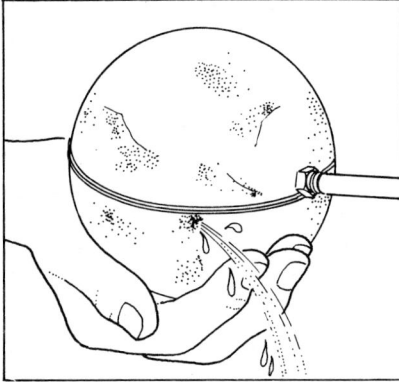

1. If there is a constant overflow from a cistern, the ball float may be leaking and must be replaced.

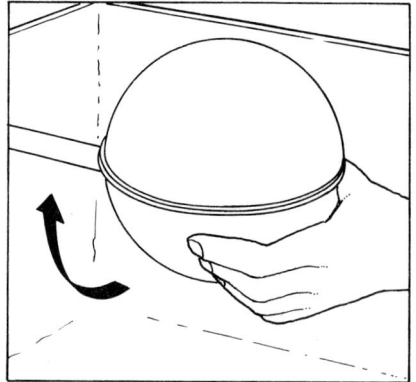

3. Fit a new ball and tighten the locknut on the arm.

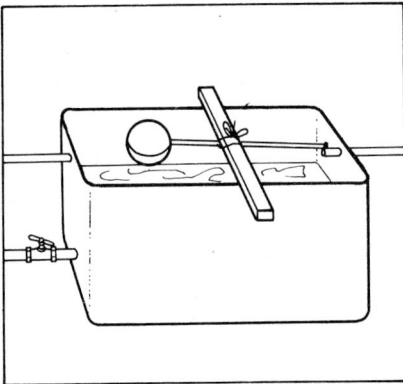

2. Tie up the arm to close the valve and unscrew the ball.

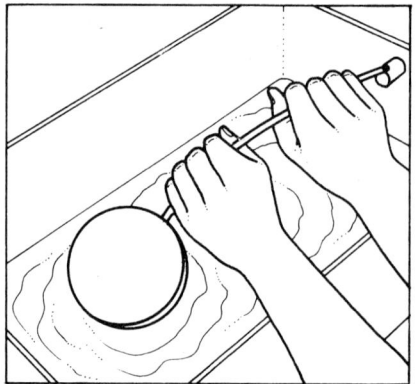

4. Untie the arm and if necessary bend it so that the water level remains below the overflow pipe.

Fitting a rubber cone to a flush pipe

You will need: adjustable spanner; push-on joint

Handy hint: If the ball float in a cistern is leaking it must be replaced, but a temporary float can be made from a plastic bottle. Drill a hole in the stopper and push it over the threaded end of the ball float arm. Use plasticine or putty to seal the join and screw the bottle onto the stopper.

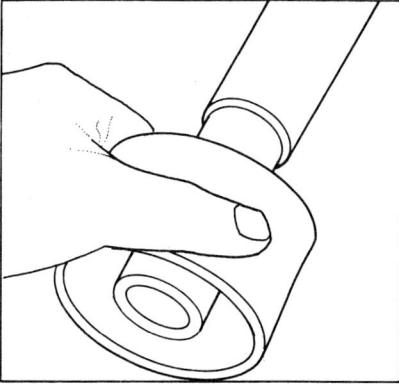

1. If a leak occurs where the flush pipe joins the WC pan, remove the old joint and push the rubber cone on to the pipe.

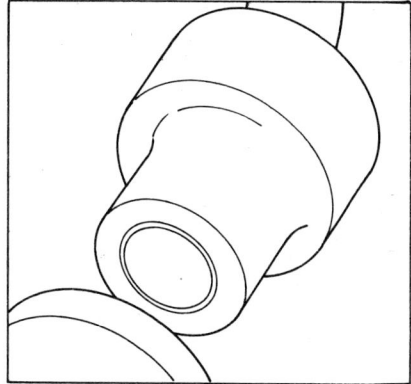

3. Insert the cone into the pan inlet pipe as far as it will go.

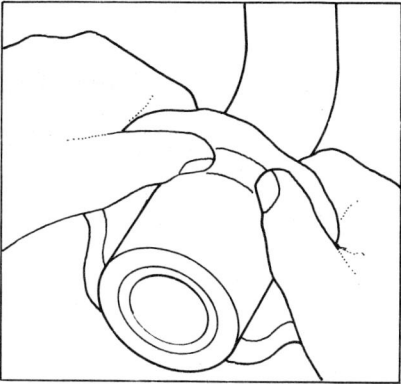

2. Fold back the cone flange so that it is inside out on the pipe.

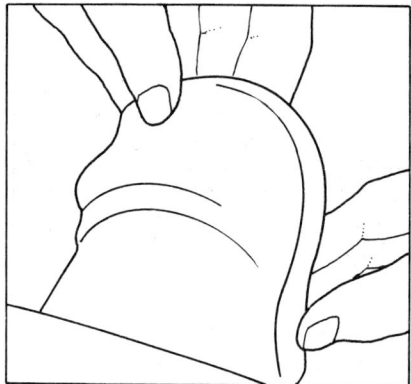

4. Fold the flange forward so that it fits snugly and evenly over the lip on the inlet pipe.

Clearing blockages in basins, lavatories and gullys

You will need: adjustable spanner; plunger; flexible wire; bowl or bucket

1. A basin blockage can sometimes be cleared with a plunger. Fill the basin with water, place the plunger over the plug hole and pump until the blockage clears.

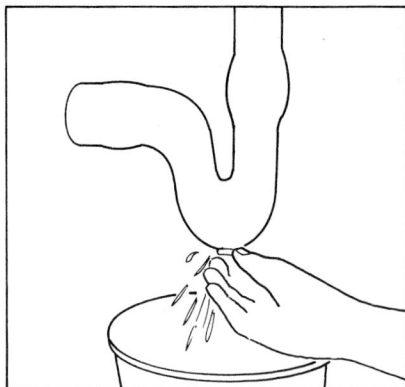

3. Place a bucket under the U bend and remove the drain plug. Run the cold tap to flush out the waste.

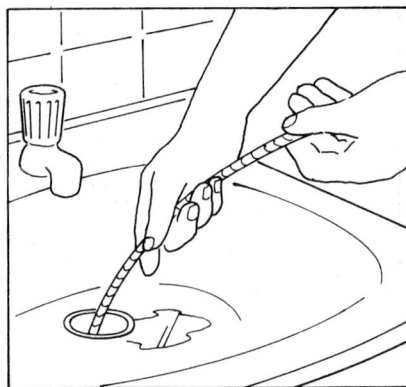

2. If using a plunger fails, insert a length of flexible wire, such as a curtain wire, into the waste hole and turn it slowly.

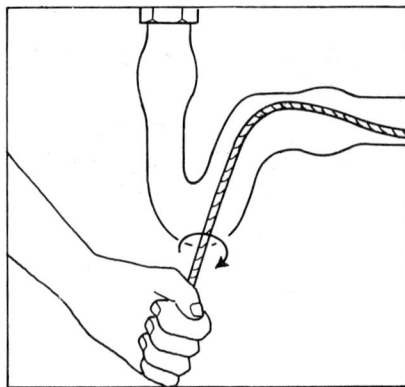

4. If the blockage is beyond the U trap, insert the wire through the drain hole and twist until the blockage clears.

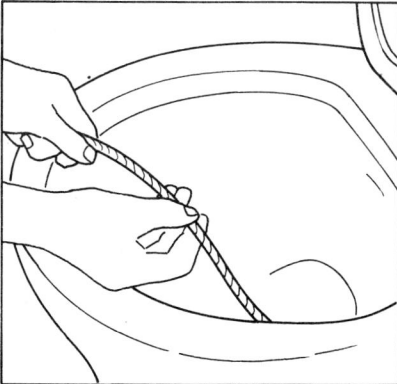

5. A curtain wire can also be used to clear a lavatory blockage.

7. Outside gullys often become blocked with leaves. First lift out the grating with a length of stiff wire.

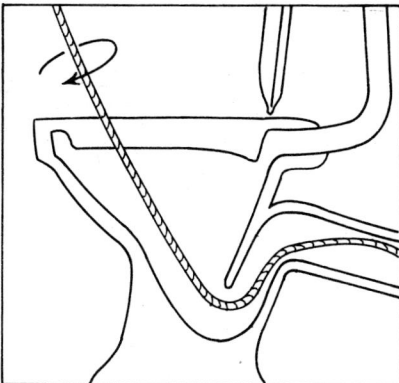

6. Push the wire well beyond the U bend and withdraw it occasionally to pull out pieces of tissue – these are the most likely cause of a blockage.

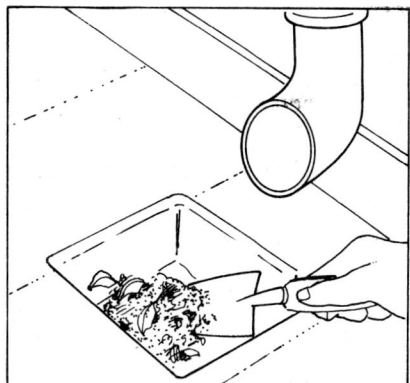

8. Use a small trowel to scoop out the obstructions. Flush several times with buckets of water and disinfectant.

Sealing gaps around sinks and baths

You will need: sharp knife; stiff brush; tube of sealant

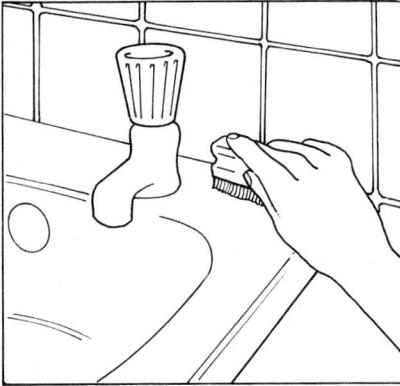

1. Small gaps can be filled with a rubber-based sealant. First clean out the gap thoroughly with a small, stiff brush.

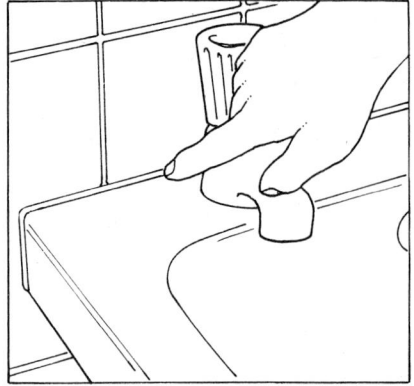

3. Run a wet finger along the sealant to get a smooth finish. Trim off any surplus with a trimming knife or razor blade.

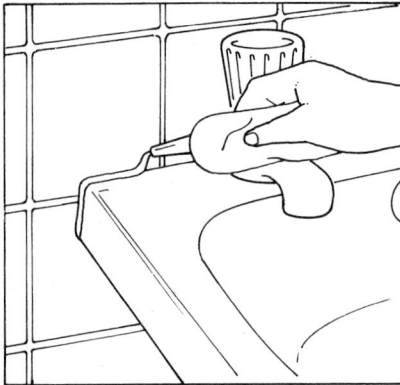

2. Wipe away any dirt and then apply the sealant. Work along the gap pressing the tube with even pressure in order to get a continuous, level flow.

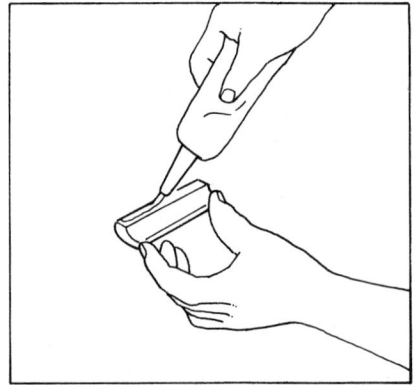

4. Cover large gaps with quadrant tiles. Use tile adhesive, applied to the two flat surfaces on the back of the tile.

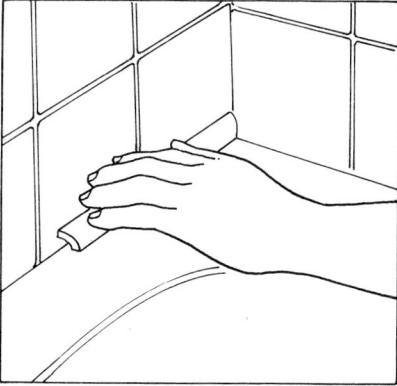

5. Start in a corner with a mitred tile, with the mitred end in the corner.

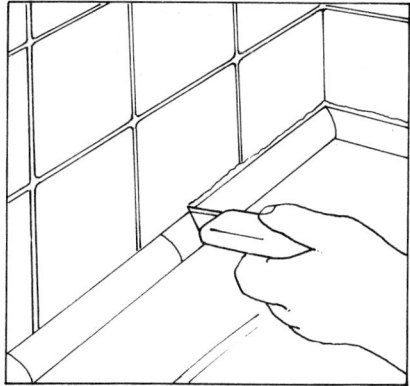

7. Work from each end towards the middle, then cut a tile to fill the gap. Trim off surplus adhesive.

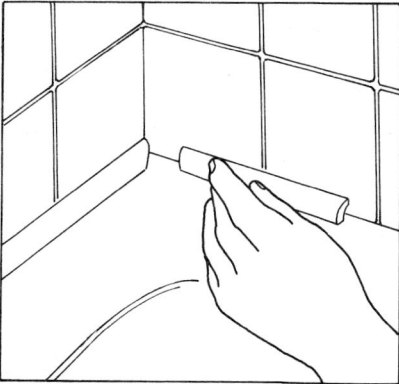

6. Fit a second mitred tile to butt against the first, with adhesive applied to the mitred face as well as underneath.

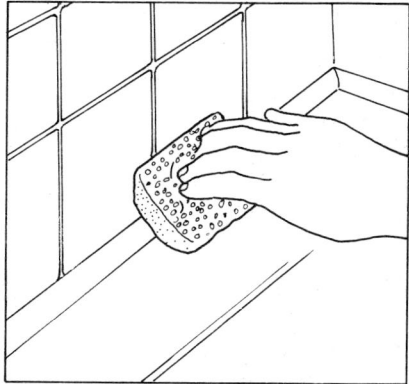

8. Use white spirit or turpentine substitute to give a final clean to the tiles. Allow 24 hours before using the bath or sink.

Enamelling a bath

You will need: 2 in (50 mm) paintbrush; sponge;
300 grit wet-and-dry paper, white spirit; bath enamel

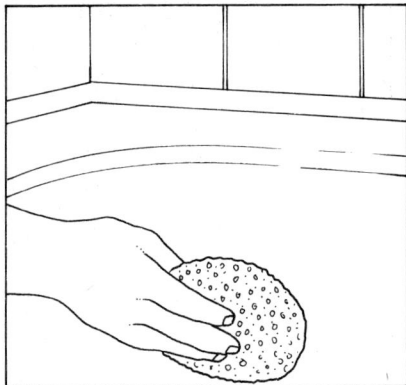

1. Chipped enamel in a cast-iron bath can be repainted with bath enamel. First of all sponge the bath thoroughly with hot water and detergent.

3. Before enamelling, tie empty tins to the taps to catch drips that will spoil the work.

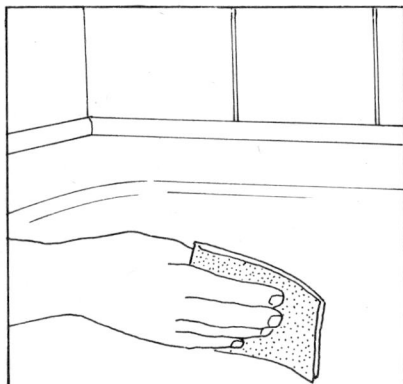

2. Use a coarse grade of wet-and-dry paper dipped in water to rub down the old enamel until it is smooth and level.

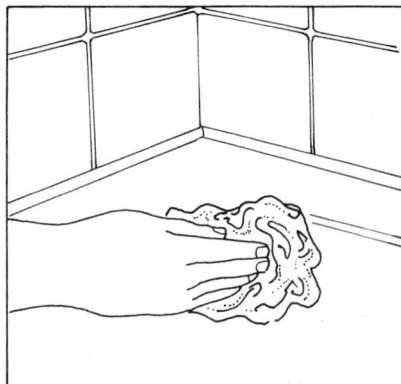

4. Give the bath a final clean with turpentine substitute or white spirit.

5. Stir the enamel thoroughly before applying with a brush. It is best to start from the bottom of the bath and work upwards with horizontal strokes.

7. Allow to dry for at least 2 days, then fill the bath with cold water.

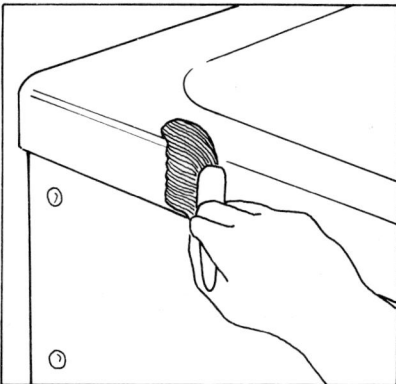

6. Finish by painting the rim, then leave to dry for 1 2 hours and apply a second coat.

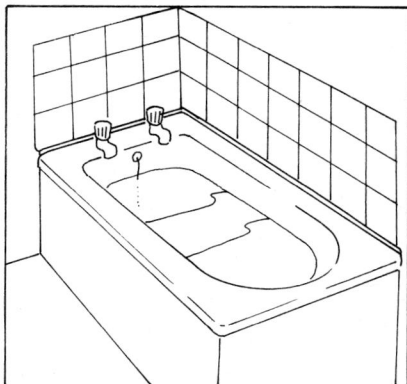

8. Keep the bath filled with cold water for another two days, then drain. When the bath is first used, run in cold water first.

Roofs

The traditional ridged roof, found in houses built before 1946, was built up from timber wall plates mounted on top of the walls. Pairs of rafters spaced at 16 or 18 in (400 or 450 mm) were attached to the wall plates and centred on a ridge board running the length of the roof. The ceiling joists were the base of this triangle. V-shaped struts gave additional support, rising from the partition wall and joined to lengths of timber called purlins. Modern roofs are usually prefabricated and are called trussed roofs.

Roofs may be covered with slates or tiles, or in some cases cedar shingles. In older houses the slates were attached to battens nailed across the rafters and with no underfelt, allowing draughts to penetrate and leaving parts of the roof open to the sky if slates were dislodged. Nowadays all roofs are underfelted with a lightweight bituminous material nailed to the rafters. Some houses also have a boarded roof.

Flat roofs are often used for extensions and garages. They are not, in fact, flat; there is a slight fall, or slope, to allow water to drain off. Construction of a flat roof usually consists of timber joists attached to wall plates on top of each wall. Chipboard or timber boards are nailed to the joists and the covering material is heavyweight bituminous felt, asphalt or sheeting.

Faults and cures

The most serious faults that can occur in a timber roof are dry rot or woodworm. **Check regularly for these dangerous diseases** – watch out for wet rot also if the roof has leaked at any time.

Slates or tiles may become loose and should be refixed or replaced as soon as possible, as should ridge tiles – the curved tiles that are cemented to the ridge at the apex of the roof.

Decorate the lower part of the roof at least once every five years, using a good weatherproof paint (see p 220). Paint the fascia boards – the boards to which guttering is attached – and the underside of the fascias, called soffits. On gable-ended houses the barge boards should also be painted regularly. These are the boards that protect the roof timbers at the gable end. Late summer is the best time to paint all outside woodwork.

Whether painting or repairing a roof, always use scaffolding if possible. Easy-to-erect scaffolding can be hired and will make the work easier and safer. **Make sure ladders are properly secured**. Never stand a ladder on uneven ground. When painting, hang the paint pot from a hook attached to a rung so as to leave one hand free for holding on to the ladder. Always use crawling boards when working on a roof – these can also be hired.

How roofs are constructed

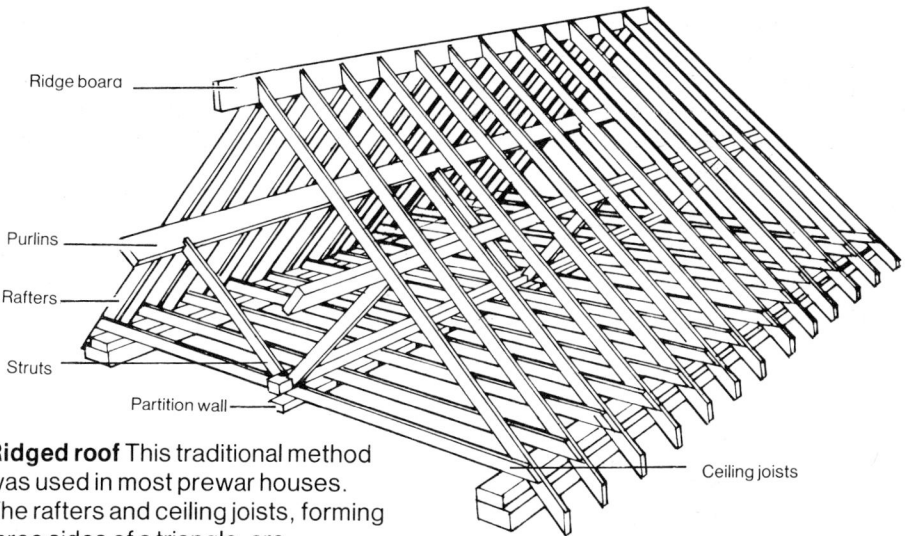

Ridge board

Purlins

Rafters

Struts

Partition wall

Ceiling joists

Ridged roof This traditional method was used in most prewar houses. The rafters and ceiling joists, forming three sides of a triangle, are strengthened by struts bearing on purlins and centred on a partition wall.

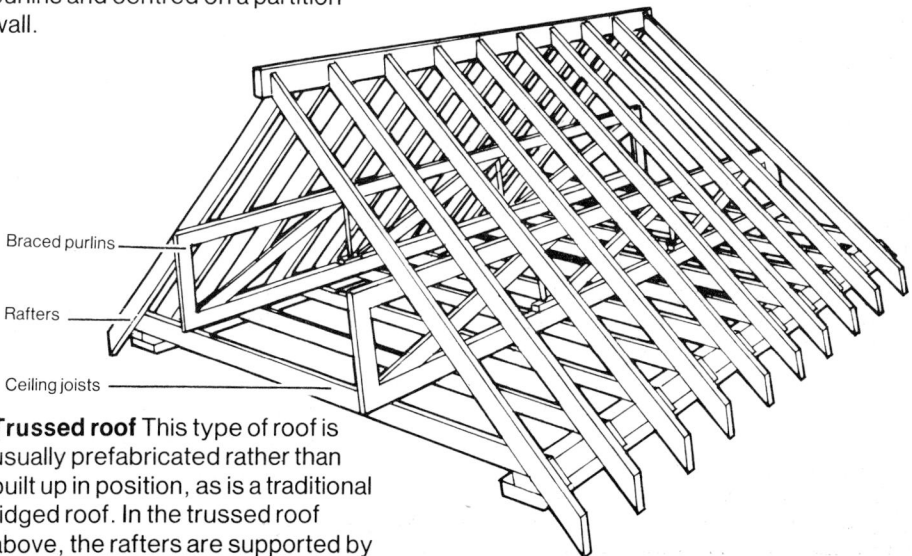

Braced purlins

Rafters

Ceiling joists

Trussed roof This type of roof is usually prefabricated rather than built up in position, as is a traditional ridged roof. In the trussed roof above, the rafters are supported by girder-like braced purlins.

133

Repairing an asbestos roof

You will need: hammer; pincers or wrench; hand-drill; galvanized nails

It is dangerous to inhale asbestos dust. Always wear a mask when cutting or drilling asbestos sheets.

1. To remove the damaged section, kneel on a piece of wood placed where the sheets overlap. Remove the nails with pincers or a wrench.

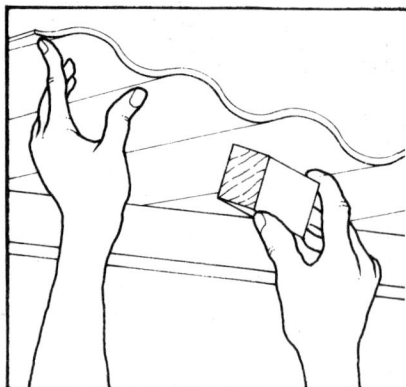

3. Slide the new sheet into position, with one edge under the raise sheet and the other edge overlapping the sheet on the other side.

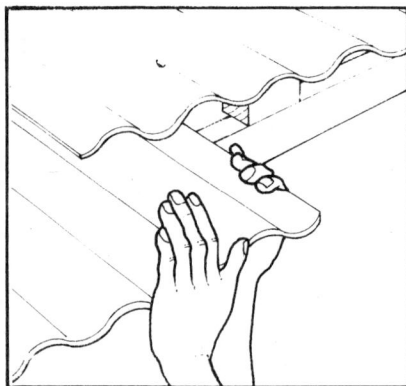

2. Slide out the sheet to be replaced and raise the adjacent overlapping sheet. Support it on wood blocks about 2 in (50 mm) square.

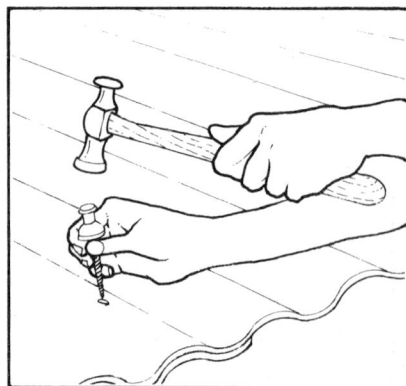

4. Drill holes in the new sheet, using the holes in the existing sheets as a guide, and nail to the joists with galvanized nails fitted with rubber washers.

Painting fascia boards and soffits

You will need: stripping knife; sandpaper; paint-brush; paint

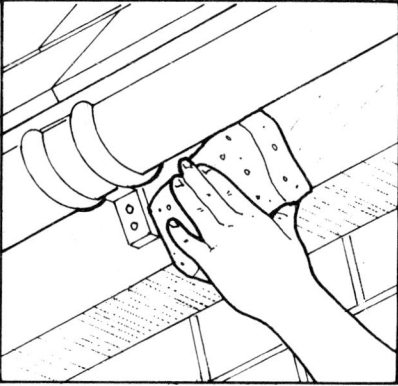

1. First wash the fascia and soffit with a strong detergent in warm water.

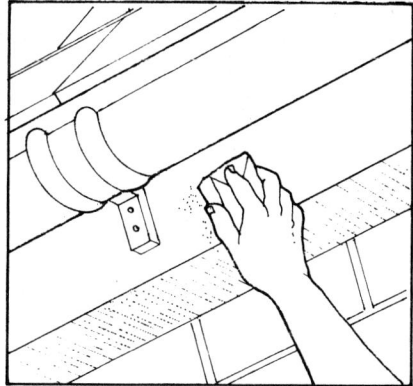

3. Rub down the edges of bare patches to bring them flush with the surrounding paintwork.

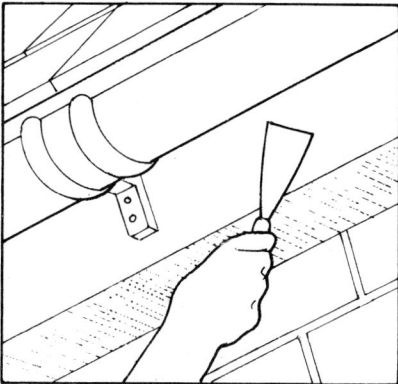

2. Use a stripping knife to remove all flaking and blistered paintwork. Paint any bare patches with primer undercoat.

4. Paint the fascia boards and soffits with a good quality oil-based paint – a non-drip paint is ideal for this to avoid splashes on the walls.

Types of slates and tiles

Slates and tiles

Slates are laid in rows, each row being staggered so that each slate partly covers two below it. The slates are nailed to battens fixed to the rafters, and a common fault on a slated roof is 'nail sickness' — when the nails rot away and the slates slip out of position. Loose slates cannot be renailed because their fixing point is covered by the slates in the row above, but they can be held by strips of lead.

Cracked or broken slates must be replaced, but natural slates are expensive and hard to obtain. Good substitutes, however, are asbestos-cement slates.

Most modern houses have tiled roofs. The tiles are pre-cast concrete and are laid in much the same way as slates, that is, in rows with each tile partly covering two below it. In most cases, however, tiles are nailed only at every third or fourth row. On the other rows the tiles are hung over the battens by projections, called nibs.

The attractive pantiles are curved and each tile overlaps the one next to it. Interlocking tiles have a channel along the underside which interlocks with the corresponding ridges on the neighbouring tile. Some tiles interlock at the sides only, others at the sides and top.

Ridge tiles are laid along the apex of the roof and are bedded in mortar. They are half round or V-shaped.

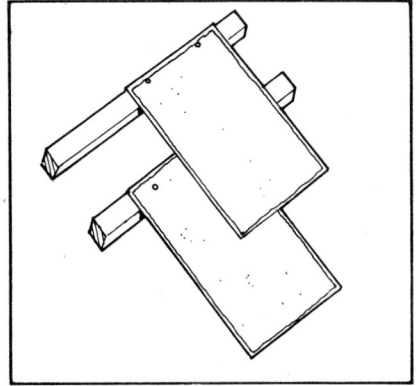

All slates must be nailed to roofing battens. The most commonly used type is the head-nailed slate, where the nails are fixed at the top of the slate.

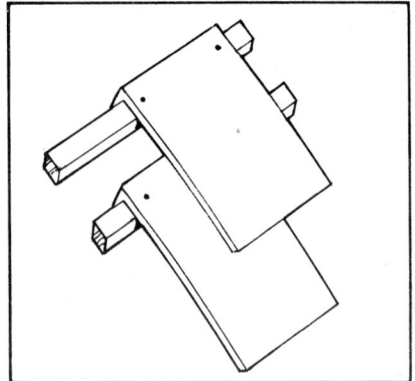

Clay tiles have small projections — called nibs — that hook over the batten. The tiles are nailed at every fourth or fifth row; in exposed areas every row is nailed.

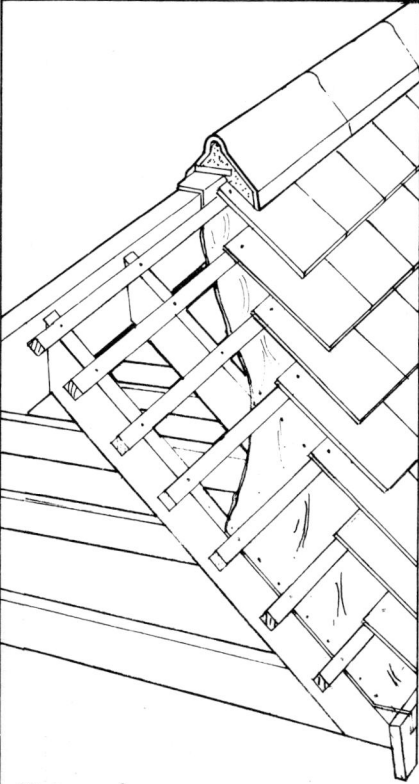

Slate roof

Many older houses have slate roofs. The slates are nailed to battens either at the top of the slate or at the centre. Each slate overlaps two below it, the amount of overlap depending on the pitch of the roof.

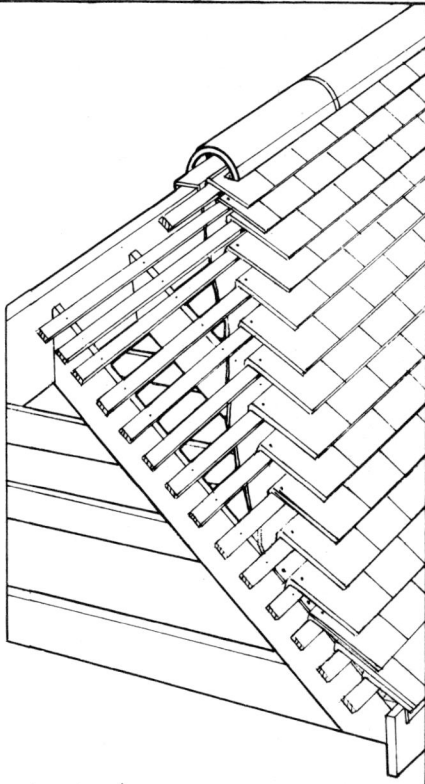

Tiled roof

Plain tiles have a hooked end, called a nib, which hook over a batten. This and the weight of the tile above is sufficient to hold it in place, but tiles are usually nailed at the ends of rows and along every fourth or fifth row.

137

Replacing a broken slate

You will need: hammer; slate ripper; slating nails; pieces of lead

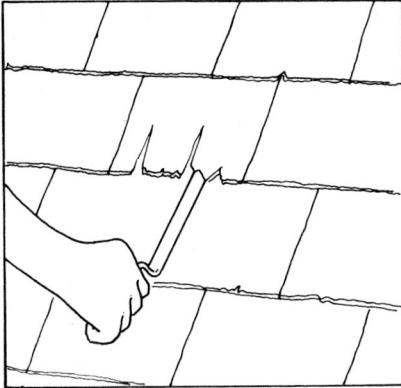

1. All slates are nailed to battens and you will need a slate ripper which can be hired. Hook the ripper under the slate and break it away from the nails.

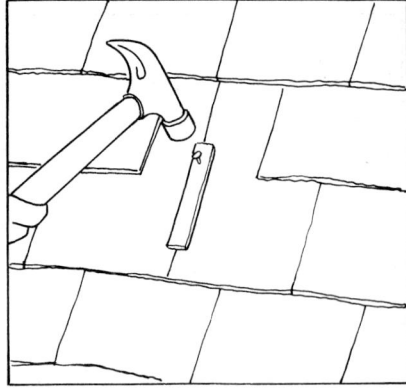

3. Nail a 1 in × 9 in (25 mm × 230 mm) piece of copper or lead between the now exposed slates.

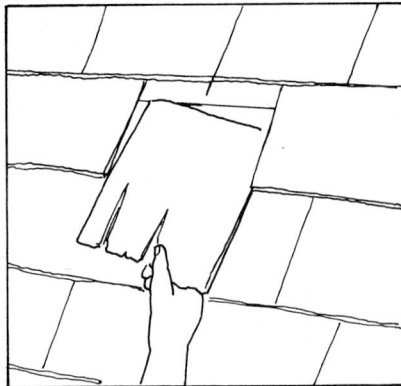

2. Take out the broken slate, making sure not to damage the adjacent slates.

4. Slide the new slate under the slates above and bend up the strip to hold the slate in place.

Replacing a broken tile

You will need: slate ripper; hammer; galvanized nails

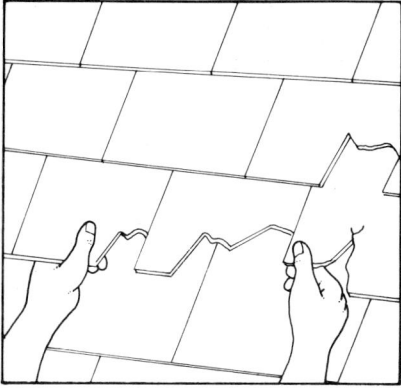

1. Lift the tile above the one to be replaced and slide out the broken pieces.

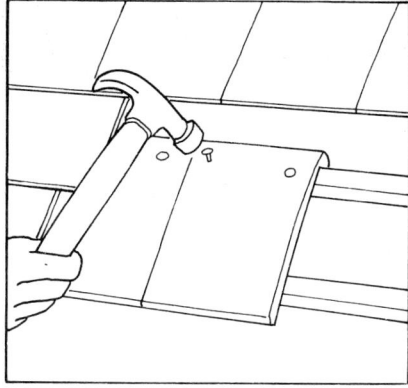

3. Release a nailed tile by twisting it away from the batten. Fit the new tile with galvanized nails.

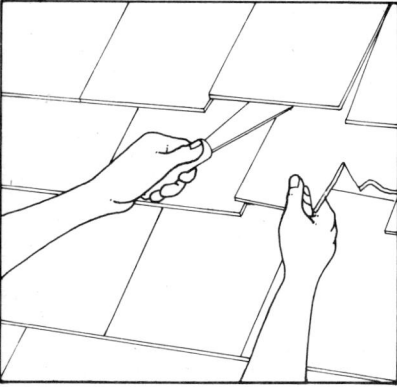

2. If the broken tile is hung on a batten, lift the tile above high enough to lift off the damaged one.

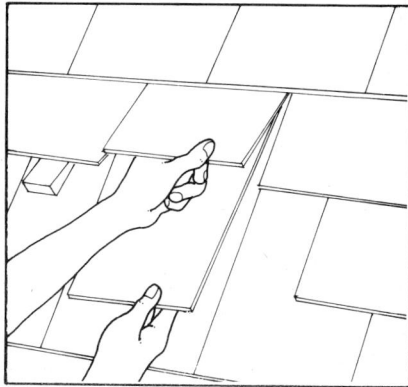

4. To replace a nibbed tile, lift up the tile above and hook the nibs of the new tile over the batten.

Fixing a loose ridge slate

You will need: hammer; cold chisel; trowel; mortar

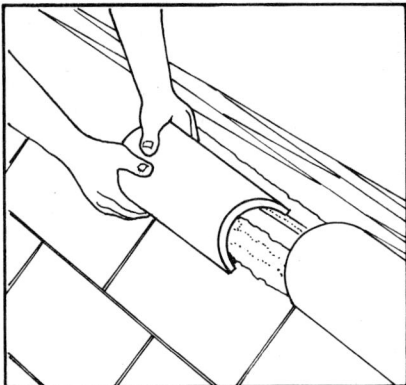

1. Take great care when removing a ridge slate; it will be heavy and is easily broken.

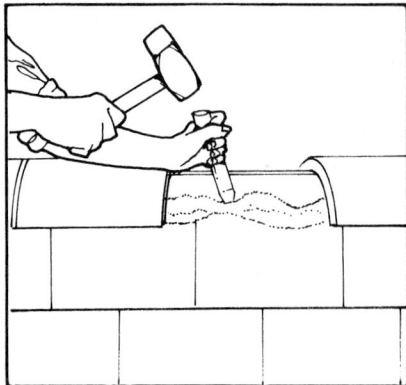

3. Remove old mortar from the ridge with a bolster chisel. Take care not to damage the roof slates.

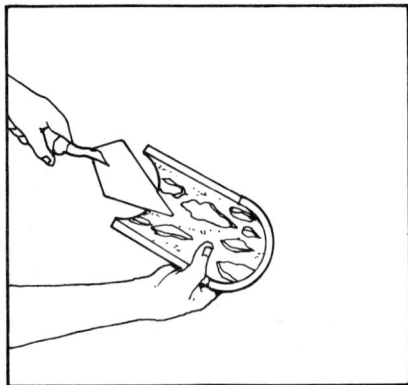

2. Use the edge of a pointing trowel to chip away old mortar. The inside of the slate must be clean or it will not sit level when replaced.

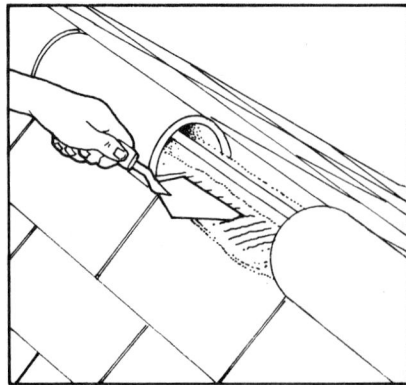

4. Mix a quantity of mortar (see pp 188-189), and lay it along the ridge.

140

Replacing a ridge tile

You will need: trowel; mortar

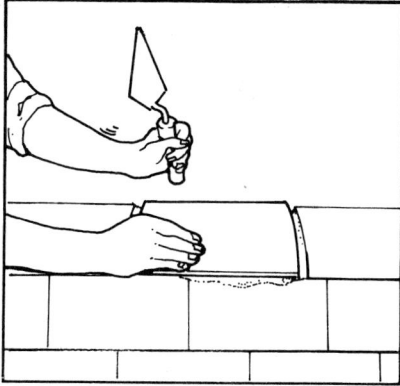

5. Replace the ridge tile, using the handle of the pointing trowel to level it with the adjacent ridge slates.

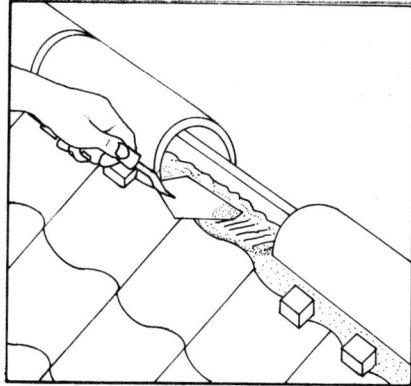

1. Ridge tiles should be refixed or replaced if they become loose. Lay a fresh bed of mortar (see pp 188-189) along the exposed ridge before fitting the tile.

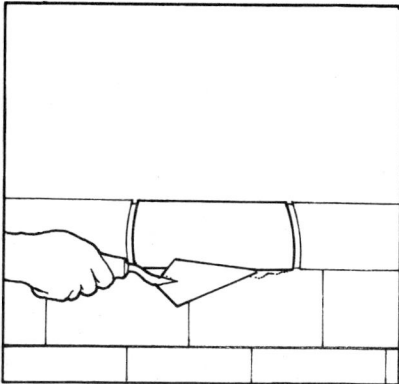

6. Fill the gaps at each end of the slate and along the bottom with mortar. Remove surplus mortar with the edge of the trowel.

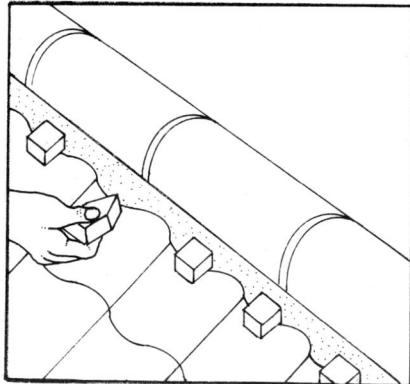

2. Lay the tile on the mortar bed, in line with the adjoining tiles. Insert triangular pieces of tile into the wet mortar to support the tile.

Replacing a shingle

You will need: slate ripper; hammer; cold chisel; hand axe; trimming knife; galvanized nails

Shingle roofs

One of the most attractive types of roofing is the cedar shingle, sometimes used on rural properties but seldom seen in towns. The shingles are made of western red cedar, and are popular in Canada and the USA. In the UK, manufacture of the cedar shingles is closely controlled to meet the requirements of the building regulations with regard to fire risk.

Shingles can be obtained in two grades, treated or untreated. Treated cedar shingles are impregnated with a preservative which, it is claimed, gives them a life of about 50 years. Untreated shingles will last for about 30 years.

Unlike tiles or slates, shingles are made in a range of widths of 4-12 in (100-305 mm) and are about 16 in (405 mm) long. They are nailed to battens spaced 5 in (125 mm) apart; no underfelt or boarding is used. Each row consists of randomly laid shingles which partly overlap the two rows below, so that there are always three thicknesses of overlap.

No special shingle is used on the ridge; instead rows of shingles are laid along each side of the ridge at right angles and are nailed to the top row on each side of the roof.

Shingles become brittle with age, and replacing one on a roof more than 15 years old can be tricky as the adjacent shingles may break. On an old shingle roof, have repairs carried out by a roofing specialist.

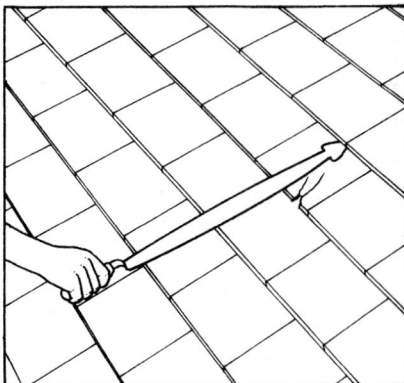

1. To replace a shingle you will need a slate ripper, which can be hired from a hire shop. Insert the ripper under the shingle above the one to be removed.

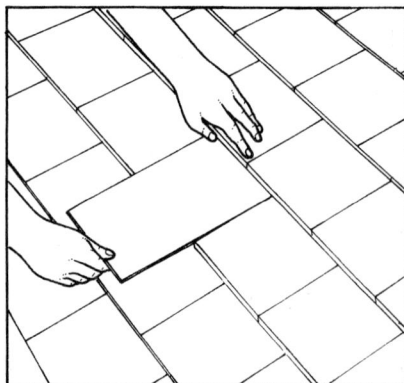

2. Pull back the ripper to shear the nails in the shingle. Then lever out the shingle and remove the nails. Fit the new shingle under the shingles above.

Construction of a shingle roof

Shingles are laid in much the same way as tiles, but no underfelt is used. The ridge is covered by shingles butted against each other and overlapping.

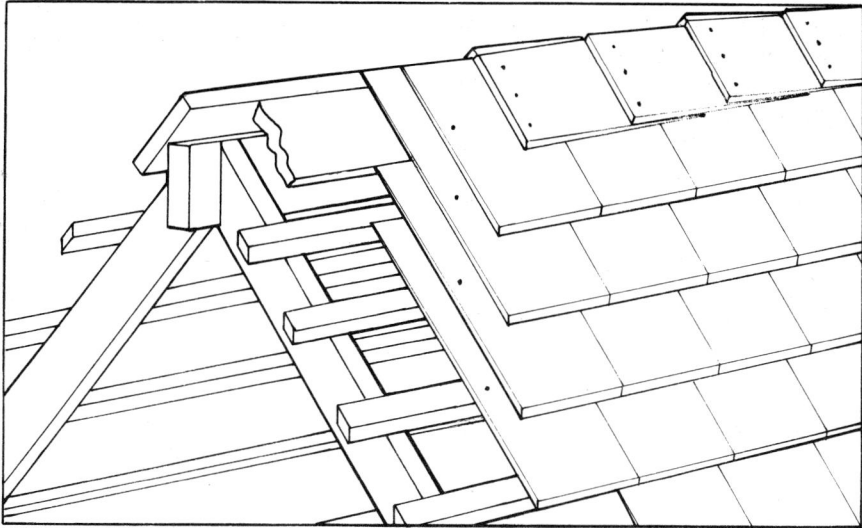

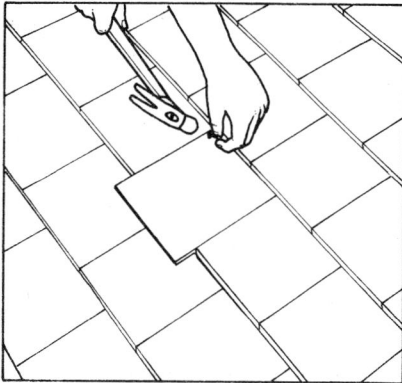

3. Nail on the shingle, using two nails placed close to the edge of the shingle above, leaving about 1 in (25 mm) of the new shingle projecting.

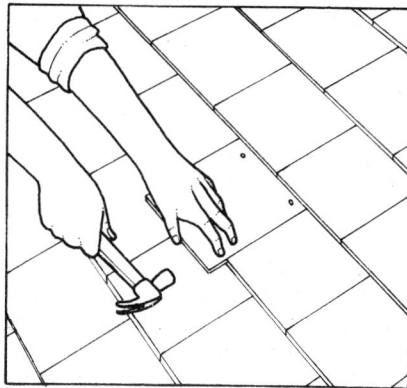

4. Gently tap the edge of the shingle with a hammer until it is in line with the other shingles and the nails are concealed.

Staircases

Two types of staircase

S taircases in a house are usually one of three types. In many 'two-up, two-down' Victorian houses the stairs are a straight flight between the walls of the rooms. In a house with a hallway the stairs may be against one wall with a balustrade on the open side, or the stairs may be centrally placed with a balustrade on both sides.

Often there is a turn in the stairs, called a dog-leg, in which the upper flight turns 90° or 180° to the landing. Sometimes tapered steps are used to turn the foot of the stairs through a right-angle.

The type of staircase used is governed largely by the space available, but all types are built on much the same principle. The steps are called treads, and each tread has a nose that projects over the vertical board below it, called a riser. On each side of the staircase are the strings — thick boards that support the treads. In some staircases the treads are set into grooves cut in the string; this is called a closed string. In others the string has steps cut into it to support the ends of the tread; this is called a cut string. In some modern houses, open-riser staircases are used where treads are set on or between the strings.

Balustrades are constructed between newel posts at the top and bottom of the stairs. A handrail is jointed into the newel posts at each end and balusters support the rail.

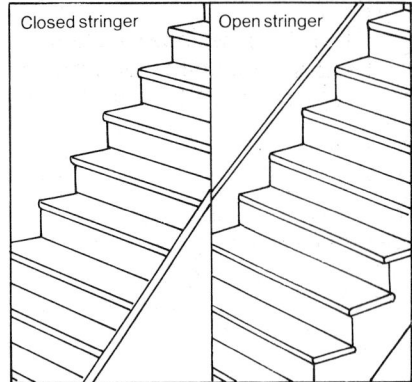

Closed stringer Open stringer

Closed and open strings The strings are the timber supports which run from one floor up to the next and carry the treads — or the steps. In a closed string construction the steps are fitted between the strings, but in an open string construction one string is cut away and the treads are fixed to the top edge.

Open risers This type of staircase is popular in many modern houses, particularly those with an open plan arrangement on the ground floor. Construction is simple, consisting only of strings and treads. The strings can be open, as shown, or closed.

144

How a staircase is constructed

The staircase shown here is of a
traditional pattern found in many
older houses. There is a closed
stringer against the wall with an open
stringer on the outer side and
supporting a baluster and baluster
rails. A newel post gives firm
support for the balustrade.

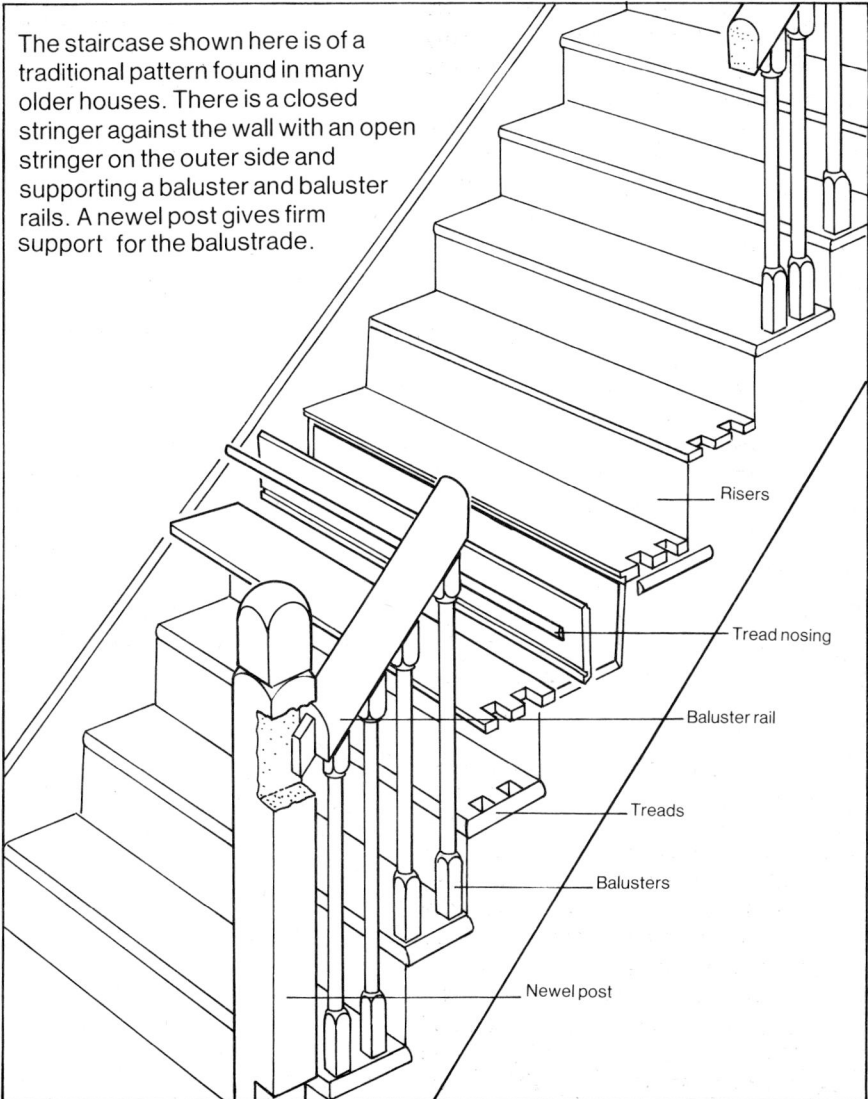

Risers

Tread nosing

Baluster rail

Treads

Balusters

Newel post

Closing a gap between treads and a string

You will need: cold chisel; hammer; saw;
wheelbrace and bit; screwdriver; screws; oval nails

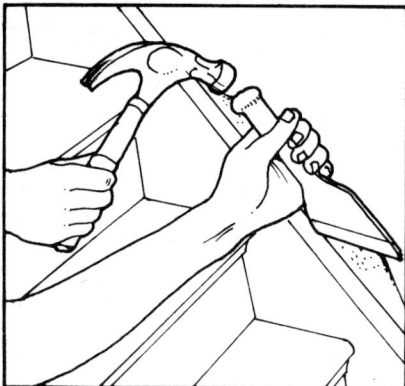

1. In old houses the steps may sag
away from the wall string, leaving
unsightly gaps. First chisel out the
wall plaster near the gap.

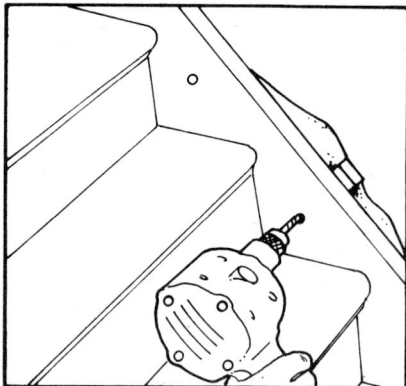

3. Drill and countersink a hole in the
string in line with each wedge.

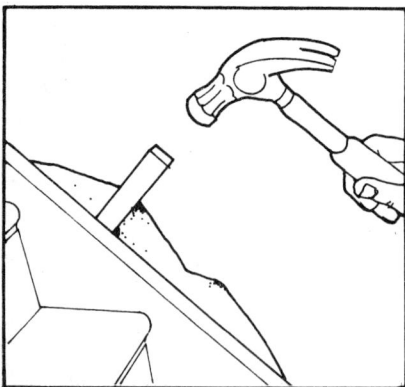

2. Make wooden wedges, about
12 in (300 mm) long and 1 in
(25 mm) thick at the thick end. Drive
the wedges between the string and
the wall until the gap closes.

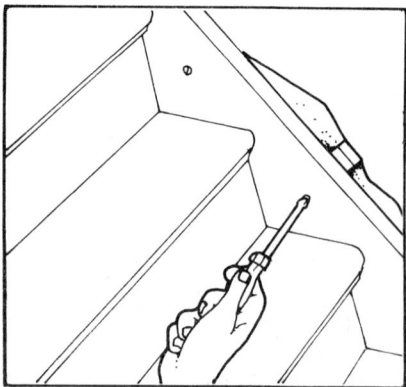

4. Screw the string to the wedges
and make good the plaster, taking it
to the stringer edge to conceal the
wedges.

Staircases

Resurfacing a worn tread

You will need: 1 in (25 mm) wood chisel; screwdriver; wheelbrace and bit; 1 in (25 mm) half-round softwood beading; sheet of $\frac{1}{4}$ in (6 mm) plywood; PVA adhesive; oval nails

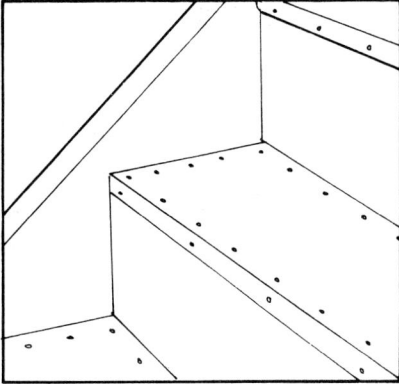

1. Cut off the nosing, using a wood chisel, and plane the face flush with the riser. Cut a piece of plywood to size and nail it onto the worn tread.

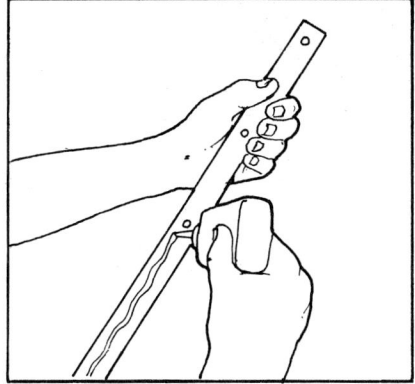

2. Make a new nosing, using the nosing on one of the good treads as a pattern. Drill three holes in the nosing – one central, the others 2 in (50 mm) from each end.

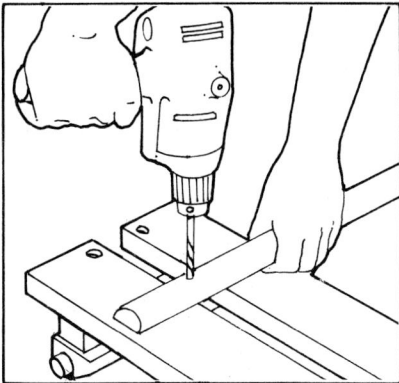

3. Countersink the holes in the nosing face. Apply PVA adhesive to the back.

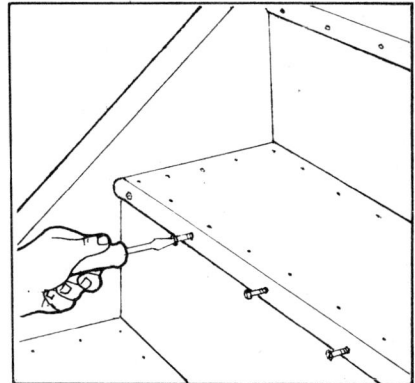

4. Press the new nosing firmly into position and screw to the tread. Wipe off surplus adhesive immediately. Fill all screw and nail head holes with wood filler.

147

Replacing a tread and riser

You will need: hammer; saw; plane; wood chisels; combination square; nail punch; hacksaw; softwood; PVA adhesive

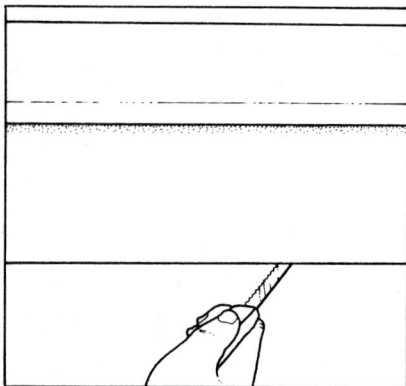

1. A worn tread can be resurfaced (see p 147), but badly worn treads should be replaced. Start by cutting through the join between tread and riser with a padsaw.

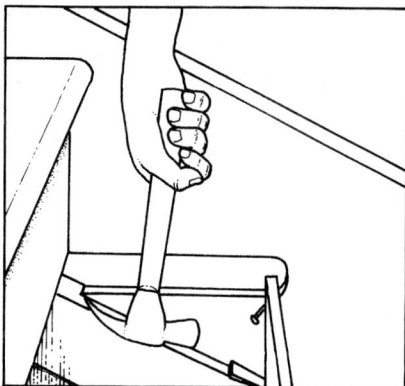

3. Slot the riser into its groove in the string. Glue a wedge beneath to raise it flush with the tread groove. Nail at an angle into the string.

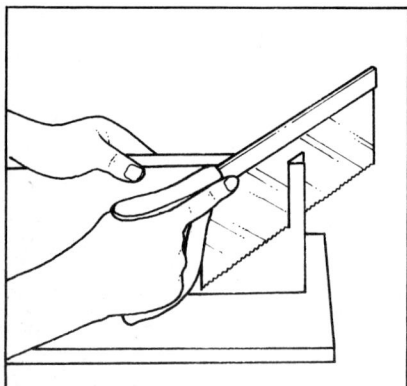

2. Make a new riser from softwood. Mitre the end that will fit against the outer string at 45°.

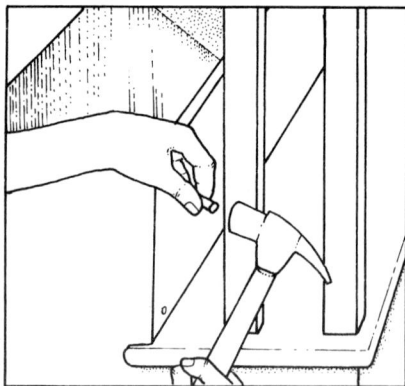

4. At the outer edge, glue and nail the riser to the cut string and sink the nailheads with a nail punch.

Handy hint: A permanent cure for squeaky stairs is described on p 151, but as a temporary remedy dust the join or crack with talcum powder. The powder will lubricate the moving edges which are causing the squeak.

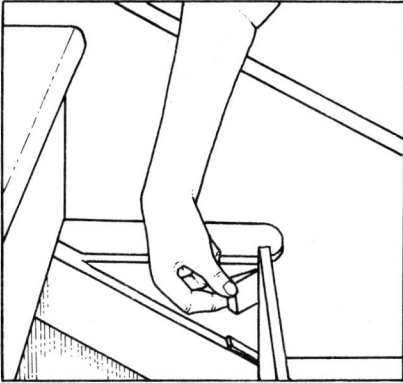

5. If necessary, tighten the join by glueing a wedge into the groove behind the riser at the inner string.

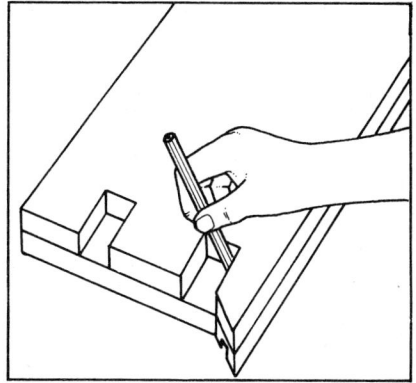

7. Using the old tread as a pattern, mark and cut out the mitred section for the side moulding. Mark also the baluster cut-outs and saw down the lines.

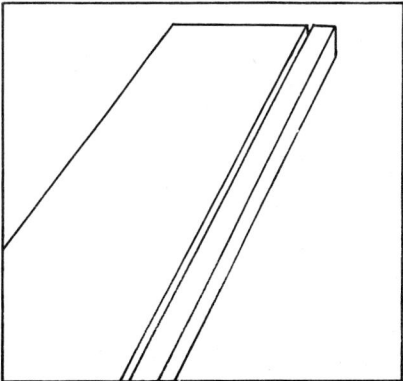

6. Make a new tread from softwood. Remove the side and underneath mouldings from the old tread. Use a plough plane to cut a groove for the underneath moulding.

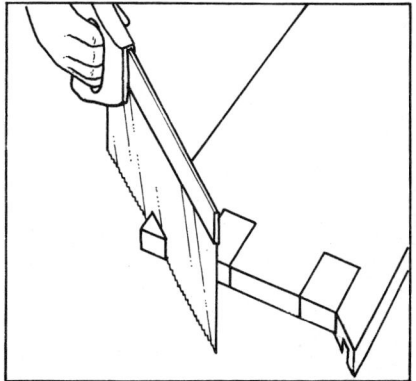

8. To ensure a good fit against the outer string, cut off one corner of the tread. *(continued)*

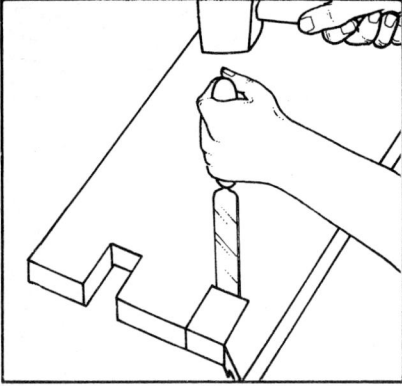

9. Chisel out the baluster cut-outs. Glue the underneath moulding into its groove with PVA adhesive.

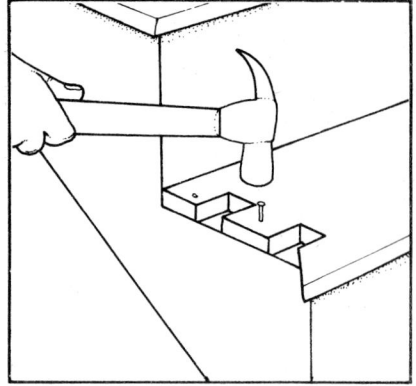

11. Use lost-head nails to secure the tread to the outer string. Sink the nails with a nail punch.

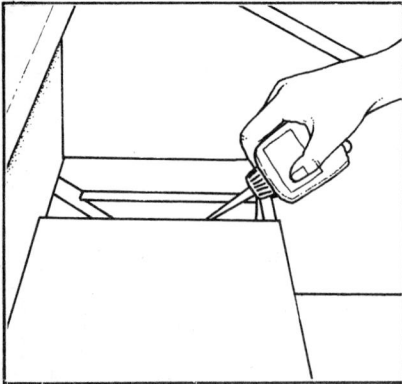

10. Apply PVA adhesive to the inner end of the tread and place it in its groove in the inner string. Tap it gently home.

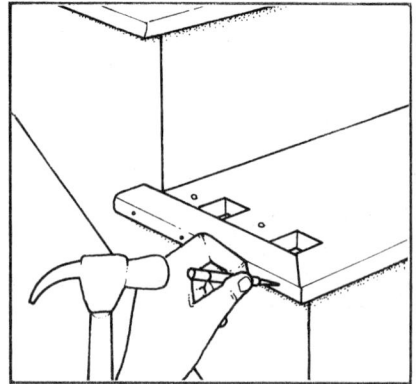

12. Glue on the side moulding and nail in three places. Sink the nails. Then fill all the nailhead holes with wood filler before painting.

Curing creaking treads

You will need: hammer; saw; wood chisel; nail punch; softwood batten, approx 2 in (50 mm) square; nails; PVA adhesive

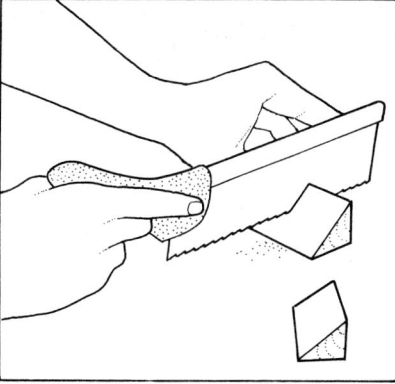

1. Creaking treads, if accessible from below, can be cured by nailing blocks to the tread and riser. Make triangular blocks 2 in × 2 in × 2 in (50 mm × 50 mm × 50 mm).

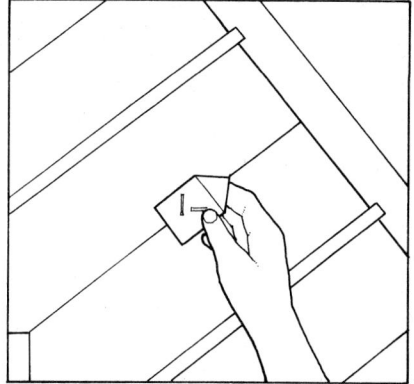

3. Apply PVA adhesive to the other two faces of the block and place it about 2 in (50 mm) in from the end of the tread.

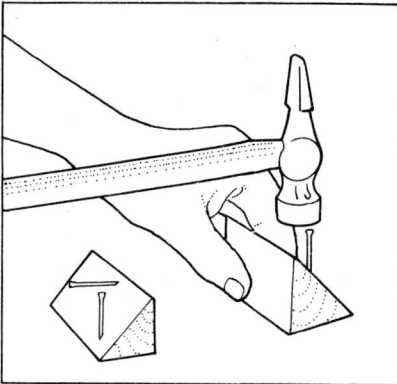

2. On one face of each block, partly hammer in panel pins at right angles to each other.

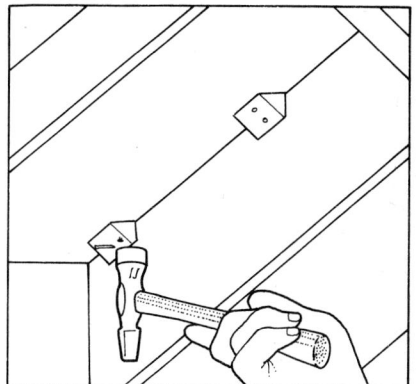

4. Hammer in the panel pins. Fix another block at the other end of the tread. If necessary add a third block midway between the two.

Replacing a worn tread edge

You will need: wood chisel; screwdriver; wheelbrace and bit; 1 in (25 mm) half-round softwood beading; nails; PVA adhesive

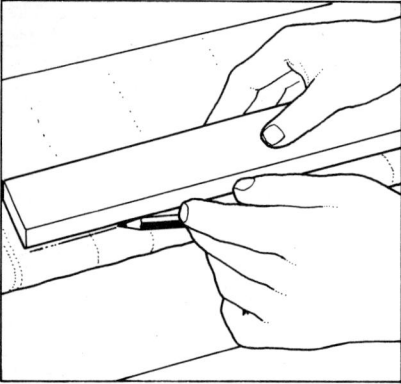

1. To replace a worn tread edge, or nosing, first mark off at each end the section to be replaced.

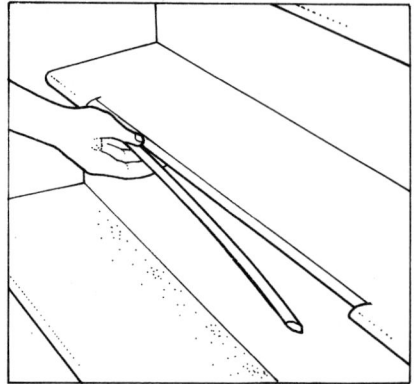

3. Cut back only as far as is necessary. Avoid cutting back as far as the riser, otherwise the tread will be weakened. Remove the cut section.

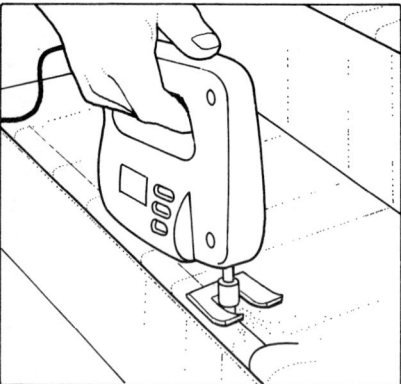

2. Cut out the worn section with a jigsaw, or use a wide bladed wood chisel. Mitre the cut at both ends.

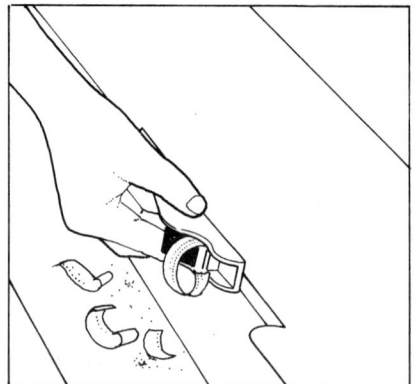

4. Use a small block plane or a shaping tool to level off the cut face.

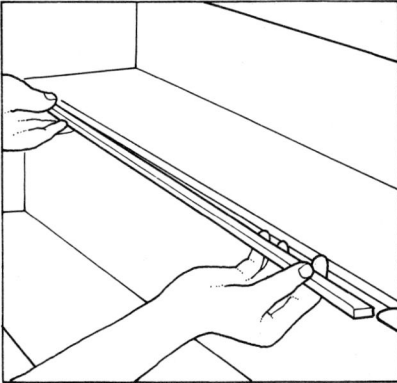

5. Cut and shape a new nosing from softwood. Mitre the ends and check that it fits the cut section.

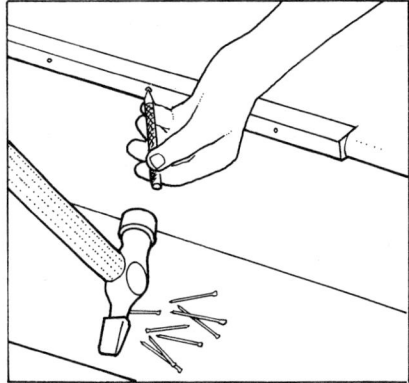

7. Nail the nosing in place and sink the nailheads with a nail punch.

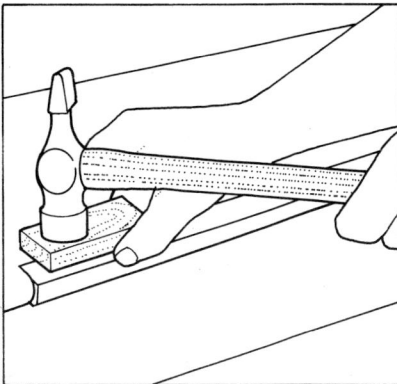

6. Apply PVA adhesive to the nosing. Tap it into place, using a block of wood to protect its surface.

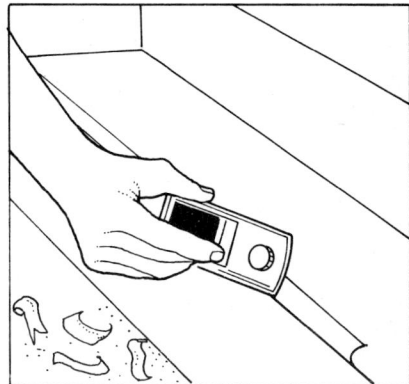

8. When the adhesive has set, use a block plane or shaping tool to blend the shape with the original profile. Finish off with sandpaper.

Fixing a loose baluster

You will need: claw hammer; cold chisel; wood chisel; saw; spirit level; softwood; nails

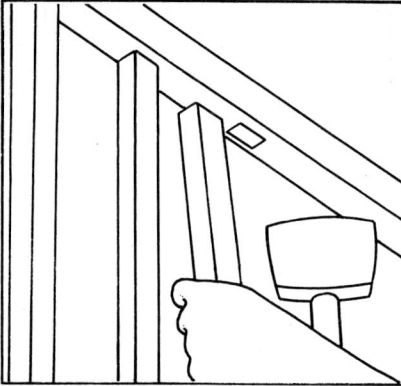

1. Balusters usually work loose when the staircase sags slightly. They can be tightened by fitting softwood under the handrail. First knock out the loose balusters.

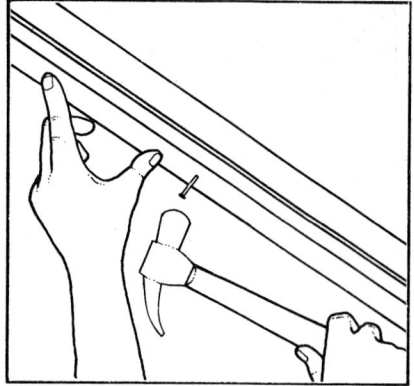

3. Fix the strip to the underside of the rail and sink the nailheads with a nail punch.

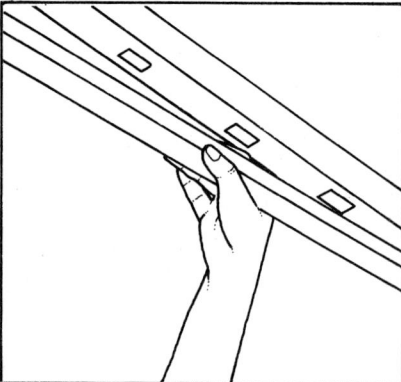

2. Measure the length of a baluster and the distances between rail and treads to find the depths of gaps. Cut a length of softwood slightly thicker than the largest gap.

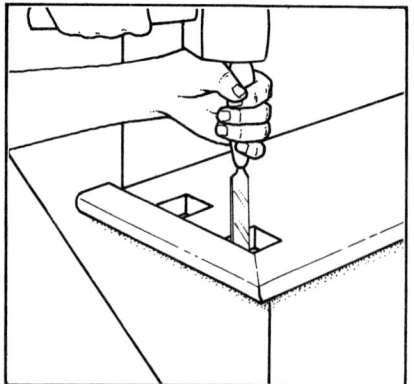

4. Clean out the baluster sockets in the treads with a wood chisel.

Staircases

Handy hint: The balustrades in some old houses are old-fashioned in design, as well as being dust-catchers. Panel over the balusters on each side with veneered or patterned hardboard. Use special hardboard nails to fix the panelling to the balusters at equally spaced intervals and cover the joins with half-round beading.

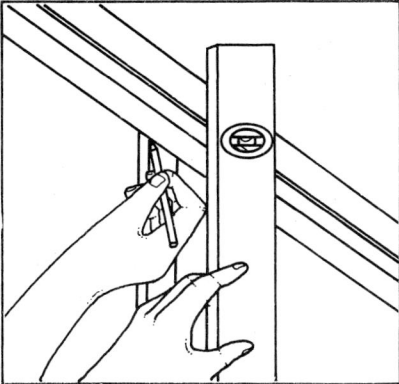

5. Fit a baluster into its socket and hold it upright — use a spirit level — against the softwood strip. If the baluster is too long, mark the extra with a pencil.

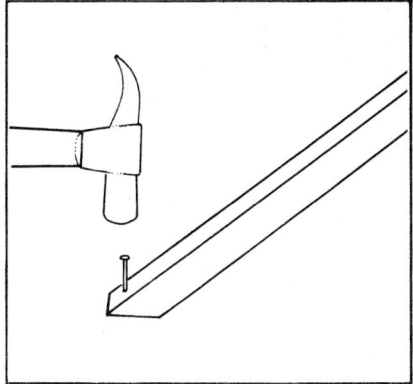

7. Hammer in a nail at an angle in the top of the baluster. Drill a hole first to avoid splitting the wood.

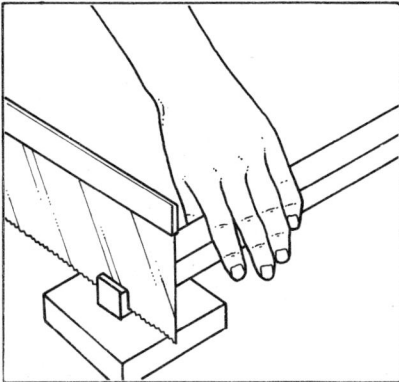

6. Remove the baluster and cut off the extra amount from the bottom end.

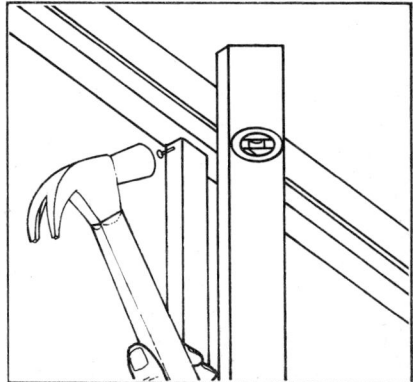

8. Apply PVA adhesive to the bottom end of the baluster and fit it in its socket. Use a spirit level to get the baluster vertical and hammer in the top nail.

155

Walls

House walls have to fulfil two important functions – they must keep out damp and insulate against cold. In addition the outer walls (and some inner walls) have to carry the weight of the roof and upper floors. These are known as load-bearing walls. Walls that divide the house into rooms are called partition walls and are usually non-load-bearing. It is important to know which is which when making any structural alterations or repairs. **Any work involving partial demolition or reconstruction of a load-bearing wall should be entrusted to a builder**.

Generally speaking, all outer walls are load-bearing while walls that are built only to the height of the first floor are usually non-load-bearing. In many houses the partition walls are built with breeze blocks or consist of a wooden frame clad with plasterboard.

Brick-built houses may have solid or cavity walls. Before the Second World War, many houses had solid walls of 9 in (225 mm) or $13\frac{1}{2}$ in (337 mm) thickness. To assist in keeping out damp the walls were often rendered with a sand and cement mix embedded with tiny stones – sometimes called pebble-dash. Cracked or flaking rendering should be repaired quickly, as water can seep behind the rendering and will soon penetrate the wall.

Most houses built since the war have cavity walls, which give good protection against damp. A cavity wall consists of two leaves; each leaf is 4 in (100 mm) thick, and there is an air gap of 2 in (50 mm) between the inner leaf and outer leaf. The inner wall is often built of breeze blocks or lightweight concrete blocks. Metal ties between the two leaves are embedded in the mortar and give the whole structure stability and strength.

The length of a brick is known as the 'stretcher' and the thickness is called the 'header'. The way bricks are laid is called the bond; the joints are staggered so that the bricks in each layer, or course, overlap the bricks in the course below. The bond used in cavity walls is called stretcher bond, because all the bricks are laid end to end.

The two most common bonds used in solid walls are English and Flemish, both being a mixture of stretcher bond and header bond, where some bricks are laid lengthwise across the thickness of the wall. In older houses using Imperial size bricks it was the type of bond which fixed the wall thickness.

A new type of outer wall recently introduced is the timber-frame. A single brick-built outer leaf is backed by a wooden frame clad on the inside with insulating board. The space within the frame is packed with insulating material, and it is claimed that this type of wall has very high insulation properties.

Construction of house walls

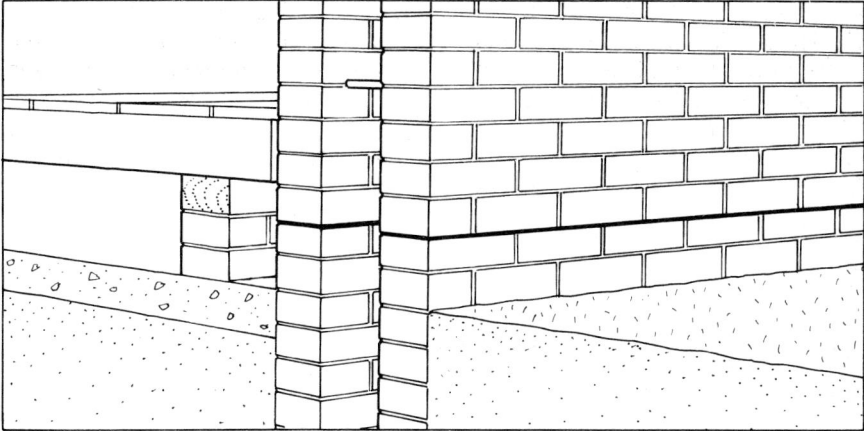

Cavity wall Most modern houses have cavity walls on the outside. The wall consists of two leaves placed 2 in (50 mm) apart and linked at intervals by metal ties.

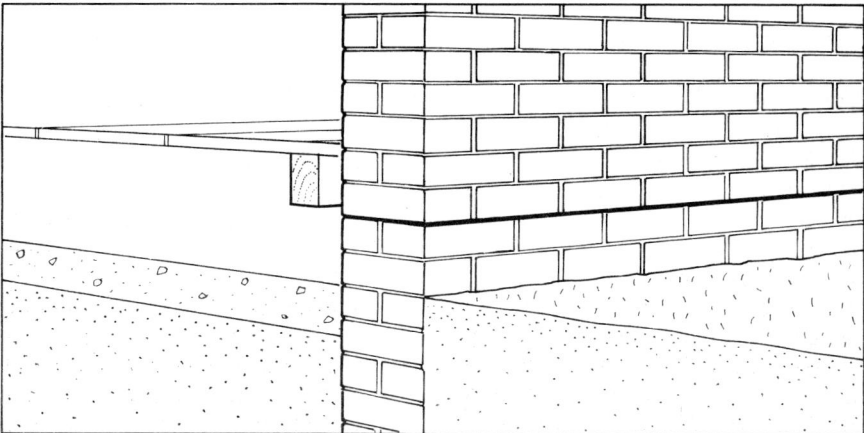

Solid wall In older houses the walls may consist of a single 9 in (225 mm) or $13\frac{1}{2}$ in (337 mm) thickness. Rendering or half rendering was often added to give extra protection against the weather.

Repointing brickwork

You will need: pointing trowel; mortar

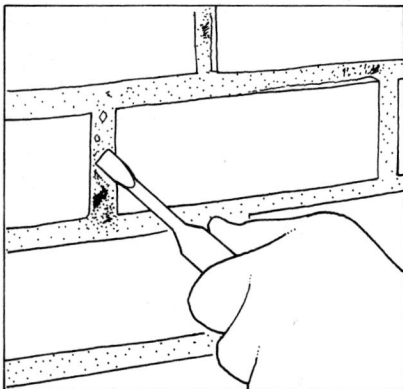

1. Crumbling mortar joints must be repointed or rain will soon penetrate. Scrape out the joint with a convenient scraper, such as an old screwdriver.

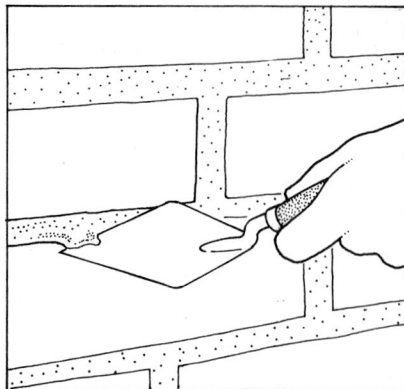

3. Fill the horizontal joints. For good weatherproofing, slope the joint slightly so that rainwater will run off.

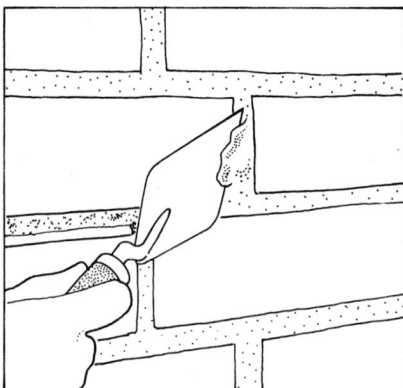

2. Mix the mortar (see pp 188-189) and apply with a pointing trowel. Do the upright joints first, applying the mortar with the back of the trowel.

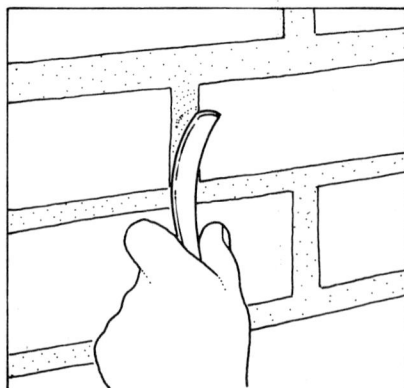

4. Alternatively make a keyed joint. This is done by rubbing the joints with a rounded tool such as a piece of old tubing. Do this before the mortar sets.

Filling cracks in rendering

You will need: pointing trowel; cement; cold chisel; hammer

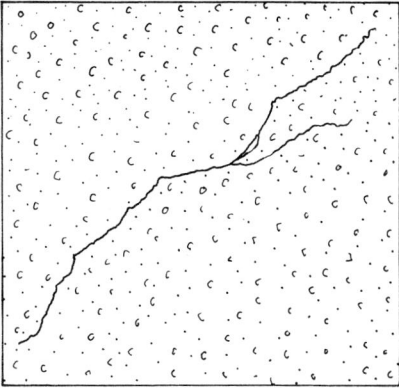

1. Repair cracks in rendering as soon as possible or water will penetrate and seep through the brickwork behind.

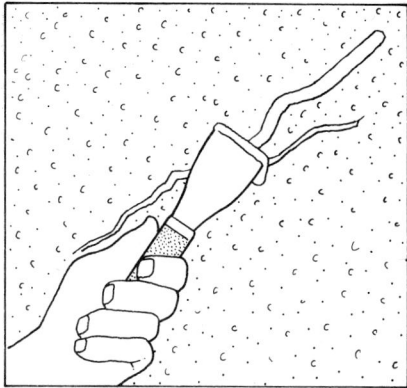

3. Brush out all loose material and then work in mortar (see pp 188-189) with a scraper.

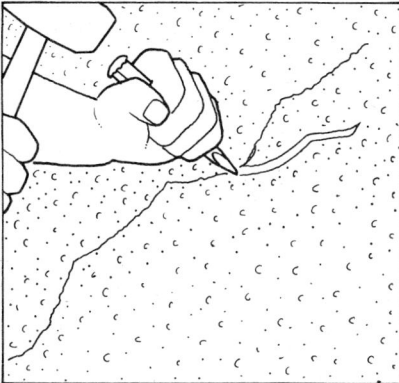

2. Open up the cracks with a cold chisel, working back to firm rendering, and cut under the edges.

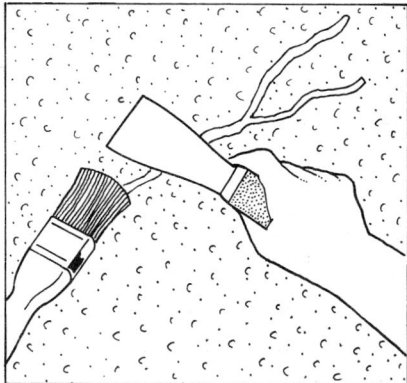

4. Smooth the mortar with the scraper, and at the same time brush away any surplus with an old paintbrush dipped in clean water.

Patching damaged rendering

You will need: plasterer's float; wooden batten; mortar

1. Cut away the damaged area with a bolster chisel and club hammer. Undercut the edges to make a good key for the mortar filling.

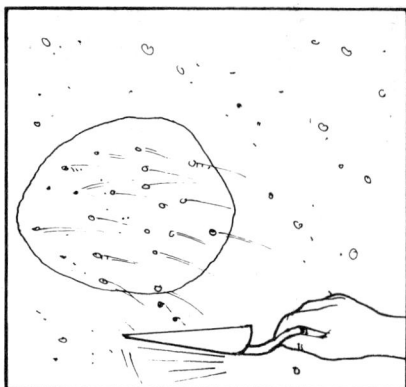

2. Make a suitable mortar mix (see pp 188-189) and apply it with a pointing trowel.

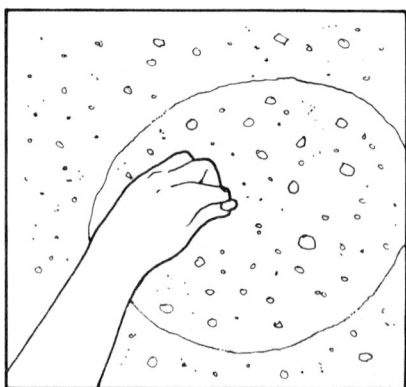

3. While the mortar is still wet, apply small stones by throwing them on the wall from the trowel at close range.

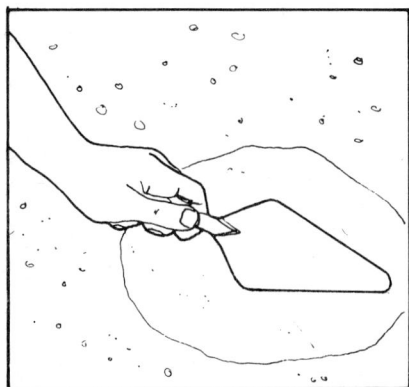

4. Though most of the stones should stick to the mortar, there may be a few bald patches. Finish off by pressing in stones by hand.

Filling cracks in brickwork

You will need: pointing trowel; cement

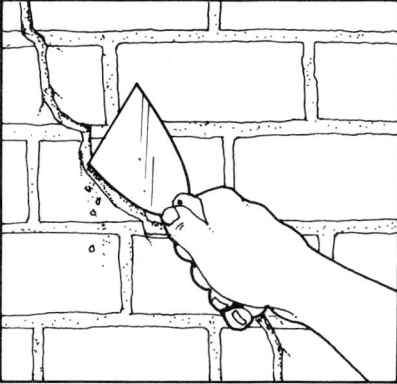

1. Where the cracks run across bricks and mortar joints, deepen and widen the cracks to provide a good key for the mortar filling.

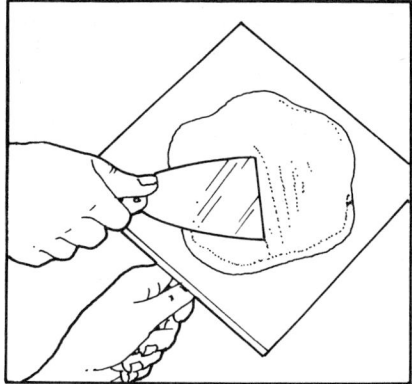

3. Mix a small amount of mortar (see pp 188-189) and add a little plasticizer.

2. Brush out all brick dust and loose mortar. Dampen the crack before filling.

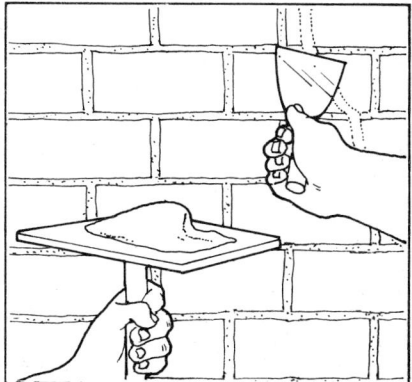

4. Use a scraper or stripping knife to apply the mortar. Press it well into the crack and wipe off the surplus.

Walls

Damp and its causes and cures

Dampness in walls can cause structural deterioration costing a great deal of money to put right if not remedied quickly. It can also lead to the growth of fungi and will ruin interior decorating – and **it is a health hazard**.

There are three main causes of damp: leaks from water pipes or cisterns; condensation; and rainwater penetration from outside. The first two can usually be spotted and rectified easily, but rainwater penetration often does not show until one of the symptoms (eg, discoloration of interior wall covering) occurs. By then a whole area of wall may be saturated.

Prevention, therefore, is better than cure and the whole house should be inspected at least once a year. As previously mentioned, cracks in rendering or bare patches will allow water to enter. Eventually it will creep behind the rendering, causing it to break away.

Where there is no rendering, pay particular attention to crumbling mortar joints and watch out for hairline cracks in the brickwork. Fill all cracks with cement and repoint faulty mortar joints. Unrendered solid walls need some kind of protection, and you may consider it worthwhile to have this type of finish. If you treat the wall yourself use a damp-proofing liquid. This can be applied by brush or it can be sprayed on.

Make sure that all cracks have been filled and that all mortar joints are sound before waterproofing or having rendering applied.

Dampness should not penetrate cavity walls. If it does the most likely cause is bridging of the wall ties. When the house was built mortar and brick debris may have fallen into the cavity and settled on the ties. In time, damp will cross the 'bridge' and appear on the inner wall. This fault is easily recognizable as the damp will show as small patches at regular intervals. The only sure cure is to clear the mortar droppings from the ties, which involves removing bricks in the outer wall so that the ties can be cleared by hand. **Such work must be carried out by a competent builder.**

Other sources of external damp include leaks from gutters and gaps around door and window openings which can be filled with a mastic sealant. Damp in the walls below window sills is almost always due to a faulty drip groove beneath the sill. The drip groove directs water away from the wall; if it is choked with dirt, scrape it clean and if necessary recut the groove with a chisel.

Even after effectively applying a cure for damp, a damp wall will take a long time to dry out. If you want to get on with renovating and redecorating the interior walls apply aluminium foil lining which will ensure that the wall dries outwards.

162

Places where a house is susceptible to damp

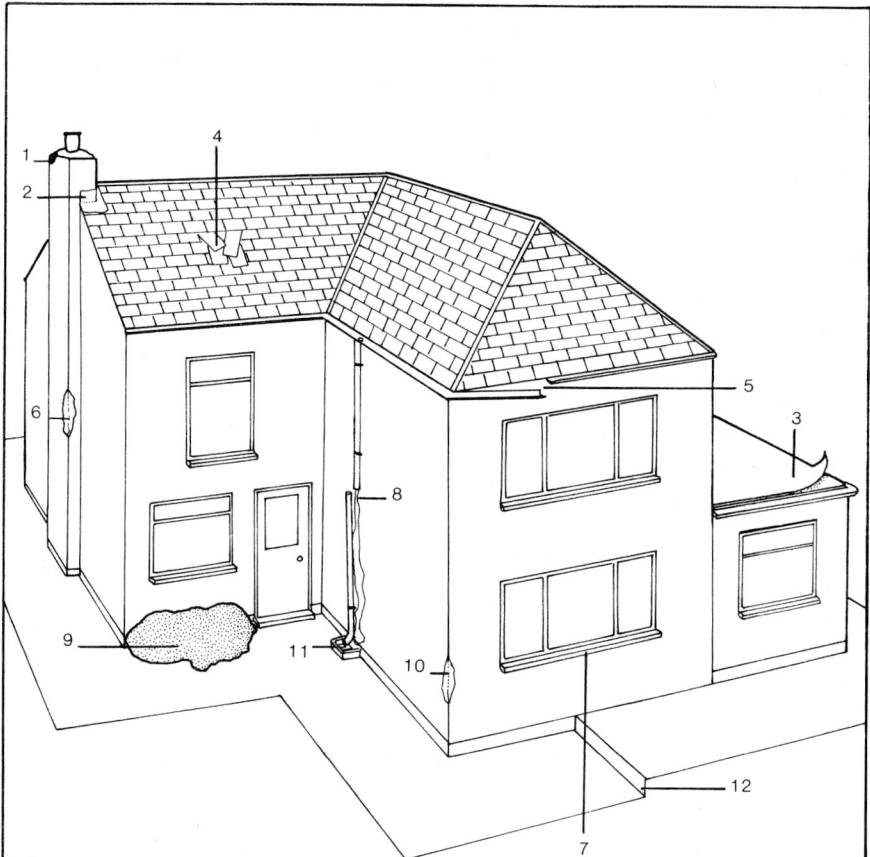

1. Damaged chimney brickwork.
2. Damaged flashing.
3. Damaged felt on a flat roof.
4. Loose tiles or slates.
5. Broken guttering.
6. Damaged rendering on chimney breast.
7. Gaps above and below window frames.
8. Broken downpipe.
9. DPC bridged by heaped earth.
10. Damaged rendering on wall.
11. Blocked gully.
12. Concrete path bridging DPC.

Lining a wall with aluminium foil

You will need: wallpapering brush; scissors; plumbline; rule; aluminium lining; adhesive

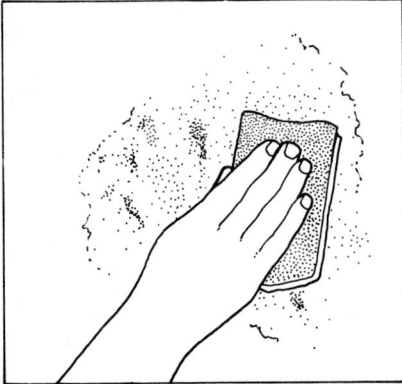

1. Aluminium foil is an excellent barrier against damp. First rub down all damp patches to remove flaking paint and fill cracks or holes with proprietary filler.

2. Wash down the wall with a solution of 1 part ammonia, 8 parts water and allow to dry. Cut the foil to length, allowing extra for trimming top and bottom.

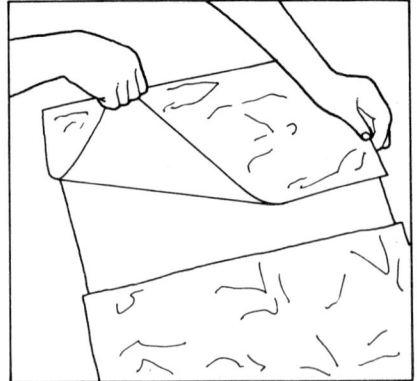

3. Lay the first sheet on a table and paste the back with a heavyweight adhesive, or as recommended by the foil manufacturer.

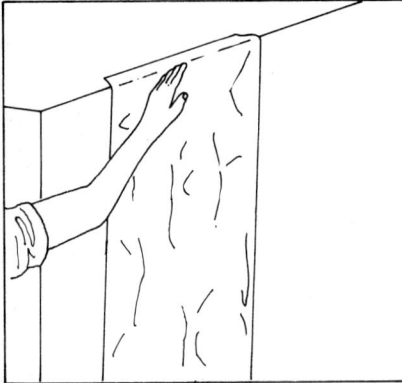

4. Fold the foil back on itself from both ends and leave it until the adhesive becomes tacky.

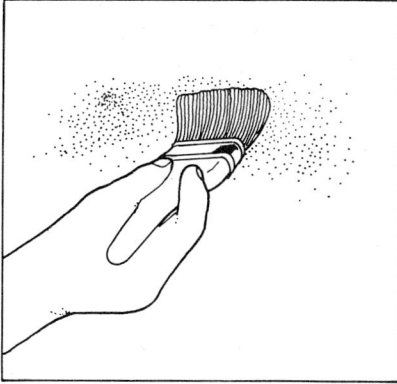

5. To ensure good adhesion, prime the wall with adhesive, covering an area large enough for the first sheet of foil.

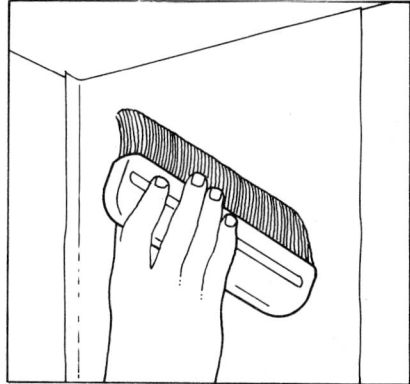

7. Pull back the lining top and bottom and trim off the excess with scissors. Then brush the lining back into place with a wallpapering brush.

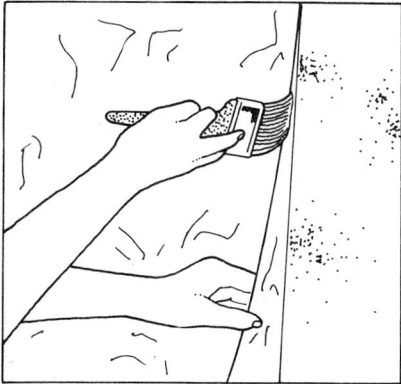

6. Mark a line on the wall, about 1 in (25 mm) from a corner, using a plumbline, and hang the first sheet to it. Brush the foil into place.

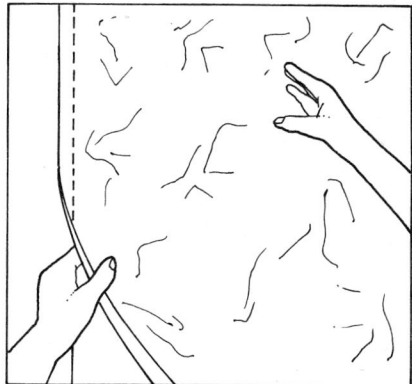

8. Continue along the wall, overlapping each sheet by about $\frac{1}{4}$ in (6 mm).

Lining a wall with polystyrene

You will need: plumbline; trimming knife; rule; wallpapering brush; lining; adhesive

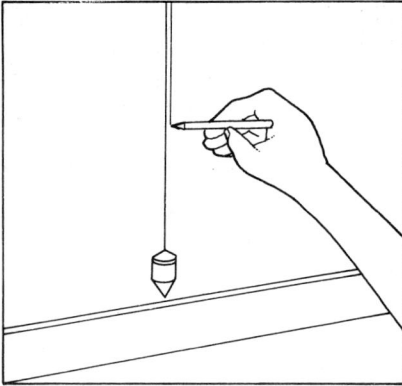

1. Expanded polystyrene sheet will insulate a cold wall and prevent condensation. Hang it like wallpaper. First find the wall centre and make a vertical line.

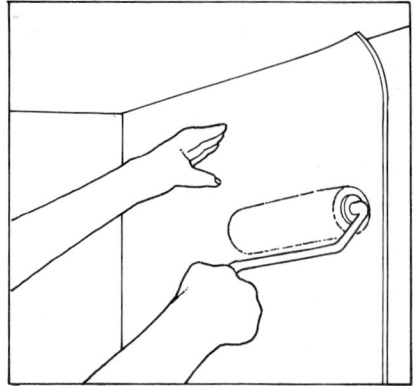

3. Use a heavyweight adhesive on the back of the sheet and place it in position. Use a foam paint roller to smooth the sheet to the wall.

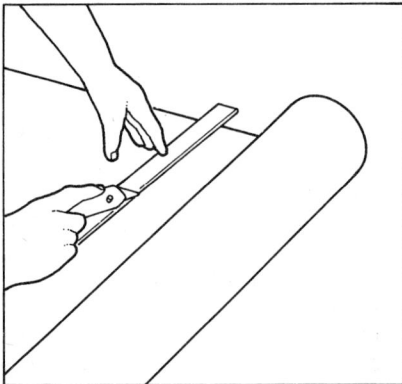

2. Measure the height of the wall and cut a length of polystyrene, allowing about 3 in (75 mm) for trimming. Use a **sharp** trimming knife to get a clean cut.

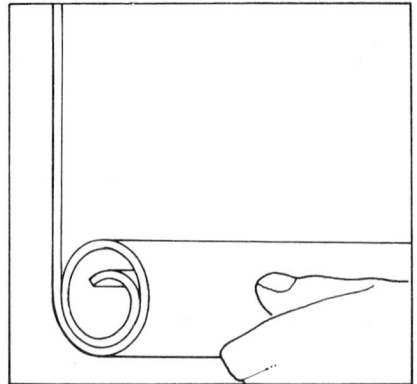

4. Hang the next sheet in the same way, with an overlap of about $\frac{1}{2}$ in (6 mm).

Handy hint: A pressurized spray and atomizer used for spraying insecticides also has its uses in the home. Filled with waterproofing liquid and then pumped to a good pressure it will reach parts of a wall that are difficult to reach with a brush, and is also more economical. Used with a fine water spray it is ideal for preparing an area of wall for plastering.

Waterproofing an outside wall

You will need: wide brush or spray gun equipment; liquid sealant

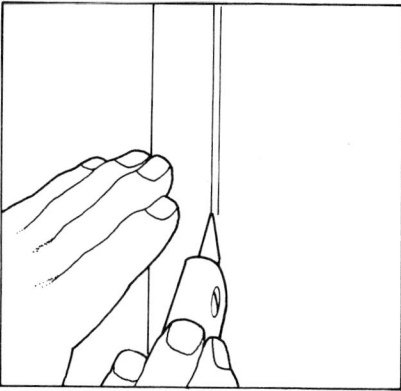

5. Use a straight edge and sharp trimming knife to trim off the overlap to get a good butt joint between the two adjacent sheets.

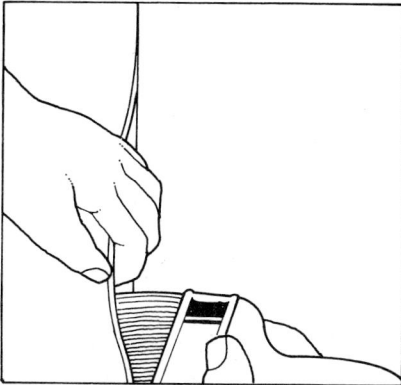

6. Lift the edges of both sheets and brush adhesive underneath. Use the roller to press the sheets firmly in position. Cover the lined wall with vinyl wallpaper.

A transparent silicon-based water-repellant can be applied to an outside wall to prevent damp penetrating bricks and mortar. This treatment is very effective on solid walls in exposed positions.

Before applying the liquid, make sure that the wall is sound; ie, repoint all crumbling mortar joints (see p 158) and fill any cracks in the brickwork (see p 161). Apply the liquid with a wide brush during dry weather. If possible, use a spray for areas difficult to reach, such as gable ends.

Most silicon-based repellants will give adequate protection for a number of years, but must be re-applied from time to time. Consult your dealer — most hardware and DIY shops are stockists — to find which makes give the longer lasting protection.

Causes and cures of rising damp

Damp-proof courses

A damp-proof course is a waterproof barrier built into house walls to prevent rising damp. Without a DPC the walls would soak up moisture from the soil like a sponge, and in many old houses rising damp occurs when the damp-proof course ceases to be effective.

Building regulations in the UK specify that a DPC must be built into the walls of all habitable buildings at a minimum height of 6 in (150 mm) above ground level. In old houses the DPC consisted of a layer of slates laid in two courses, and it is this type that is most susceptible to failure. Over the years, as settlement takes place, the slates crack and moisture seeps through.

Modern houses have a flexible material in the DPC, which may have a core of lead, aluminium or copper. Sometimes plain copper or lead is used, but the most common material has a fibre or asbestos base and is laid between two layers of bitumen. In cavity walls there is a DPC in both leaves and vertical DPCs at doors and windows.

Rising damp is easily distinguishable from other forms of damp — it appears low down on the inside of the wall, rising in an uneven line to 2 ft (61 cm) or more depending on the severity of the DPC breakdown. There are a number of ways to treat it, all requiring the attention of specialist firms.

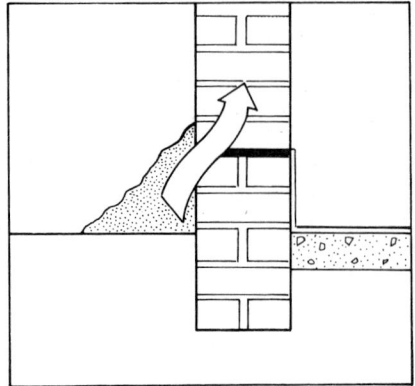

1. Anything that bridges the damp-proof course will cause rising damp, such as earth banked against the wall as shown above.

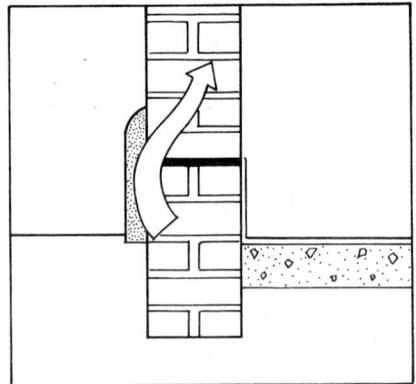

2. A cemented skirting on an outside wall will form a path for damp to rise if it is taken above the DPC.

Handy hint: A simple way to identify a solid or cavity wall is to measure across the wall thickness at a window opening; allowing for rendering and internal plastering a cavity wall is above 10 in (250 mm) thick whereas a solid wall is either 9 in (225 mm) or 13½ in (337 mm).

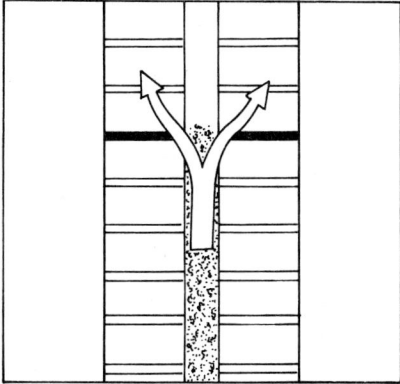

3. In a cavity wall, brick rubble and mortar droppings may bridge a wall tie, or may fill the cavity to above the DPC level, as shown.

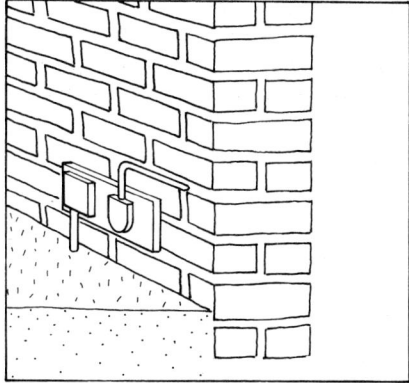

5. Damp rises due to the difference in electrical charge between wall and ground. A copper strip earthed by metal rods (a method called electro-osmosis) overcomes this.

4. One method of curing rising damp is called siphonage. Porous clay tubes set in the wall increase the moisture evaporation rate and control the rising damp.

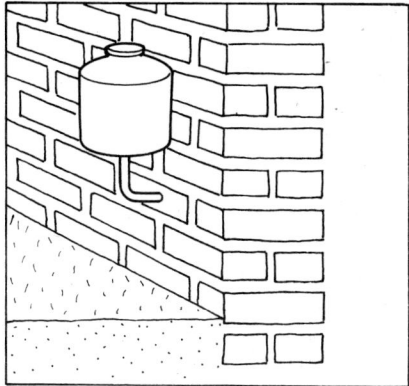

6. A silicon solution injected into a wall stops rising damp. The liquid, injected from bottles, spreads through the brickwork, providing an effective barrier.

Replacing a damaged wall tile

You will need: cold chisel; hammer; tile; adhesive; grouting cement

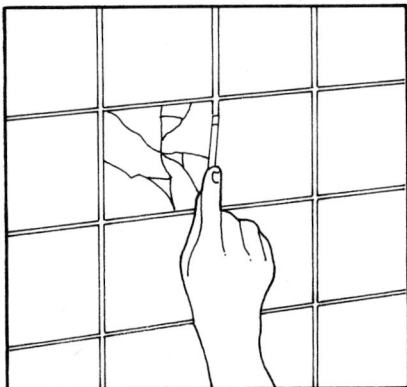

1. Remove the damaged tile without damaging those adjacent to it. First dig out the grouting cement with a sharp tool such as a gimlet or pointed scraper.

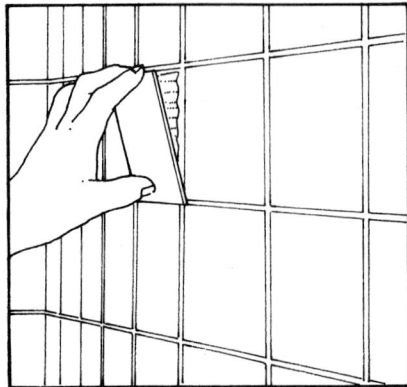

3. Clean out all the old adhesive. Apply fresh adhesive to the back of the new tile and press it into position.

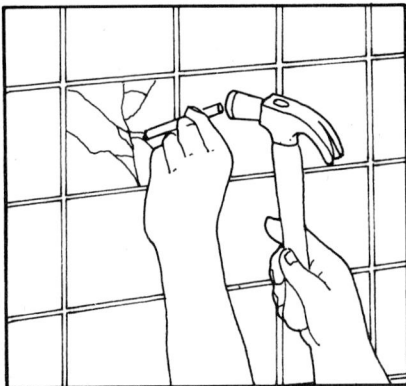

2. When all the surrounding grouting has been removed, chip away the tile with a chisel. Work from the centre to the corners.

4. Go over the joins with grouting cement. Allow the grouting to dry and wipe off the surplus with a wet sponge.

Repairing a chipped corner

You will need: filler knife; filler; sandpaper; stiff brush

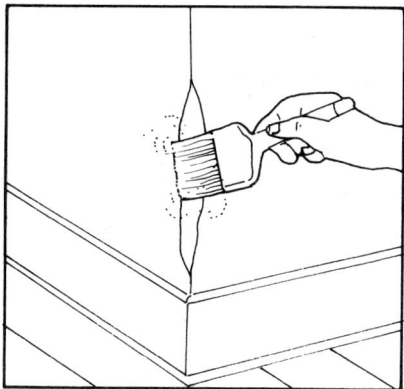

1. A corner projecting into a room, such as on a chimney breast, is easily damaged. If only the plaster is chipped, a repair can be made with cellulose-based filler.

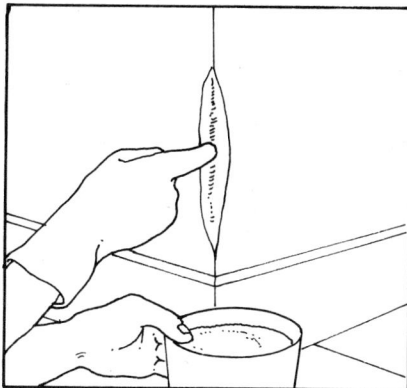

3. Before the filler sets, shape it with a wetted blade (an old kitchen knife or a scraper). Round off the corner with a wet finger.

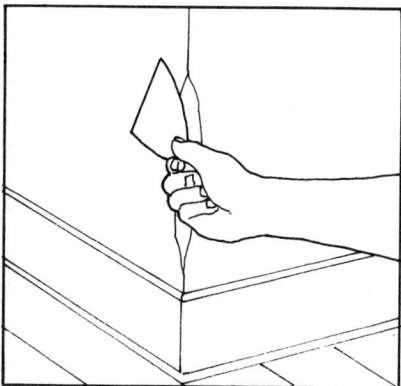

2. Chip away all loose plaster and brush clean. Make a stiff mix of filler and apply it until it is proud of the corner.

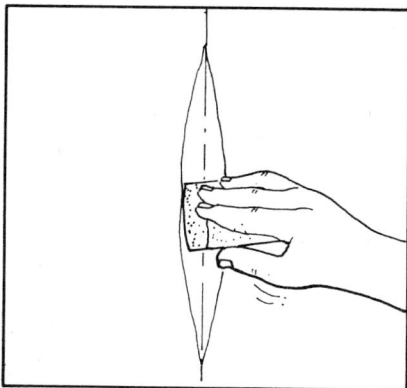

4. Give the filler plenty of time to set (following the maker's instructions) and rub down with sandpaper to blend the repair into the corner.

Windows

Windows, like doors, need special care and attention if they are to give long and good service. Two types are commonly used, the casement window and sliding sash.

Casement windows are hung on hinges which may be at the side, top or bottom — some modern designs have a central pivot so that the window opens vertically or horizontally. One of the advantages of modern casement windows is that they come in a variety of combinations.

The frames may be of metal or wood — aluminium is a popular material as it needs virtually no maintenance. Timber frames, on the other hand, will not attract condensation and if painted regularly will last for many years.

Sliding sash windows, often found in older houses, have two advantages over casement windows — they do not project outwards when open and they can be set to give just the right amount of ventilation. They are, however, more prone to sticking and in time the sash cords are liable to rot and break, which can be dangerous.

The way a sash window works is through a simple mechanism concealed in the framework. The sashes, the upper and lower sections of the window, are attached to weighted cords running in recesses. The weights counterbalance the weight of the sash, so that it will stay in any position when raised or lowered. The cords run on pulleys which can be seen at the point where the cord enters the frame. The pulleys should always be kept free; avoid getting paint on them when redecorating the window and apply a few drops of thin oil to the pulley spindle from time to time.

As with doors, the hinges on casement windows should be kept oiled and the fixing screws checked from time to time for tightness. Do not, however, oil the pivots on centrally pivoting windows — they have to be semi-stiff so that the window stays open in any position.

Keep locks and latches free; it is also a worthwhile investment to fit security locks on all downstairs windows and any upstairs that are adjacent to a drainpipe or above a porch.

There are several types of security lock available for both sliding sash and casement windows; the most effective for sliding sash is a bolt that secures the two sashes together and is locked in position by a special key; for wooden casement windows there is a similar device which locks the casement to the frame; and for metal framed windows there are locks which fit over the locating peg on the stay arm. Most effective, perhaps, is a cylinder lock incorporated in the handle of the window catch.

Two types of window

Casement window In its simplest
form a casement window has a
single pane in a side-hung frame.
Variations include a top opening
light, as shown. Casement windows
may have a wood or metal frame.

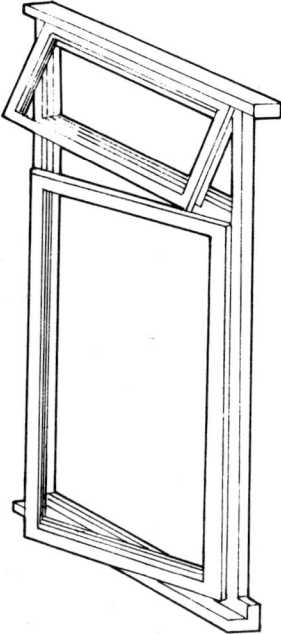

Sash window Most sash windows
are double-hung, as shown, the two
sashes being counterbalanced with
weights and pulleys. They are found
in many older properties, particularly
Victorian and Edwardian.

Replacing a sash cord

You will need: claw hammer; wood chisel; pincers; trimming knife; new cord

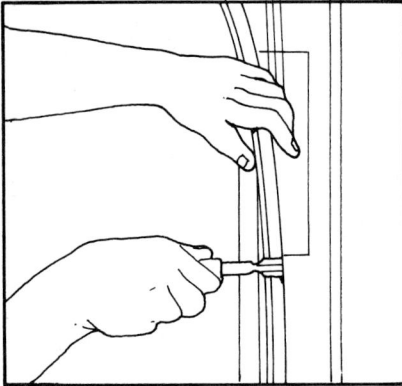

1. Use a chisel or wide-bladed screwdriver to prise off the outer beading fitted on the inside of the window.

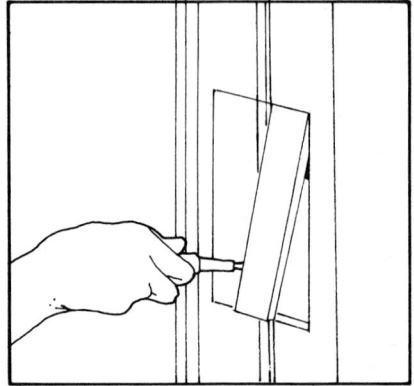

3. Prise out the pulley trap. This is a section slotted into the hollow frame.

2. Lift out the lower sash. Cut the sash cord if it is attached.

4. With the trap removed the sash weight can be seen at the bottom of the weight compartment.

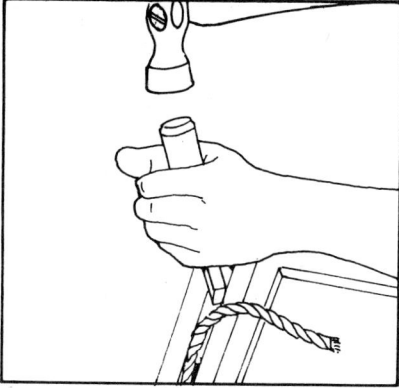

5. The sash cord is nailed to the sides of the sash. Cut it off with a chisel or take out the nails by using pincers.

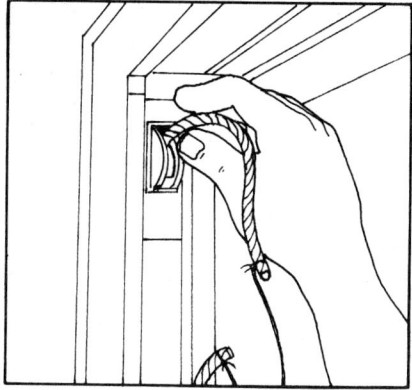

7. Tie a small weight, such as a bent nail, to a piece of string. Attach the string to the new cord and feed it over the pulley.

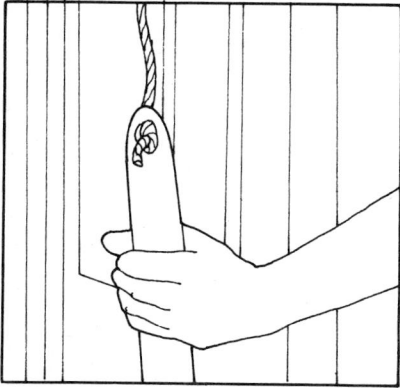

6. Lift out the weight from its compartment and disconnect the old cord.

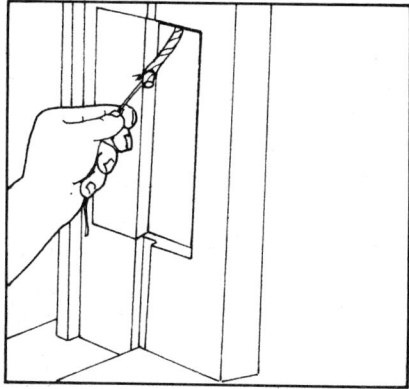

8. The weight will feed the cord down to the trap. *(continued)*

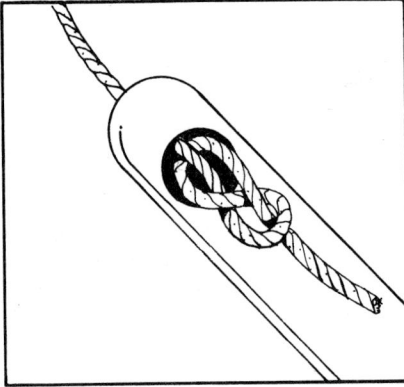

9. Remove the small weight and string. Tie the sash cord to the weight with a non-slip knot.

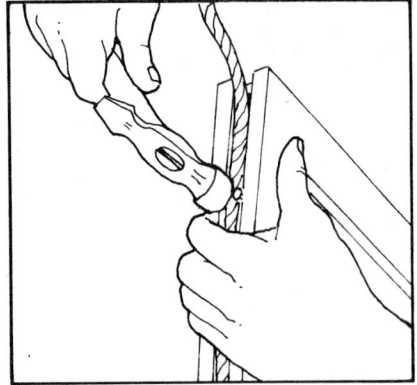

11. Remove the sash and nail the cord in the groove, below the mark. Use clout nails and nail along 12 in (30.5 cm) of the cord.

10. Knot the other end of the cord. Hold the lower sash at the top of the window frame and mark on the position of the top pulley with a pencil.

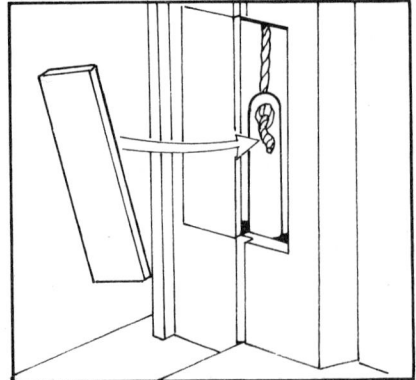

12. Slide the window back into the frame. Replace the pulley trap and beading.

176

Repairing a rotted wood sill

You will need: chisel, hard-setting mastic sealer

1. Wet rot in a wood sill can be repaired by removing the rotted area and filling with a hard-setting filler.

3. Brush out all the wet-rot fibres and dust.

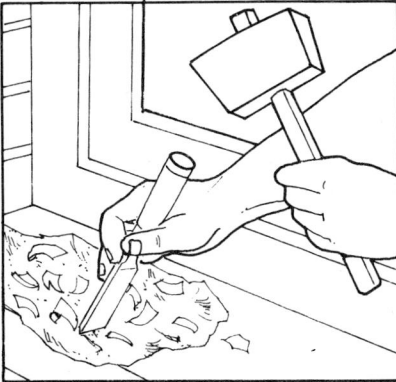

2. Chisel out all the affected area back to where the wood is firm and dry.

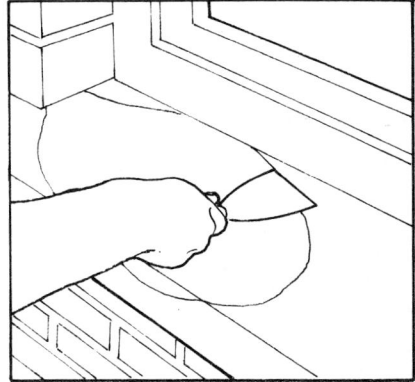

4. Fill the cavity with a proprietary filler, following the maker's instructions. When the filler sets, level off and shape with a shaping tool; repaint the sill.

Filling gaps around a frame

You will need: putty knife; small hammer; wood chisel; pincers; rule; filling knife; paintbrush; paint; putty

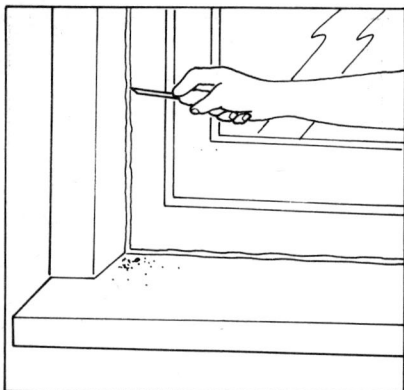

1. Gaps around a wood frame can be filled with putty to which gold size has been added. First rake out the gap with a scraper or old screwdriver.

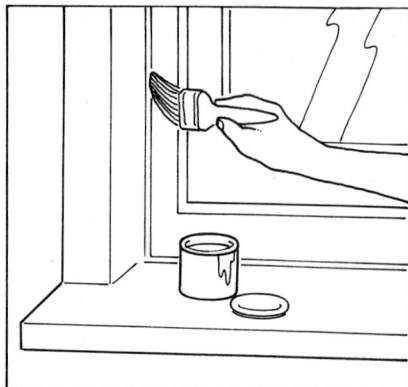

3. Brush gold size into the gap, making sure it penetrates deeply.

2. Make up a small amount of putty with a putty knife which has been dipped in gold size.

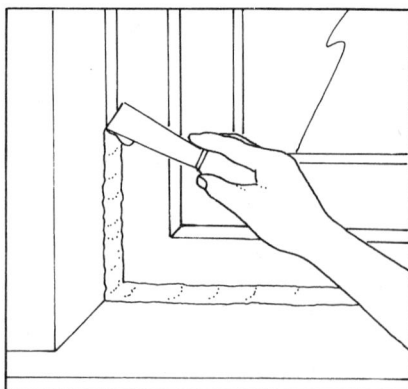

4. Fill the gap with the gold-size/ putty mix and finish off with a putty knife to get a flat, smooth bead. Paint when set.

Replacing a broken window pane

You will need: hammer; chisel; pincers; knife;
putty knife; paint-brush; putty; paint; brads

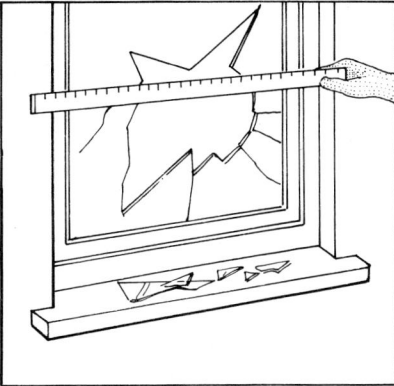

1. Before buying a new pane,
measure the frame accurately.
Include the thickness of the putty
and from this measurement
subtract $\frac{1}{4}$ in (6 mm) overall.

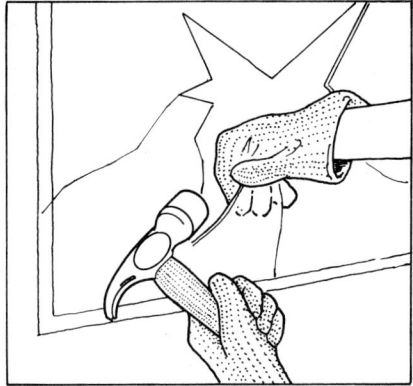

3. Remove the broken glass. Try to
ease out sections by hand. If using a
hammer to break the glass, wear
protective goggles or an old pair of
glasses.

2. Wear thick and strong gloves and
chisel away the old putty all around
the frame.

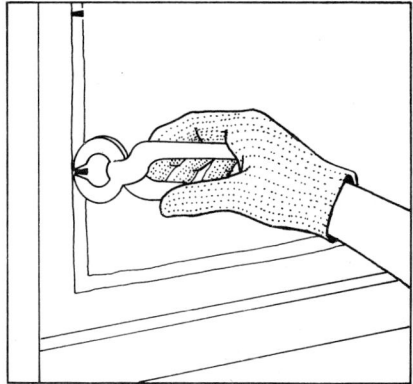

4. Pull out the brads around the
frame with a pair of pincers. *(continued)*

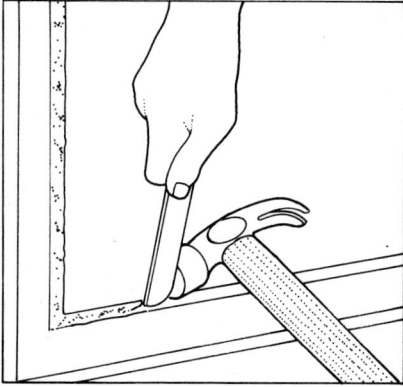

5. Clean out all the old putty with a strong knife. The frame must be perfectly clean before fitting the new pane.

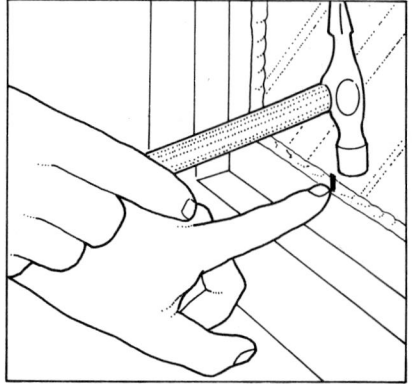

7. Gently press the new pane into the putty. Then hammer in brads at about 6 in (150 mm) intervals.

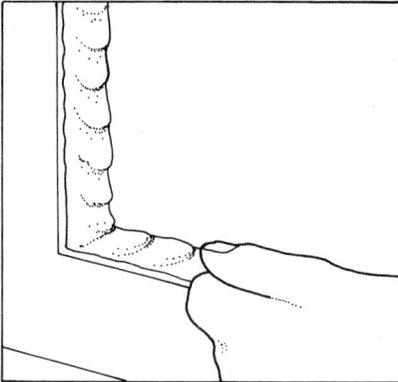

6. Lay a bed of putty around the frame, pressing it firmly into the rebate.

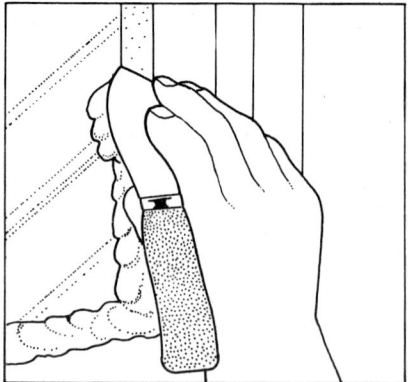

8. Apply putty to the frame with a putty knife, using the straight edge of the knife to bevel the putty.

Replacing old putty

You will need: trimming knife; putty knife; putty

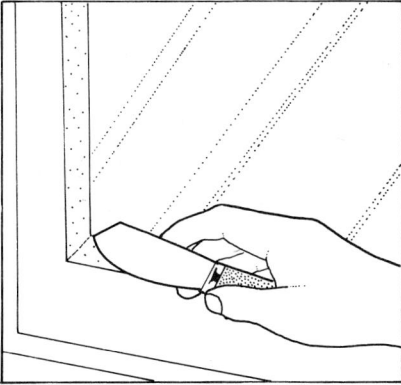

9. Again, making use of the straight edge of the putty knife, level off the top edge of the putty so that it is flush with the top of the rebate.

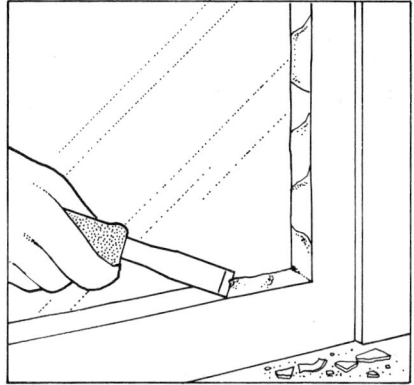

1. Putty sometimes goes brittle with age, especially if it has not been painted, and may cause windows to rattle. Remove all the old putty with an old chisel.

10. Allow about four weeks for the putty to harden and mature. Then paint with a good quality oil-based paint.

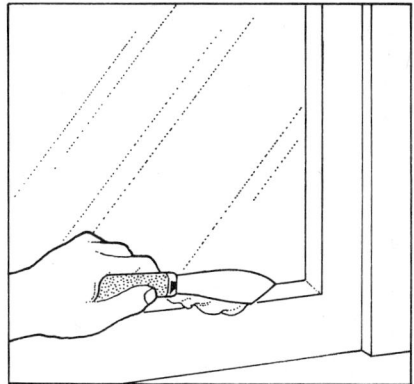

2. Press in new putty, working it well into the rebate with your thumb. Level off with a putty knife or trimming knife. Paint after about four weeks.

Repairing a concrete sill

You will need: hammer; cold chisel; trowel; wood
batten; plasterer's float; cement

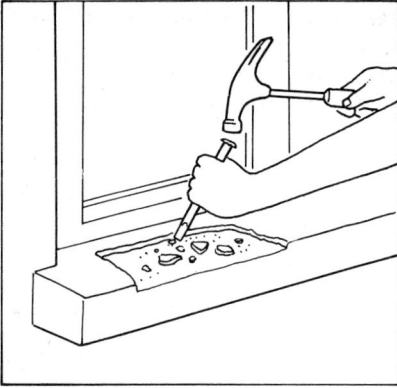

1. A badly cracked or flaking sill can
be resurfaced with mortar. First chip
away the damaged area to a depth of
2 in (50 mm) with a cold chisel and
club hammer.

3. Hold a batten against the sill and
spread the mortar to the edge of the
batten.

2. Wet the surface thoroughly with
clean water and cover with a mortar
mix of 4 parts sand, 1 part cement
and 1 part lime.

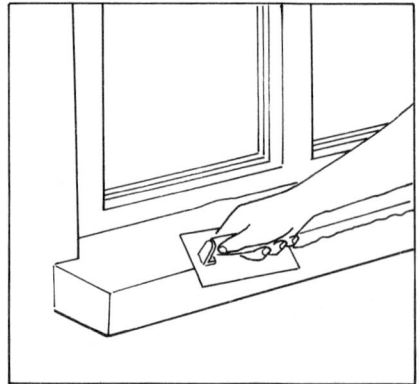

4. Remove the batten and smooth
the mortar so that it slopes slightly to
the front edge of the sill.

Painting sequences for windows

You will need: large and small paintbrushes; masking tape; paint

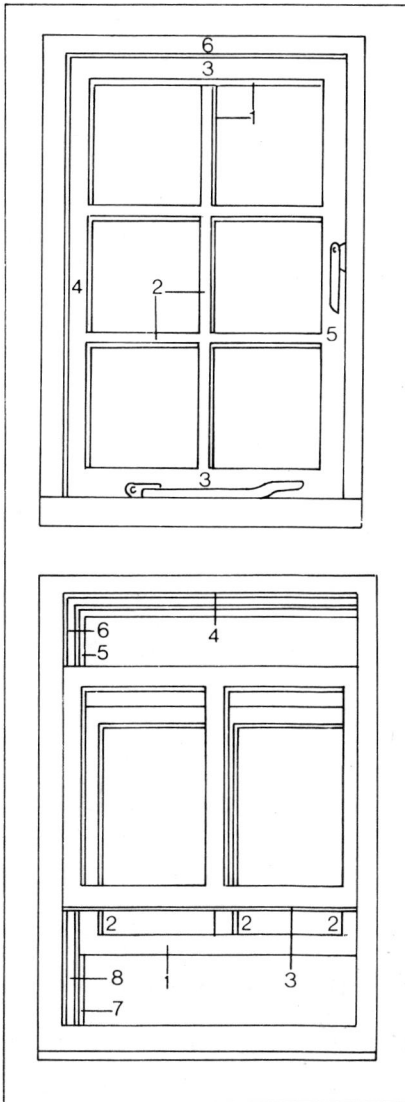

Painting sequences for windows
Always paint windows in sequence as shown by the numbering in the illustrations. This is particularly important with sash windows where the sashes have to be positioned and repositioned while some painted parts are still wet.

If you are repainting a window with its original colour, sequential painting will ensure that no parts are overlooked.

Adhesives and their Uses

In recent years, modern adhesives have far outstripped the animal glues that were once used for jobs around the house. Now there are adhesives for specific tasks and so a wide range exists.

There are a dozen or more different types of adhesive, and many are so sophisticated in their application that it is essential to follow the instructions rigidly. Before attempting any repair, therefore, make sure that you have the right adhesive for the job; that the surfaces to be joined are clean; and that you have clamps or weights ready for slow-setting adhesives.

Though superseded for many jobs, **animal glues** are still used in furniture making and are supplied in powder form ready to be mixed with water or in solid bars which are melted and the glue applied hot. Animal glues make a strong joint but are not waterproof; for outside repairs to woodwork use a **synthetic resin (urea)** which has good all-round properties. **Epoxy resins** are two-part adhesives which harden when the ingredients are mixed. Because they do not rely on air for setting they are useful for making joins under water. **Polyvinyl acetate (PVA)** is an easy-to-use adhesive that will stick paper, leather, china and wood. It makes a strong bond but is not waterproof and is suitable only for indoor jobs. A good general-purpose adhesive is the **cellulose-based type** which sets quickly, is waterproof and fairly strong.

One of the most useful adhesives is **contact cement** which bonds immediately, though some brands have a 'slip' time which allows a few seconds for the user to finally position the two surfaces. It is used chiefly for sticking laminates, ceramic tiles, hardboard and metal to wood. This is an adhesive which has to be applied to both surfaces and is almost dry before the two sections are brought together.

For polystyrene repairs there is **polystyrene cement** which softens the two halves to be joined and welds them together when it hardens. Its use is limited strictly to rigid polystyrene and cannot be used on expanded foam or on nylon and polythene.

For flexible materials such as carpets and curtains, use white **latex-based adhesive** which can be washed in hot water. **Wallpaper** adhesives are based mainly on vegetable extracts such as starch or dextrine, though some are a cellulose paste. All are mixed with water and there are various grades for types of wallcovering such as anaglypta and lincrusta.

Finally there are the superglues — **cyanoacrylate** — which bond instantly and will virtually stick anything to anything. **There is no solvent for this glue and it should be used with extreme care.**

Types of bond

Adhesive	Characteristics	Setting time	Uses
Animal glues	Made of bone, hide and sinews. Includes 'Scotch' or fish glues	4 – 6 hours	Woodworking
PVA (woodwork)	Clean to use and unlike animal glue has little smell and dries clear	20 – 60 min	All woodworking jobs
PVA (building)			An additive to aid bonding of cement
Epoxy resins	Hardens by chemical action and supplied in two parts, glue and hardener, which are mixed just before use	8 – 24 hours Fast-setting type 30 – 60 min	Will bond most materials but is expensive for large jobs
Contact cement	Bonds immediately when two coated surfaces are joined. Ideal for jobs where clamping or applying weights is difficult or impossible	Immediate, but some brands have a few seconds 'slip' time	Laminates, plywood etc
Urea (synthetic resin)	Two part adhesive or mixed with water Joint is waterproof and heat resistant	4 – 6 hours	Woodworking and general use
Cellulose	Makes a flexible joint, is quick-drying and waterproof	10 – 15 min	Leather and fabrics, china, glass
Casein glues	Supplied in powder form and is mixed with water. Will set at low temperatures	4 – 6 hours	Furniture and other woodworking repairs
Latex	Washable but will not withstand dry-cleaning	1 – 2 hours	Fabrics, particularly carpets and curtains
Rubber resin	Solvent based synthetic rubber	2 – 4 hours	Floor tiles, linoleum rubber, felt
Cyanoacrylate	One of the new 'wonder' glues. Used in minute quantities	instant	Mostly small repair jobs such as crockery, ornament etc

Concrete

Concrete consists of cement mixed with gravel and sand, called aggregates, and bound together with water. The gravel, or sometimes crushed stones, is known as a coarse aggregate and the sand is fine aggregate. Portland cement is used for most concretes, though there are fast-setting cements available which should be used if there is a risk of heavy frost before the cement has had time to harden. Frost is concrete's worst enemy, it will cause it to disintegrate and it is advisable not to carry out any concreting work during the winter unless absolutely necessary.

When buying aggregate, ask for 'all-in' which has the sand and stones already mixed. For small jobs you can buy ready-mixed aggregate and cement — all you need to do is add the water.

It is important that only clean, fresh water is used — rainwater may contain impurities which will affect the setting. The amount of water, too, is important — too much will produce a weak concrete that will shrink and crack as it sets.

The aggregate and cement should be mixed in proportions suitable for the work to be done. For heavy duty work (such as repairing a driveway, floor or fence posts) use 1 part of cement to $4\frac{1}{2}$ parts of all-in aggregate. Paths can be repaired with a mix of 1 part cement to $3\frac{1}{2}$ parts of aggregate. It is the coarse aggregate that gives the concrete body and strength, but this is not needed for filling cracks and holes and a mix of 1 part cement to 3 parts of coarse sand is sufficient for this work.

When mixing concrete measure out the aggregate first, then add the cement. Try not to make more than is necessary for the job — as it is better to make several mixes than to overestimate and have concrete left over. Add water in small amounts until you have a workable mix with no dry aggregate. For the best results use a watering can fitted with a rose; this will ensure an even spread of water.

Concrete made with Portland cement takes about four days to set in warm weather, but it should not be allowed to set too quickly. Cover it with damp sacking or polythene sheets or a layer of damp sand. Boards placed on bricks and laid across a concreted path or driveway will prevent dogs, cats and birds leaving their footprints.

For mending cracks in a concrete path or drive, use the 1 part cement, 3 part sand mix and add a PVA bonding agent that will give a good bond between the old and new concrete.

For concreting a very large area, such as a long path or drive, you can hire a concrete mixer complete with ready-mixed concrete. This will take a lot of the hard work out of the job.

How to mix concrete

You will need: spade; sand; cement; watering can and rose; bucket; water

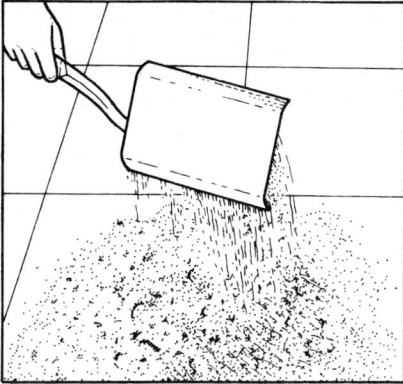

1. First mix the sand and aggregate in the correct proportions. Then measure out the cement and add it to the heap.

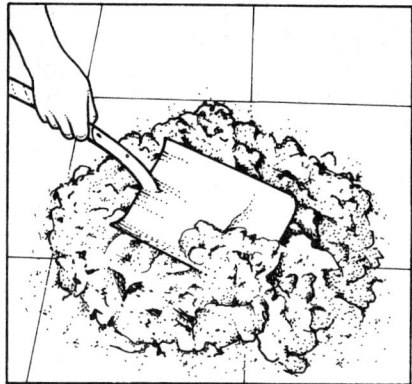

3. Mix well with a spade, turning the mix constantly until it is fully wet.

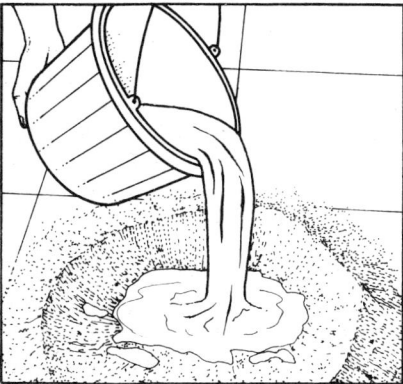

2. Make a crater in the middle of the heap and pour in water as required.

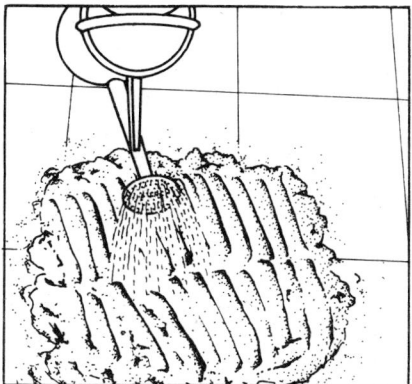

4. The mix should be stiff enough to hold ridges made with the edge of the spade. If more water is necessary use a watering can and rose.

Mortar

Mortar is used chiefly for bricklaying and repointing; that is, repairing crumbling joints in brickwork. It is also used for rendering outside walls.

The ingredients for brickwork mortar are graded sand, Portland cement or lime, and water. Choosing the right ingredients is essential for making a good mortar — sand, for example, should be well graded, which means that the grains vary in size from coarse to fine. Well graded sand gives a strong mortar mix, whereas uniform sand (where the grains are all of equal size) results in a weak, porous mix.

A sand/cement mortar mix, though strong, tends to crack as it dries out. A sand/lime mix sets slowly and does not crack but it makes a weak joint. A compromise, therefore, is to use all three ingredients. Another ingredient, particularly useful for rendering, is masonry cement. It makes a highly workable mix with good plasticity.

A mortar with good plasticity is smooth and therefore easy to mix and point. Plasticizers are available in powder or liquid form and break down surface tension. They can be added to cement/sand mixes.

Another additive that can be used when pointing is a vegetable dye or ready-mixed coloured compound for picking out the joints against the colour of the brickwork.

A golden rule for using mortar is that the mix should be no stronger than the materials with which it is to be used. For brickwork, laying and pointing, the usual mix is 1 part cement, 1 part hydrated lime and 6 parts of sand. When adding water, avoid too wet a mix as it will be difficult to pick up on the trowel and will slide off.

Mix the cement, lime and sand thoroughly before adding water. Try to make the mix close to where it is to be used and avoid making more than you will need for each part of a job. The area should be clean — a large piece of chipboard or a square of timber makes an ideal mixing base — so that the mix is not contaminated with particles of soil or dust.

Add water sparingly from a watering can fitted with a rose and keep turning the mixture until it is evenly wet. From time to time, stick a trowel into the mix to test it — when it is withdrawn the impression should stay; if the mortar crumbles it is too dry, if it disappears rapidly it is too wet. Adjust accordingly. If you are using plasticizer or colouring, follow the manufacturer's instructions.

When you are ready to use the mortar, transfer some of it to a hawk. This is a bricklayer's tool which you can make yourself; it consists of a piece of board about 12 in (305 mm) square with a vertical handle beneath. Hold the hawk in one hand, using the other hand to lift mortar with a trowel and apply it.

How to mix mortar

You will need: spade; trowel; sand; cement;
lime; watering can and rose; water

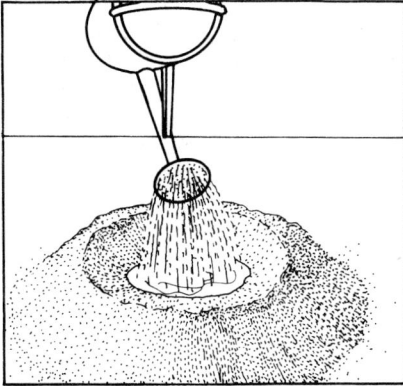

1. Mix the ingredients – sand,
cement and lime if required – and
make a crater in the top of the heap.
Add water from a watering can and
rose.

2. Mix thoroughly until all parts of
the heap are consistently wet. The
mix should be stiff enough to be
sliced with a trowel.

Mortar mixes

Use	mix	Use	mix
Bricklaying or pointing on an external wall	For summer (no frost risk) 1 part cement; 2 parts hydrated lime; 9 parts sand (Winter) 1 part cement; 1 part hydrated lime; 6 parts sand	Internal walls	1 part cement; 2 parts hydrated lime; 9 parts sand
		Block walls (External)	1 part cement; 1 part hydrated lime; 6 parts sand
Garden walls	2 parts cement; 1 part hydrated lime; 9 parts sand	Block walls (internal)	1 part cement; 1 part hydrated lime; 9 parts sand
Rendering	1 part masonry cement; 5 parts sand		

Plaster and plastering

Plastering a large area, such as a complete wall, requires a skilled technique which is beyond the scope of the average handyman. It is possible, however, to repair small areas and to fill large cracks or splits, such as might occur when fitting a new electricity power socket.

Plaster consists of burnt gypsum with various additives which determine the setting and hardening times and there are several different grades. It can be bought from a builders' merchant who will advise you on the grade to use. For large areas you need two types of plaster, one for the undercoat and one for the top or skim coat. Skim coat plaster is a neat powder which gives a smooth finish; undercoat plaster is mixed with sand to coarsen it so that it will key well to the wall.

For filling small holes and cracks there are proprietary fillers available which work well and are easy to use. They set quickly (in about 30 minutes) and can be mixed with emulsion paint to match the colouring of the surrounding plaster. Mix plaster in a bucket, putting the powder in first and then adding water and stirring at the same time. Aim for a doughy consistency and be ready to use the plaster within half an hour of mixing. If this is not possible, make a creamier mix. Plaster sets rapidly but takes a long time to fully dry out; do not paper over it or paint for at least six months, except with emulsion paint which will not seal the finish.

Prepare the area to be plastered by breaking away all loose plaster and brushing the hole and edges clean with a soft brush. Chisel out the old plaster until the surface beneath is bare.

If it is smooth bricks or concrete blocks, scratch the surface with the chisel to provide a good key for the undercoat. Immediately before you apply the plaster, soak the area with clean water from a soft brush. Use a trowel to apply the undercoat, pressing it well into the hole. Do not worry too much about the finish at this stage – it will be covered by the skim coat and the undercoat's main objective is to provide a firm base.

Allow the undercoat to set before applying the top finish. Gypsum plaster is light brown in colour which darkens when mixed with water; as it sets it will lighten to a pale chocolate colour.

Before you apply the skim coat, have ready a large sponge and a wood batten which is about 6 in (150 mm) longer than the widest part of the area being plastered. Apply the top coat with a trowel and smooth it gently, trying to get a level, unbroken finish. When the whole area has been filled, place the batten flat on the wall and draw it across to level the surface. Fill any areas which are hollow. Then dampen the sponge and wipe it gently over the plaster to get a smooth finish.

How to mix plaster

You will need: trowel; bucket; plaster; water

1. Use a scoop or garden trowel to measure out sufficient plaster for the work to be done. Use a plastic bucket for mixing.

2. Add clean water slowly, stirring all the time until the plaster is a creamy texture. Use the plaster immediately.

There are many different types and grades of plaster, each with different characteristics and formulated for different jobs. Some are suitable for use by the amateur and some are not; the chart (right) will serve as a guide.

Type	Use	Characteristics
Anhydrous; hard burnt	For top coats	Sets to a smooth, hard finish
Anhydrous; moderately burnt	For both top and under-coats. This is one of the easiest plasters for the handy-man to use because it can be smoothed with a wet sponge or trowel	Dries slowly and so gives time for mistakes to be rectified
Retarded hemihydrate	Used as an undercoat and for finishing plasterboard	Sets quickly
Hemi-hydrate	For moulding and repairs to cornices and ornate ceilings	Sets quickly

Bricklaying

Bricklaying is a skill that comes with much practice and experience, and it would be a difficult task for the average handyman to take on a large job such as building a garage or a house extension. Nevertheless there are small jobs (eg, bricking in a fireplace) which can reasonably be undertaken.

All brickwork, whether a wall or filling in a fireplace, must be bonded. This means simply that the bricks are laid in such a way as to give the structure strength and stability. A wall built with bricks stacked one on top of the other would quickly fall down. For most small jobs requiring a single thickness of bricks, stretcher bond is adequate (see p 156). Each row of bricks is called a course, and in each course the bricks overlap those in the course below.

Two other bonds, called English and Flemish, are used in large structures, but there is also the English Garden Wall bond used as the name implies. This bond is not as strong as English or Flemish but is attractive to look at. It consists of three courses of stretchers alternating with one course of headers. In a header course the bricks are laid across the wall.

Another attractive garden wall is made by Open bond. This consists of courses laid in stretcher bond but with spaces the width of a quarter of a brick, called a quarter-bat. A garden wall will need a foundation, which can be made by digging a trench about 1 ft (30.5 cm) deep and filling it with concrete (1 part cement; 4 parts mixed aggregate). When bricking-in a fireplace the bricks can be laid directly on the hearth.

If the courses are to be laid to a height of about 2 ft (61 cm), you will need to check constantly for level and straightness with a spirit level. Getting the correct level depends largely on using the right amount of mortar between courses, and a little practice may be needed. After mixing the mortar (see pp 188-189), scoop up enough to load a trowel and make a bed about $\frac{3}{8}$ in (9.5 mm) thick and lay the first brick flat side down. Butter the end of the next brick to the same thickness and lay it against the first brick. Continue along the course and check for level, tapping down any bricks above the level with the handle of the trowel.

Lay the next course in the same way, trowelling mortar into the hollowed top (called the frog) of each brick in the course below.

At some point you may need to cut a brick, especially when bricking-in a confined space. This is done with a bolster chisel; measure off where the brick is to be cut and mark a pencil line. Hold the bolster at a slight angle along the line, leaning towards the waste section of the brick. Make the cut with a sharp, single blow with a club hammer.

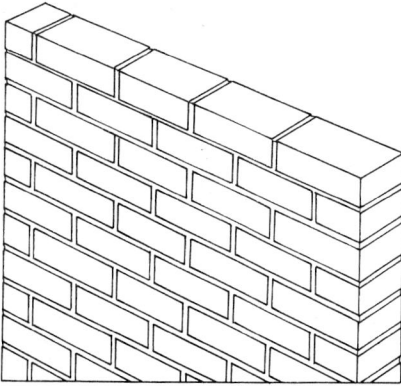

1. Stretcher bond Used in single 4 in (100 mm) walls and in cavity walls. The bricks are laid with their long side exposed.

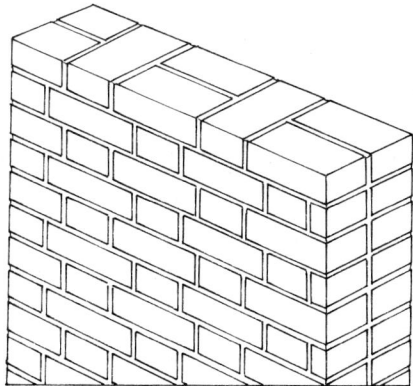

2. English bond Makes an $8\frac{1}{2}$ in (215 mm) wall. The bond consists of alternate rows of stretchers and headers, the end faces of the bricks.

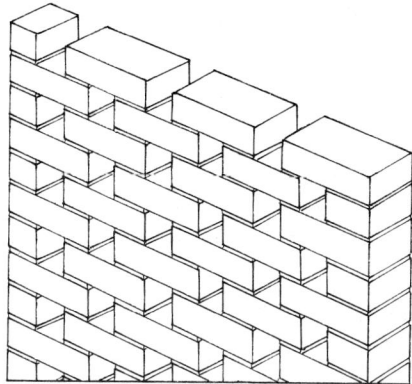

3. Flemish bond Similar to English and makes the same thickness wall. It has pairs of stretchers laid with headers between them. Weaker than English due to continuous vertical joints.

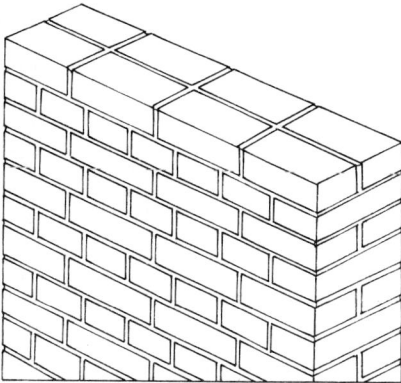

4. Open bond Purely decorative, this type of wall is basically a stretcher bond with spaces between the bricks. Each space is equal to a quarter of the brick length.

Basic bricklaying

You will need: trowel; mortar

1. Lay a bed of mortar and flatten it with a trowel so that it is level and about $\frac{3}{8}$ in (9.5 mm) thick.

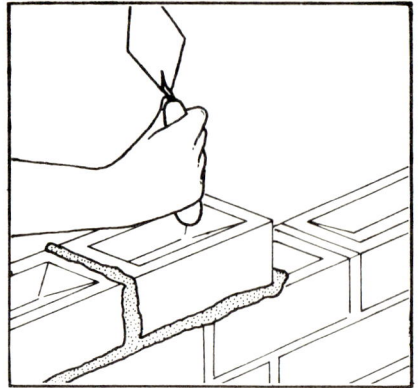

3. Lay the brick frog-side (the indented side) uppermost and tap it into position with the trowel handle.

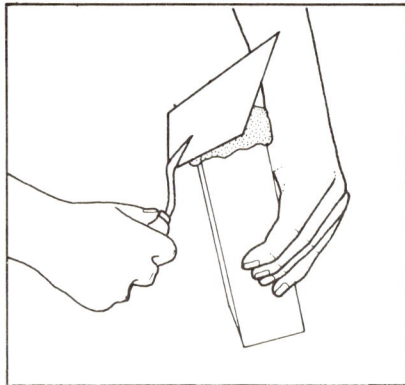

2. Butter one end of a brick with mortar, levelling it off to about $\frac{3}{8}$ in (9.5 mm) thick.

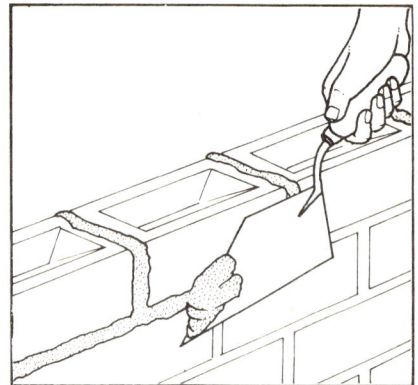

4. With the edge of the trowel, clean off all surplus mortar to leave the joints absolutely flush with the surface of the wall.

Additional tips

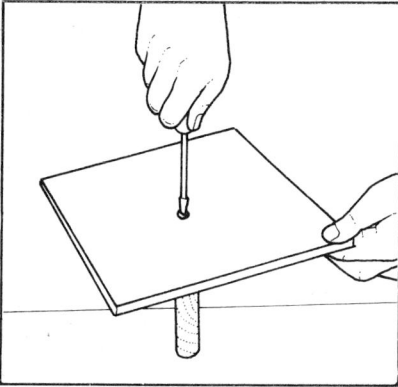

Making a hawk
A hawk is used to hold mortar while bricklaying. Make one from a piece of plywood about 12 in (30.5 cm) square with a short length of broom handle fixed underneath.

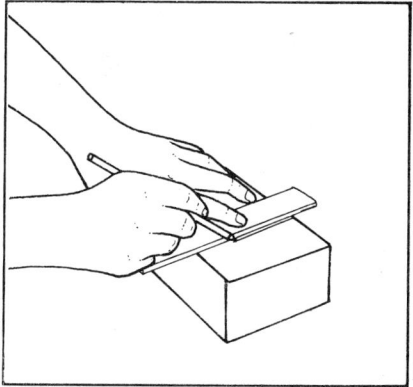

Cutting a brick
1. Place the brick with its flat face uppermost. Mark off the end to be cut with a pencil and rule.

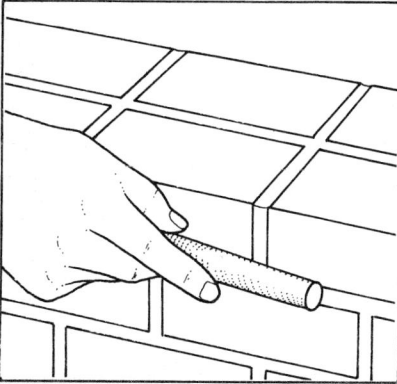

Rubbing mortar joints
For a neat finish to a mortar joint, rub the joint while it is still wet with a piece of pipe to make a concave impression.

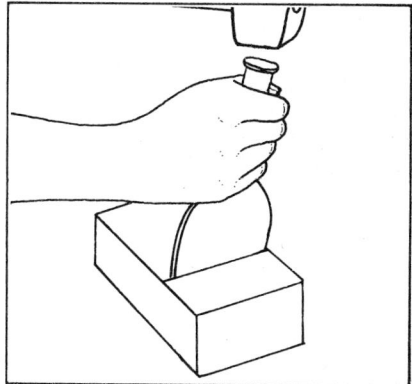

2. Make the cut with a bolster chisel. Tilt the chisel handle towards the waste end of the brick and give it a single, sharp blow with a club hammer.

Woodworking

For most jobs around the home the basic techniques of woodworking will suffice; some skill in sawing and planing; making simple joints and using the correct fixings (ie, screws and nails).

Some knowledge of the materials you are working with — softwood, hardwood, plywood, chipboard etc — and their characteristics is also essential. Softwood comes from coniferous trees, and the most commonly used is deal — another name for Scots pine. It can be bought ready planed, is easy to saw and drill and can be shaped with a rasp or Surform. If used outside it must be protected with a preservative or a quality paint.

Hardwood is superior to softwood in many ways — it is less prone to shrinkage, can be used outdoors without protection and has a tougher surface. Oak, mahogany, teak and walnut are popular hardwoods.

Plywood consists of several veneers bonded in odd numbers, for example three-ply, five-ply etc. The veneers are laid with their grains at right angles to each other to give a tough though relatively thin sheet. It is perhaps the most popular of manufactured woodworking materials, but it is important to choose the right type and grade for certain jobs. For outside use there is a waterproof bonded ply which is marked EXTERIOR WBP. There are also grades in accordance with the quality of the outer veneers. A clear unblemished plywood is grade A; blemished plywood is B and BB is plywood which has had the blemishes removed.

Chipboard is made from chips of softwood bonded together under pressure. It is cheap to buy and there are grades for interior and exterior use. One of its disadvantages is that it is heavy, also if it is subjected to loads without adequate support it will bow. Chipboard will not hold ordinary wood screws, but inserts can be bought which are similar to wall plugs.

For making corner joints there are simple corner pieces available from DIY shops — the pieces are in two sections, which are screwed in the angles and then bolted together.

The simplest type of carpenter's joint is the lap joint; two pieces of wood are placed together, one overlapping the other, and fixed with screws. It makes a useful joint for light framework. For a stronger joint, the halving joint is made by cutting a channel into each piece of wood, to half its thickness, and interlocking the two pieces. A good joint for shelving is the housing joint; one piece of wood has a channel cut into it to the thickness of the shelf which is glued and pinned into the groove. Such a joint can carry a considerable weight, but for lightweight shelving support blocks screwed to support the ends of the shelf are sufficient.

Basic woodworking joints

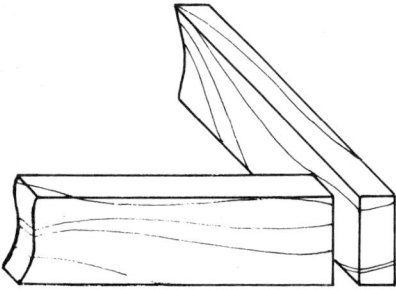

1. Butt joint Two plain ends joined in this way can be secured by screws, nails or glue.

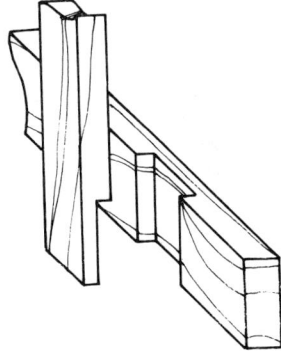

2. Halving joint The two joined sections are halved to give flush surfaces.

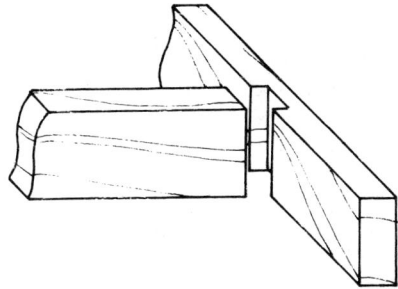

3. Cross halving joint This is used where two joined members cross at right angles.

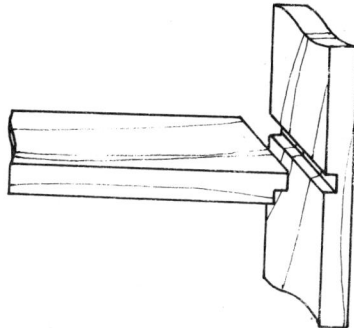

4. Halved housing joint This is a variation of 2 and 3.

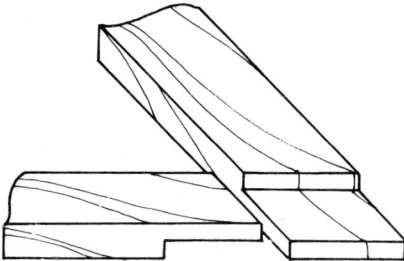

5. Housing joint One piece of wood is 'housed' in a section cut in another.

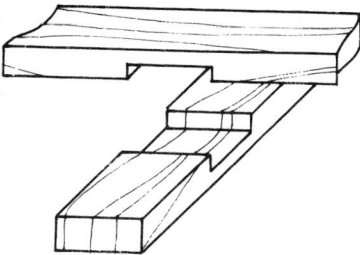

6. T halving joint Used to join to members as a T piece.

Woodworking

Basic tips on the use of tools

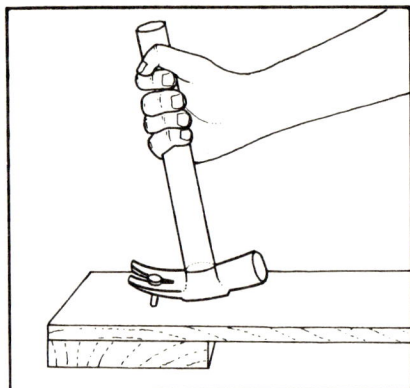

To extract a nail, use a claw hammer. Hook the claw under the nail head, pull the handle towards you and finish with the handle vertical.

Use a coping saw for cutting irregular shapes. Adjust the blade so that it is taut in the frame.

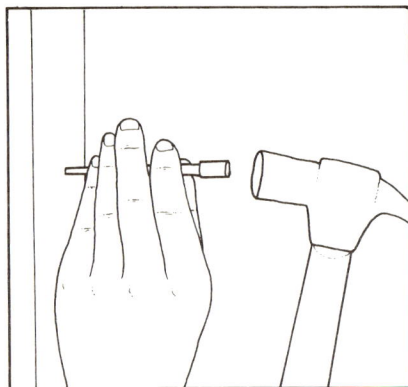

Where nail heads are exposed, use a nail punch to sink the head below the surface. Fill the hole with a wood filler.

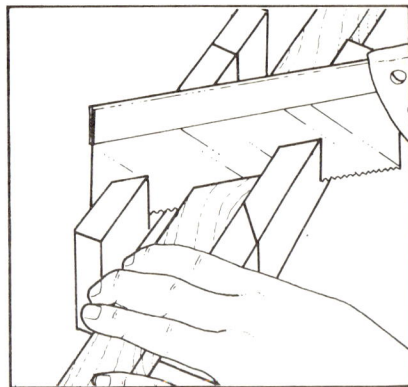

To make accurate mitred joints use a mitre block and tenon saw. Choose the angle required, insert the piece of wood and cut through the guide slots.

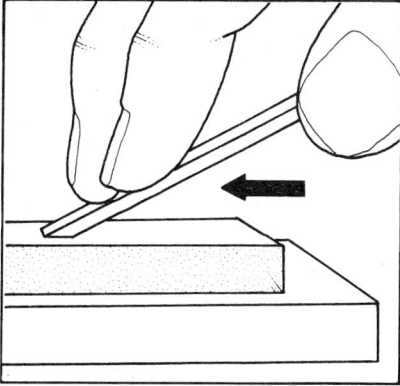

Keep chisels sharp with a carborundum oil stone. Hold the chisel with its face flat and work backwards and forwards along the stone.

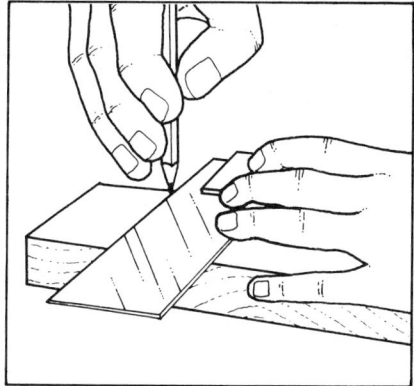

Use a try square for marking a line at right angles to one side of a piece of wood. Hold the handle firmly against one face and scribe the line.

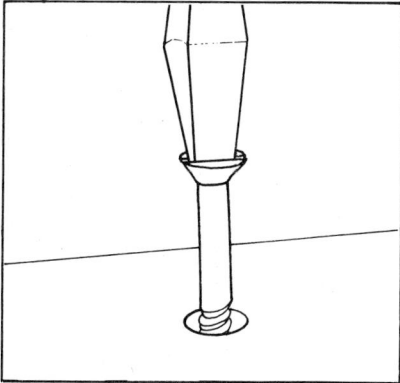

Always use the correct screwdriver, especially when screwing into a finished surface. The blade should be a snug fit in the screw slot.

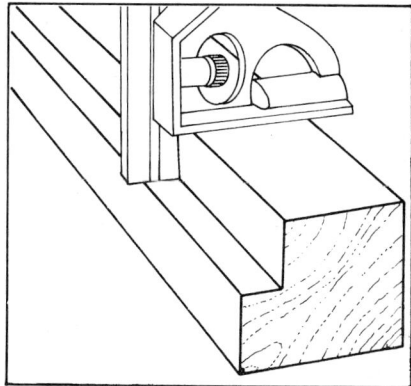

A combination square can be used for marking 45° and right angles. Used on a rebate, as above, it will give perfect squareness on three faces of the work.

Wood diseases

Most houses, and especially old ones, have a considerable amount of timber in their construction and are prone to wet rot, dry rot and woodworm. It is essential to know and recognize these diseases.

Perhaps the most dreaded of woodwork pests is **woodworm** — infected timbers usually have to be completely replaced once this deadly menace spreads. The most common type of woodworm, affecting the softwood timbers in rafters, joists and floors, is the furniture beetle. Often only a few holes appear on the surface, but below the woodwork is riddled with honeycomb-like passages.

There are woodworm-killing fluids available, and if the condition does not appear to be serious they can be effectively used. It is best, however, to treat woodworm only on areas which are non-structural, such as skirting boards or picture rails. **In roofs and floors, take no chances**. Get advice from a specialist firm.

Dry rot also is a disease that will spread rapidly if not checked, though in this case prevention is better than cure. Dry rot thrives in damp, unventilated places and a common cause is poor underfloor ventilation due to blocked air bricks.

Dry rot is recognizable in several ways; often a reddish dust appears or there may be a thin, grey-white covering with lilac or yellow patches.

The fungus throws out strands which can penetrate brickwork and mortar in search of the moisture on which it thrives. As a result of dry rot the timber breaks up and crumbles.

Like woodworm the treatment of dry rot is either drastic or limited. In structural timbers the advice of a wood preservation specialist should be sought, but almost certainly the work will involve complete replacement of all affected wood. In non-structural timber you can cut back the affected area to well beyond the extent of the fungus and replace the wood after giving it two coats of fungicidal fluid. Also apply two coats to to all woodwork within 5 ft (1 m 52 cm) of the area.

Wet rot is also a fungus, but is less serious than dry rot as it does not spread. Its fungus appears as thin, yellowish-brown lines which turn to dark brown or black. When probed with a knife blade, wet rot breaks into soggy fibres. Treatment is much the same as for dry rot. In largely affected timbers they must be replaced with fungicidal fluid-treated timbers and the adjacent area should also be treated. In non-structural timbers, however, such as a window sill or door sill, a patch of wet rot can be cut back to dry timber and filled with a proprietary wood filler or hard-setting mastic. Rub down and shape the filler after it has set and paint the whole sill.

Dry rot

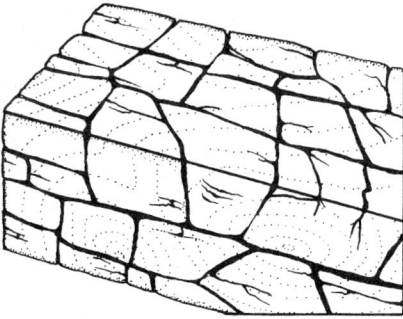

1. Dry rot, the most serious of the two rot diseases, is easily recognizable. The wood crazes into cube-like pieces and crumbles when probed.

Woodworm

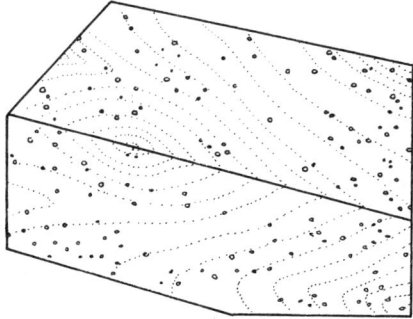

3. On the suface, woodworm appears as holes – called flight holes – where the hatched beetle has burrowed its way out. At this stage the damage has already been done.

Wet rot

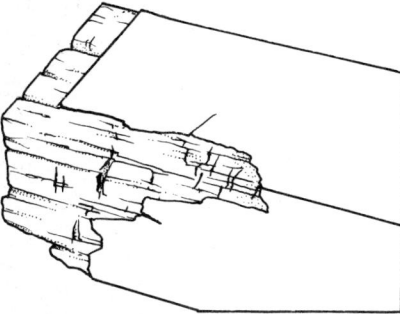

2. Wet rot can be detected by its fibrous appearance. When probed the wood is soft and spongy.

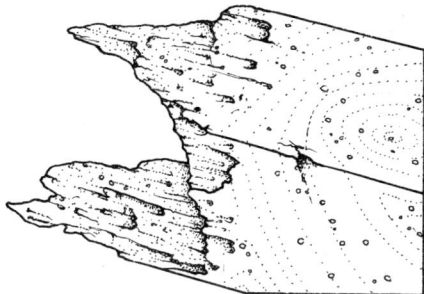

4. Beneath the surface, dozens of passageways mark the progress of the woodworm grub. The wood becomes brittle and breaks easily.

Soldering

Soldering is an effective way of joining two metals with a molten alloy – usually tin and lead. Joints unlikely to be subjected to strain, such as wires in an electrical appliance, can be joined at a temperature of about 250–480° F (120–240°C) using an electric soldering iron; this is called soft soldering. Joins needing greater strength are soldered at a higher temperature, about 1100–1650° F (590–900°C); this is called hard soldering which must be done with a blow torch and an alloy of copper, silver and zinc.

Most metals can be joined by either method, particularly brass, copper, lead, zinc, tin and pewter. **Steel, aluminium and cast iron cannot be soldered**.

To assist the solder alloy to flow a flux is used, but for small soft soldering jobs there are wire solders already cored with flux which makes the job much simpler. Otherwise a stick of solder must be used and a flux paste. Electric soldering irons can be bought with several inter-changeable bits – the copper tip – for large or small jobs. When soldering the heat from the iron must transfer to the work pieces, so do not try to solder large pieces of metal with a small iron or bit as the heat will dissipate too rapidly. An alternative to an electric iron is a gas blow torch with a special soldering attachment.

To get a good, clean soft-soldered job, first make sure that both the soldering bit and the pieces to be joined are clean and bright. Use a fine file or glasspaper to do this. Heat the iron and coat it with a thin layer of solder, then heat the work piece by holding the iron against it and coat the surface – this is called tinning. Finally apply the iron again and run solder on to the join. Allow a few moments for it to harden before testing the joint for strength.

The flux used for hard soldering is borax, and can be used in either paste or powder form. It must be brushed on to the work piece after it has been cleaned ready for soldering and before heat is applied. You will need two hands for hard soldering, so it may be necessary to devise some sort of clamping arrangement across the parts to be joined. Make sure, however, that the clamp is clear of the joining area, or you may solder the clamp to it. You will also need a heatproof base to work on, such as a sheet of asbestos or a couple of house bricks placed side by side.

Adjust the blow torch to get a blue, pencil-thin flame and heat the work piece until it glows dull red. Apply the solder and allow it to run well into the joints before removing the flame. Let the joint cool naturally, then wash off the surplus flux with hot water.

Making a soldered joint

You will need: blowtorch; paint-brush; soldering iron; solder

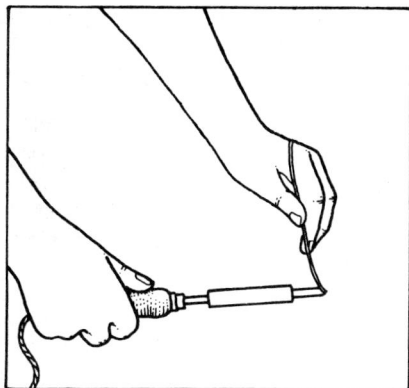

1. To make a soft soldered joint, first 'tin' the heated bit with a piece of flux-cored solder. Apply more solder when the bit is in contact with the joint.

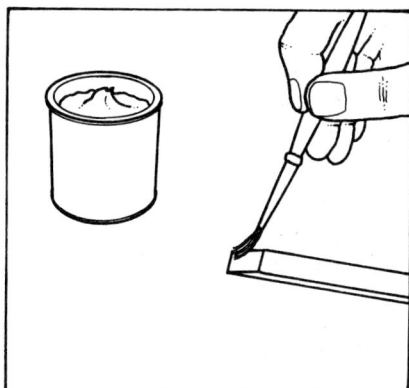

3. To hard solder, or braize, a joint apply flux to the two faces of the workpiece.

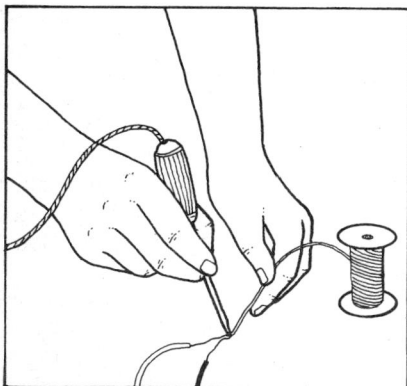

2. For small work, 'tin' the bit and bring the workpiece to the soldering iron. Hold the iron steady and move the piece away when the solder has flowed.

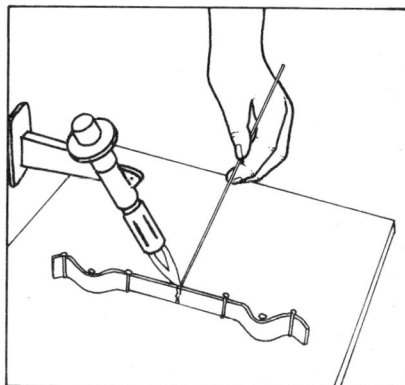

4. Clamp the two pieces together and use a blowtorch to heat the metal until it glows red. Apply solder or braizing rod to the joint

Dictionary of useful tools

Good tools will last a lifetime, so always buy the best. Below is an ABC guide to the basic tools needed to carry out most jobs around the house, and a few tips on how to use them.

Bradawl

A sharp-pointed hand-tool used for making a starting hole for a wood-screw. A similar tool is the gimlet which has a corkscrew-like end. Both tools are simple to use, but must be held straight when starting a hole otherwise the screw will go in at an angle.

Chisels

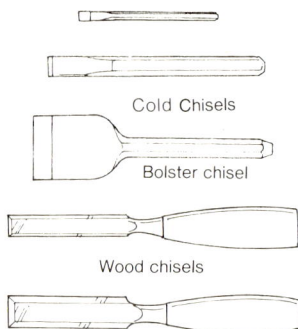

Cold Chisels

Bolster chisel

Wood chisels

Cold chisels are used for chipping bricks, concrete, plaster etc, and two at least are needed – one large, one small. A bolster chisel has a wide blade and is useful for removing large areas of concrete or plaster, as well as its intended function, lifting floor-boards. The most useful wood chisels for general work are the bevel-edge type. Two sizes, a $\frac{1}{4}$ in (6 mm) and a $\frac{3}{4}$ in (19 mm), should be adequate for most jobs. When using a chisel to remove wood, such as cutting into a door to fit a mortise lock, always start well inside the marked line and work out to it.

Drills and bits

A good power drill will take the effort out of many jobs such as drilling into walls, and there are many useful attachments available including sanding discs, circular saws, hedge trimmers and polishing mops. Choose one with a $\frac{1}{2}$ in (13 mm) chuck, the adjustable jaws that hold the twist bit, and with two drilling speeds. For light drilling jobs such as for woodworking, and especially where a very small diameter bit is being used, a hand-drill will give better control.

A set of twist bits, $\frac{1}{32}$ in-$\frac{1}{4}$ in (0.5-6 mm), will suffice for most jobs and can be used for drilling metal or timber. Masonry bits for use on brickwork or concrete have a specially hardened tip and are sold in sizes corresponding to wall plug sizes. A power hammer drill is useful for masonry work – the bit is moved in a rapid hammering action as it revolves. Attachments are available

Breast drill

Hand-drill

Power drill

Countersink

Twist bits

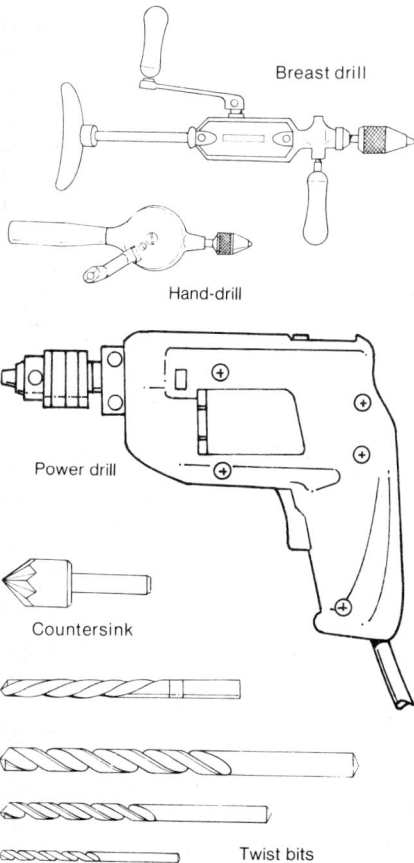

for converting an ordinary power drill to a hammer action.

When drilling masonry, use the slower speed of a two-speed drill. Drill in short bursts, removing the bit from the hole frequently to prevent clogging and overheating.

Files and rasps

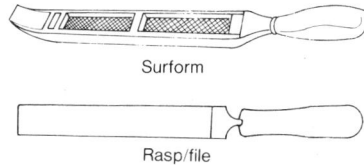

Surform

Rasp/file

Files are made in several grades — rough, bastard, second cut, smooth and dead smooth — and it is best to have one of each. The most commonly used shapes are flat, round and half round. Rasps have individually formed teeth and are used for shaping soft metals and wood. A handy tool is the combination rasp/file which has file-cut teeth on one side and rasp-cut teeth on the other. Another shaping tool which can also be used for planing carries the brand name surform and can be used on wood or metal

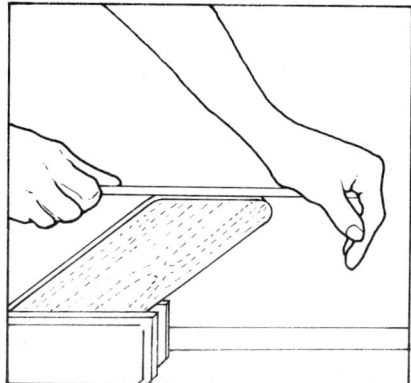

When filing, hold the file by its handle

in one hand and grip the end of the blade with the other. Make firm, forward strokes keeping the file blade level.

Hammers

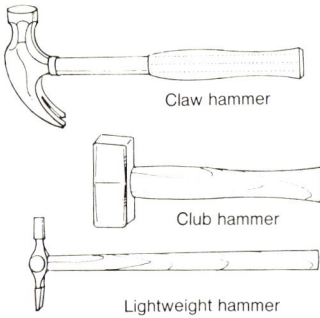

Claw hammer

Club hammer

Lightweight hammer

A must in any tool kit. A claw hammer with a metal shaft and rubber grip is a good all-purpose tool – the claw is used for pulling out old nails, or ones you didn't hammer in straight. You

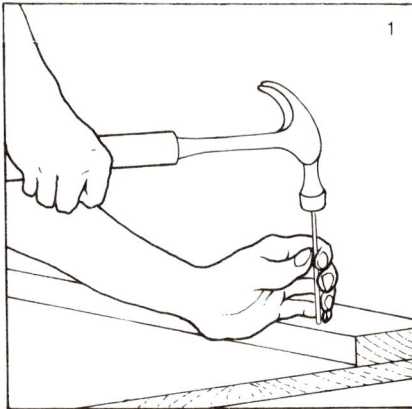

will also need a lightweight hammer for small jobs such as pinning and tacking, and a club hammer for heavy work such as breaking concrete and for use with a bolster chisel. When hammering in nails, start the nail with a few light taps first then drive it home with firm strokes keeping your eye on the nail head(1). The hammer

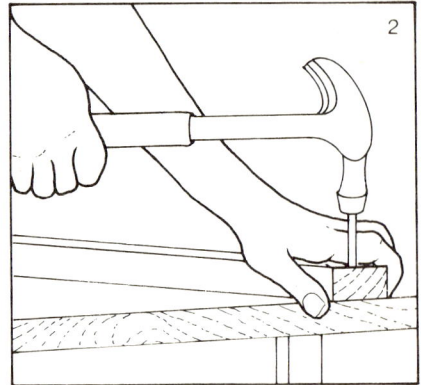

handle should be at right angles to the nail at the moment of impact(2).

Knives

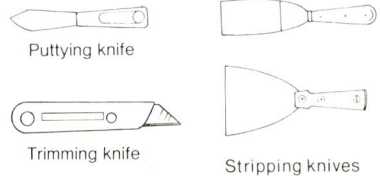

Puttying knife

Trimming knife

Stripping knives

Not all knives are for cutting, and there are several that will serve more than one purpose. A stripping knife, for example, is used for stripping wallpaper and loose paint, but it will also serve as a filling knife for applying filler to cracks in plaster. The blade should be flexible and springy – a 3 in (75 mm) wide blade is ideal for most jobs. For puttying it is best to use a special puttying knife which is shaped for trimming and bevelling the putty. It, too, is useful for small filling jobs. Trimming knives have replaceable blades and can be used for all types of trimming jobs. Special blades are available, for example a hooked blade for cutting sheet vinyl.

Paint brushes, rollers and pads

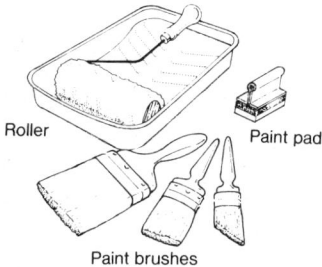

Roller   Paint pad

Paint brushes

For most indoor painting, apart from walls and ceilings, a 2 in (50 mm), 1 in (25 mm) and $\frac{1}{2}$ in (13 mm) will suffice. For walls and ceilings use a 4 in (100 mm) or 6 in (150 mm) brush. Rollers are available with lambswool, mohair or foam covering. Lambswool rollers are the longest lasting if cleaned thoroughly after use, but a low-density foam roller should be used for textured paint.

Paint pads are less wasteful on paint than rollers, and are ideal for use on flat surfaces such as skirtings and window frames. They are obtainable in sizes up to $2\frac{1}{2}$ in (63 mm) wide.

Proper care of brushes, rollers and pads will lengthen their life. Clean them with a proprietary brush cleaner, or if used for emulsion paint wash them in warm, soapy water.

Pincers and pliers

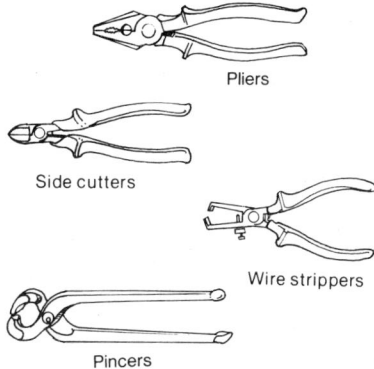

Pliers

Side cutters

Wire strippers

Pincers

Pincers are used for pulling out nails that a claw hammer cannot tackle – for example nails which have only a small head such as panel pins and 'lost head' nails. A good pair of pliers is essential, preferably with insulated handles for electrical work. The side cutter can be used for snipping wire and for stripping back the insulation on electrical wire. A small pair of snipe-nose pliers will be useful for small jobs in awkward places.

Planes

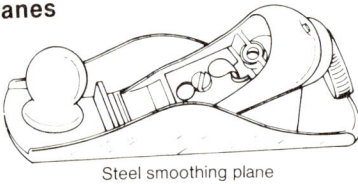
Steel smoothing plane

The carpenter's chief tool. For the average handyman a steel smoothing plane with a 2 in (50 mm) blade will do most jobs such as removing wood to cure a sticking door or gate. Always use a plane with the blade set just deep enough to remove the wood in fine shavings. Do not be tempted to increase the depth in order to remove more wood at each stroke as this may result in gouging.

Punches

Nail punch

A nail punch for sinking the heads of nails in timber, such as floorboards, and a centre punch for marking metal before drilling a hole should be enough for most household jobs.

Saws

There are saws for almost every kind of cutting job – and you will need several. For most woodworking jobs, however, a multi-purpose saw with interchangeable blades will do the work of most wood saws. Small sawing jobs where curves have to be followed can be coped with, appropriately, a coping saw(1). A

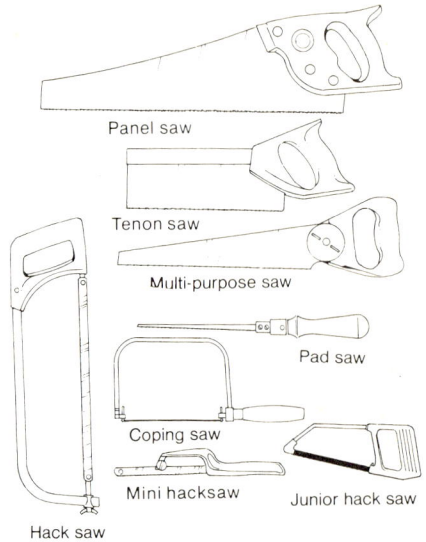
Panel saw

Tenon saw

Multi-purpose saw

Pad saw

Coping saw

Mini hacksaw   Junior hack saw

Hack saw

padsaw will tackle jobs that are impossible with other saws, such as cutting keyholes. For metal work use a 12 in (30.5 cm) hacksaw, and a small junior hacksaw for light jobs.

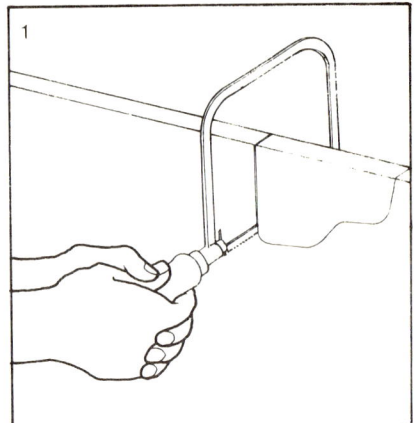

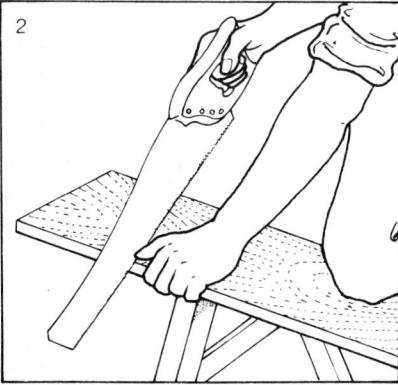

When sawing wood or metal, keep the saw at an angle of 45° to the work and saw in long, forward strokes and work slightly outside your guideline(2). Level down to the line afterwards with a plane, on wood, or file.

Screwdrivers

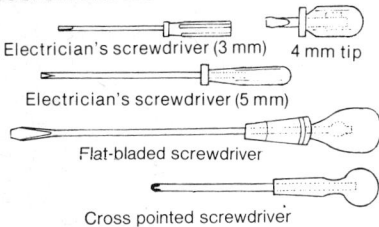

Electrician's screwdriver (3 mm)   4 mm tip

Electrician's screwdriver (5 mm)

Flat-bladed screwdriver

Cross pointed screwdriver

There are two main types of screwdriver — the flat-bladed for use with slotted screws and the cross-pointed for cross-head screws. You will need several sizes of both types, and it is useful to buy them in sets ranging from a small electrician's screwdriver, for such jobs as wiring a

plug, to a strong carpenter's screwdriver with an oval handle and a $\frac{3}{8}$ in (9 mm) blade.

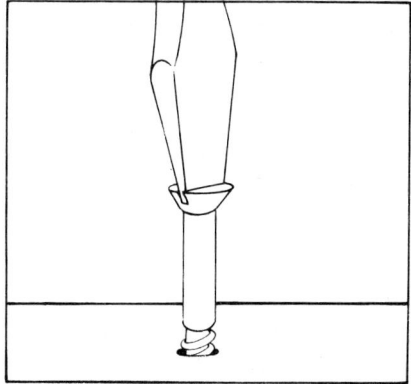

Always use the right screwdriver for the job, that is, one with a blade or cross-point that fits snugly into the screw head. Keep screwdriver and screw in line at all times, whether you are fitting or removing a screw.

Spirit levels, steel rules and squares

A spirit level is essential for getting things straight, and the most practical kind are the type that can be used both vertically and horizontally. A 3 ft (90 cm) spirit level is the most suitable for the handyman; a small, horizontal level is handy for checking short lengths. For measuring and marking materials before cutting, use a 12 in (30 cm) steel rule graduated in both imperial and metric measure. A flexible steel tape, at least 6 ft (1.8 m) long and also with

Spirit level

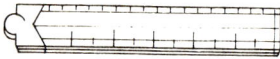
Joiner's boxwood rule

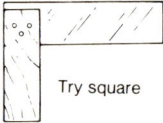
Try square

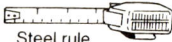
Steel rule

plaster on to a wall. It is an essential tool for plastering large areas in order to get a smooth and level finish (see pp 190–191).

Workmate

metric and imperial graduations, will be needed for many large jobs, but will not be accurate enough for small work.

A try square is used for checking a right angle, but a combination square is a worthwhile investment as it will also deal with angles of 45° as well as internal and external right angles.

Trowel and float

Pointing trowel

A bricklayer's pointing trowel can be used for most jobs involving cement or mortar, such as filling external wall cracks and repairing crumbling mortar joints. Its sharp point is used for finishing off mortar joints – called pointing.

A plasterer's float is a flat piece of metal with a handle mounted in the centre, and is used to 'float' wet

This handy device made by Black and Decker combines all the uses of a carpenter's bench and vice. It is portable and folds for stowage. The flat top opens like a vice and there are special inserts for gripping a length of wood while sawing or drilling, thereby leaving both hands free.

Wrenches and spanners

One of the most useful of tools is the self-locking wrench, or mole-grip. Its jaws are adjustable and a lever inside the grip arms locks the jaws on to a pipe, nut or bolt. A pipe wrench, or stillson, looks like an adjustable spanner but its jaws are serrated for grip. It works in one direction only; pulling against the jaws causes them to bite into the metal and the harder you pull the more the jaws grip. Do not use these wrenches on hexagon-headed bolts or on nuts unless they are exceptionally difficult to remove. A good adjustable spanner opening up to about 3 in (75 mm) should be adequate for tackling most nuts and bolts you are likely to encounter around the house.

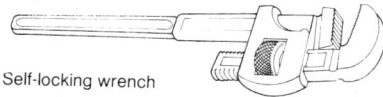

Self-locking wrench

Fasteners

Nails, screws and wall fixings

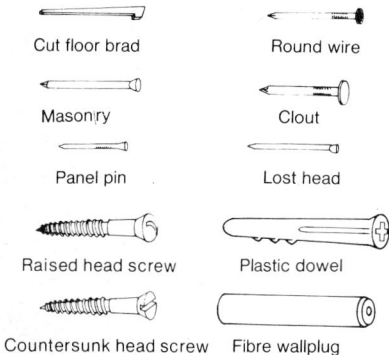

Cut floor brad

Round wire

Masonry

Clout

Panel pin

Lost head

Raised head screw

Plastic dowel

Countersunk head screw   Fibre wallplug

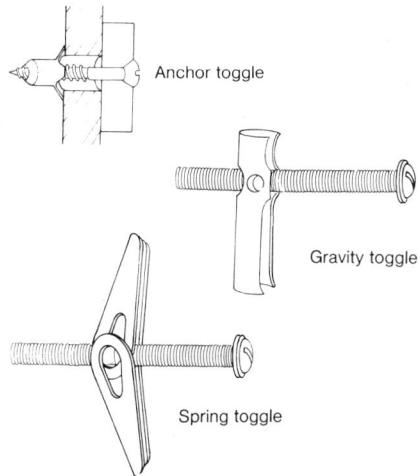

Anchor toggle

Gravity toggle

Spring toggle

Nails come in various sizes, shapes and lengths and all are designed for a particular purpose. They are sold by weight, but most DIY shops have them in handy packs of small quantities. For general purposes, such as fixing fences, the round wire nail gives a firm fixing but is liable to split wood. For jobs where the wood is liable to split, use oval wire nails driven in so that the oval shape is in line with the grain. Where it is important that the nail heads should not protrude, use lost head nails which can be punched just below the surface and the hole filled. This is a useful nail for floorboards, but the correct nail for that job is the cut floor brad. The smallest nails you are likely to need are panel pins which have a small head and fine gauge. They are useful for small tacking jobs such as wood mouldings.

Outside the house the masonry nail is designed for fixing to brick, breeze block or concrete. For roofing felt, window sash cords and wire fencing use clout nails which have a wide head.

Nails should not be used where a heavy and constant load is applied to the fixing. In those circumstances use screws. For general woodworking the countersunk screw is used. Its head can be driven flush to or just below the surface. Countersunk screws are available with slotted or cross heads. For work where the screw head will show, such as on door handles, use nickel or chrome plated raised head screws. For hardware fittings where the hole is not countersunk use round head screws which are also available either nickel or chrome plated.

Screw sizes are graded in numbers (the larger the number the larger the screw) and the number 8 is a convenient size for many jobs. The length of the screw is measured from the rim of the head to the tip of the thread.

The most widely used wall fixing is the wall plug; a fibre or plastic dowel which fits into a bored hole and expands as the screw is driven in. They are sold in sizes relevant to the screw size. Some plastic wall plugs are tapered and have forward facing serrations, and once in position are difficult to withdraw. So always make sure you have drilled the hole deep enough before inserting this type of fixing.

For really heavy work, such as fastening timber beams to a wall, use masonry bolts which have a strong insert that expands as the bolt is screwed home.

There are three types of fastener useful on thin panelling or ceilings, where access to the rear of the panel is difficult or impossible. One is the gravity toggle; it has a swivel toggle that drops into a vertical position when pushed through the hole. A similar fixing is the spring toggle which has two spring loaded arms which expand behind the panel after being pushed through the hole. The third type is the nylon or plastic anchor which has gripper arms that expand behind the panel as the screw is tightened.

Power tools

There are numerous attachments for power drills. These however, may overwork the tool if too many are used and often it is better to buy the right power tool for a particular work.

One of the most useful is the sander, which is more practical for large areas, and simpler to control, than the rotary sanding disc attachment for a power drill. Sanding sheets of all grades are available. A circular saw with a 1150 Watt motor will tackle timber and man-made boards up to a depth of 2 in (50 mm). Most power drills have only a 350 Watt motor and circular saw attachments can cope only with up to about 1 in (25 mm). A jig saw, so-called because its blade 'jigs' rapidly up and down, will deal with sawing jobs outside the scope of a circular saw, such as following curves. It is light and easy to use and the blade can be angled for mitred cuts. There is also a power plane for taking the hard work out of planing.

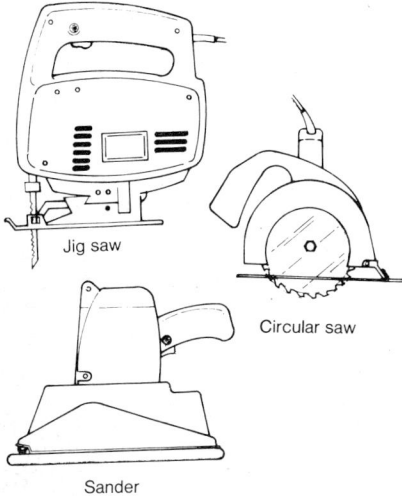

Jig saw

Circular saw

Sander

Hiring tools

Few people except for the devoted DIY man will want to face the high outlay involved in purchasing the full range of power tools, but most are available from hire shops. The hire business is very competitive and charges vary enormously, so it is wise to shop around when hiring tools. Many shops charge a daily rate, but some will hire for a period of as little as four hours. It pays, therefore, to estimate the amount of time you will need the tool, and to organize the work to avoid paying for the equipment when it is not in use.

Check also the shop's business hours so that you can return the tool as soon as you have finished with it.

When hiring, make sure that you understand the hire terms. A deposit is usually required and this may be withheld if the tool is not returned in good order. The hirer may also make an additional charge if the tool is returned in dirty condition. Before you sign the contract, ask to see the tool working. If you are not sure how to use it, ask for a demonstration. Quite often an electrical appliance has a seal fitted to the plug, and once this seal is broken the equipment is deemed to have been used. You cannot then claim that it was not in working order when it was supplied.

Other equipment you may want to hire includes ladders, scaffolding, paint sprayer or concrete mixer. Such large items can be delivered to your home at an additional charge — the hire period ends when they are collected by the hire firm. If you are hiring equipment for outside work it is as well to allow an extra day in case you are held up by bad weather. The hirer may not be able to extend your hire time at short notice.

Handy tips for around the home

The bulk of this book is devoted to looking after the structure of a home – the walls, ceilings, windows and doors etc, all of which need regular attention to keep the property habitable and at the same time to maintain its value. But furniture and furnishings also need to be cared for.

Below is a list of some of the jobs you can do easily and cheaply, often with little more than a few tools and using materials found in most kitchens.

Cleaning

Carpets and rugs When anything is spilled on a carpet or rug, mop it up quickly with a damp cloth. With luck you will avoid leaving a stain. Otherwise use one of the methods listed below:

Beer stains Clean with a mild detergent to which has been added 1 eggcup of white vinegar and 1 pint (0.56 litres) of water.

Blood Sponge with a saline solution of $\frac{1}{2}$ teaspoon of salt to 1 pint (0.56 litres) of water.

Chocolate or cocoa Place a basin under the carpet (only if it is not rubber or foam backed) and sprinkle borax powder on the stain. Then pour hot water through the stain, followed by a cold rinse.

Coffee Use borax powder, as for cocoa; coffee stains can sometimes be removed with fizzy lemonade that has gone flat.

Fruit juice Rub gently with methylated spirits.

Grass stains Use methylated spirits or eucalyptus oil.

Grease (butter, oils, fats) Sprinkle with an absorbent powder such as talcum or French chalk. Press the powder firmly into the stain and then brush or vacuum about half an hour later. Follow up with a proprietary dry cleaner.

Hair lacquer Clean water may do the trick, if not use methylated spirits.

Milk Rinse in lukewarm water. If the stain persists, use borax powder as for chocolate.

Paint For oil-based paints use turpentine or a proprietary paint remover such as brush cleanser. Emulsion paint can be washed away with cold water if the stain is fresh, otherwise use methylated spirits.

Spirits (whisky etc) Sprinkle with talc or French chalk and blot with tissues. Sponge with clean water and then apply carpet shampoo.

Tea Rub in a solution of equal parts of glycerine and warm water. Allow to dry and then rinse lightly with cold water. Finally clean with a carpet shampoo.

Wine As for spirits.

Floors

Stains on wooden floors Rub with wire wool soaked in white spirit.

Linoleum Use wire wool and liquid paraffin.

Wallpaper
Use a mild detergent in warm water to remove stains on washable wall-paper. For obstinate grease spots use a proprietary cleaner. On non-washable wallpaper, spray the stain with an aerosol dry cleaner, leave it to dry and then brush off the dried powder. Some household materials that will aid spot removal are: glycerine for fruit juice, bottled sauces and wine; peroxide mixed in equal parts with water for beer, coffee, tea, wine and spirits; turpentine substitute for ink, tar and wax polish; enzyme detergent for blood, cocoa, egg, jelly and starch.

Warning Before applying any type of cleaner, whether a proprietary brand or a home made solution, always test first on an unused area to see that it will not attack or discolour the fabric. For proprietary cleaners, always follow the maker's instructions carefully.

Furniture repairs
Cigarette burns Rub with fine glass-paper and touch up with wood stain to match.
Dents in furniture Scrape away polish from the dent. Make a pad of cotton wool wrapped in a soft cloth. Soak in boiling water and apply to the dent. Keep the pad hot and continue treating the dent until it has disappeared. Allow to dry thoroughly and

then sand down with fine paper.
Loose chair or table legs If the legs are held by screws, remove them and pour a little PVA adhesive into the holes. Refit the screws or ones a size larger if the screws will not tighten. If there are no screws, ease the legs out of their joints, scrape out old adhesive and refit with PVA adhesive. Clamp or bind the join until the glue has set.
Scratches Light scratches in wood can be removed with paper dipped in linseed oil.
Sticking drawers Rub the sides of the drawer, or its runners, with candlegrease or a bar of soap.
Uneven legs Don't try to level by cutting the legs to get them even — you may end up with a footstool! Build up the short leg with thin pieces of wood glued together with PVA adhesive and attached to the foot with panel pins.
Veneers Slight blistering can be repaired by pressing with a hot iron on top of layers of blotting paper. Alternatively, slit the blister with a trimming knife, insert PVA adhesive under the blister and apply a warm iron.

A severe blister can be removed. Cut around with a trimming knife and scrape off the old glue. Apply PVA adhesive to both surfaces and replace the cut-out piece. Stand a heavy weight, such as an electric iron (cold), on the repair overnight.

What to do in an emergency

Even in the best-run homes, accidents will happen. And the statistics for accidents in the home are horrifying — $1\frac{1}{2}$ million people annually are treated in hospitals for burns, cuts and more serious injuries sustained in their homes.

A major hazard is fire, often made worse by people trying to deal with it in the wrong way or by panicking and making the situation worse. Most fires can be tackled with water, but **not** fat fires such as a blazing chip pan or frying pan. Water will cause the flames to spread. If fat or oil catches fire in the kitchen, first turn off the source of the fire — the gas flame or electric ring — and then smother the flames with a saucepan lid or a damp towel.

Electrical fires also must not be tackled with water, though water can be used on a fire started by an electrical fault once the power has been turned off at the main supply. When dealing with a fire always make sure you have a clear escape route should the fire get out of hand, and always call the fire brigade and make sure everyone is out of the house before attempting to put out the blaze. **Do not continue to fight the fire once it has got out of control**.

As a precaution it is a good idea to have at least one fire extinguisher in the house — preferably two, one upstairs and one down.

Taking sensible precautions is the best way to lower the risk of fire: always have faulty wiring replaced immediately; have electrical appliances checked regularly; make sure that correctly rated fuses are fitted; keep all inflammable materials such as paint, paint stripper, impact adhesives, paraffin and methylated spirits outside the house. Before going to bed at night, have a final look around to see that open fires are doused or safe, electrical appliances are switched off and that no cigarettes have been left burning. For extra protection, fit smoke detectors in each room. These are fitted to the ceilings and trigger an alarm when smoke enters the unit.

If you or anyone in your home suffers burns, cool the burned area with water. **Do not try to remove clothing which has stuck to the area and cover the burns with a clean dressing**. Send for a doctor or ambulance immediately if the burns appear serious, but in any case have them treated as soon as possible.

Apart from the risk of fire there are numerous accidents which may occur in the home and may require immediate treatment. In all cases of serious injury, send for the doctor or ambulance first and then apply first aid. Keep calm, a panic-stricken call will only cause delay in getting an ambulance to you.

Giving first aid

Electric shock In some cases of electric shock the victim becomes paralyzed and cannot let go of the electrical appliance. **Do not touch them or the shock will be transmitted to you**. Switch off the supply at the mains. If this is not possible try to pull the victim away with a non-conductive item such as a walking stick. If the victim is not breathing give artificial respiration – the kiss of life – and continue until medical help arrives.

Place the individual on his or her back, and clear any obstruction from the mouth. It is important to pull the head back and lift the chin up. Pinch the nostrils together, **except in the case of a child**.

Cover the mouth with your own and blow gently. **In the case of a child cover the mouth and nostrils**.

Check to see if the chest is rising; if not pull the head further back and blow again. Remove your mouth and wait until the chest falls. Repeat this every five seconds until help arrives.

Fractures A broken bone must be treated quickly by a doctor. While waiting, keep the victim still and stop any bleeding. Do nothing else unless the victim is in a state of shock, in which case keep him or her warm with blankets and try to give reassurance. Do not offer stimulants such as brandy or whisky in case an anaesthetic is needed later.

Eye injuries Something in the eye, such as a piece of grit, can often be removed with the corner of a clean handkerchief. But if the object is embedded in the eyeball, cover the eye with a gauze pad and get the patient to a doctor or hospital casualty department.

Acid or any other irritant fluid in the eye should be washed away with clean water. Bathe the eye under cold running water and send for medical help immediately.

Cuts For a bad cut, where bleeding is excessive, apply pressure to the cut to stem the bleeding and bandage firmly. **Get medical help as soon as possible**. A minor cut should be washed with soap and water and then dabbed with a disinfectant. Allow to dry and cover the cut with a clean dressing.

Choosing the right paint

There are two main types of paint for household work — oil-based and emulsion. Oil-based paints are made with alkyd and other resins to give a tough, hard-wearing finish. They usually need an undercoat when applied to bare wood, but some non-drip paints will cover in one coat. Non-drip paint (or thixotropic to give it its correct name) is a gelled paint which will not run or drip. It is easier to apply than liquid paint and more economical to use. The thinning medium for oil-based paints is white spirit, but non-drip paint should not be thinned nor should it be stirred.

Also in the oil-based range is polyurethane paint, which gives a hard surface that resists water and heat and protects against scratching. It is available in gloss and semi-gloss finishes. Polyurethane varnish will give the same protection to wood finishes, the varnish is clear and can be bought in matt, semi-matt or gloss finishes.

You can see oil-based paints on almost every type of surface; it is especially useful for outside work where good weather protection is needed. If using a liquid paint, always use the manufacturer's recommended undercoat and make sure to prepare the area to be painted. If you are painting on top of old paint, rub it down thoroughly to remove flakes and blisters and then wash down with white spirit. Oil paint takes several hours to dry, depending on the temperature, so do not paint outdoors in cold weather or in unsettled conditions. To keep gloss paintwork looking smart and clean, wash regularly with warm water and a mild detergent.

Emulsion paints are water-based and have largely taken the place of distemper. Some contain vinyl or acrylic resins and are available in matt or silk finishes. Gloss emulsions are also available, but the gloss does not compare with that of oil-based paints. Most emulsions are for plastered walls and ceilings, though some can be used on wood, and can be applied by roller or brush. Water is used for thinning and for washing brushes, rollers etc. Emulsion paint dries quickly; in a warm room it will be dry enough for a second coat within about half an hour. All emulsion paint finishes are washable.

Do not use emulsion paint for exterior work; instead use masonry paint which, though water-based, will give a durable finish to brickwork, cement or a pebbledash rendering. It can be applied direct to painted or unpainted surfaces.

Metric conversion table

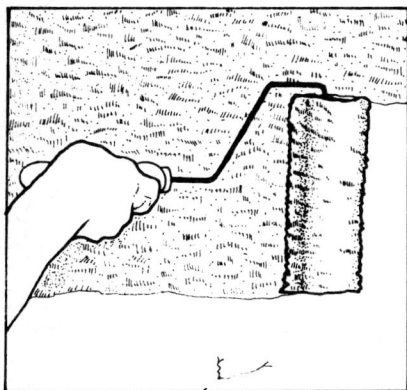

Textured paints have become popular in recent years. The paint is plastic based and is spread liberally in a thick, even coat. The textured finish is obtained in several ways; a low-density foam roller run over the surface will pick up the paint to give an attractive stipple effect, or a sponge can be used to make irregular patterns and whirls. Dabbing the surface with a paint brush will also produce a variety of patterns. Because it is applied thickly, textured paint is messy to use and will drip heavily when used on a ceiling. Make sure, therefore, that floors and furniture in the room are well covered.

Length	
$\frac{1}{64}$ in	0·397 mm
$\frac{1}{32}$ in	0·794 mm
$\frac{1}{16}$ in	1·587 mm
$\frac{1}{8}$ in	3·175 mm
$\frac{1}{4}$ in	6·350 mm
$\frac{1}{2}$ in	12·700 mm
$\frac{3}{4}$ in	19·050 mm
1 in	25·400 mm
12 in (1 ft)	304·800 mm
36 in (1 yd)	914·400 mm

Area	
1 sq in	6·452 sq cm
1 sq ft	929·030 sq cm
1 sq yd	0·836 sq m

Capacity	
1 fl oz	2·841 cl
1 pint	0·568 l
1 gallon	4·546 l

Weight	
1 oz	28·350 g
1 lb	0·454 kg
1 cwt	50·802 kg
1 ton	1·016 metric tons

Index

Punches 208—9

R

Radiators 18—21
  blocked 21
  clearing an air lock 21
  valve 18—19
Rainwater drainage 52—7
Rasps 205
Rendering 188—9
Repointing brickwork, of fireback 32
  walls 158—9, 188—9
Risers 144—5
Rising damp, causes and cures 168—9
'Rodding' 50—52
Roofs 52—7
  cedar shingle 132—143
  construction 142—3
  dry rot, wet rot and woodworm 132
  ridge slate 140—41
  slate 137
Rubber resin 184—5

S

Saws 208—9
Scaffolding 53, 132—3
Screwdrivers 209—10
Screws 212—3
Settlement 84—5
Sewer, main 50—52
Shed 86
  recovering felt roof 98—9
Shingle roof, replacing 142—3
Sill, repairing wet rot 177
  replacing 48—9
Single stack system 50—52
Sinks and baths, gaps around 128—9
Skirting board, replacing 80—81
Slates and tiles 136—141
  fixing a loose ridge slate 140
  replacing a slate 138
  slate roof 137—8
Sleeper walls (below floor level) 72
Sliding sash window 173
  replacing sash cord 174
Slow-setting adhesives 184—5
Soakaway 53

Soffits 135
Softwood 196
Soil pipe 50—52
Soldering 202—3
Solid wall 157
Spanners 211—2
Spirit levels, steel rules and squares 210
Stains, removing various 216—17
Staircases, construction and repair 144—155
Stopcock 102—6
Stop valves 113
Storage tank 113
Strings (staircases) 144—5
Supataps 113
Superglues 184—5

T

Taps 112—16
  capstan 112
  pillar 112—13
  supataps 113—14
Thermostats 18—19
Tiles, replacing in fireplace 27
  roof ridge 141
  roofs 137—9
  walls 170
Tools and how to use them 204—215
Treads, staircase 144
  curing creaking 151
  replacing 147—9
  worn edge 152
Trees and settlement 84—5
Trowel 211
Two stack system 50—52

U

Urea, synthetic resin (glue) 184—5

V

Vegetable die (for use when pointing) 188—9
Vent pipe 51
Victorian houses, stairs in 144

W

Wallpaper, removing 216—17

Index